I0812440

IMAGES
*of America*

# THE MILLINGTON-ARBELA AREA

1854–2004

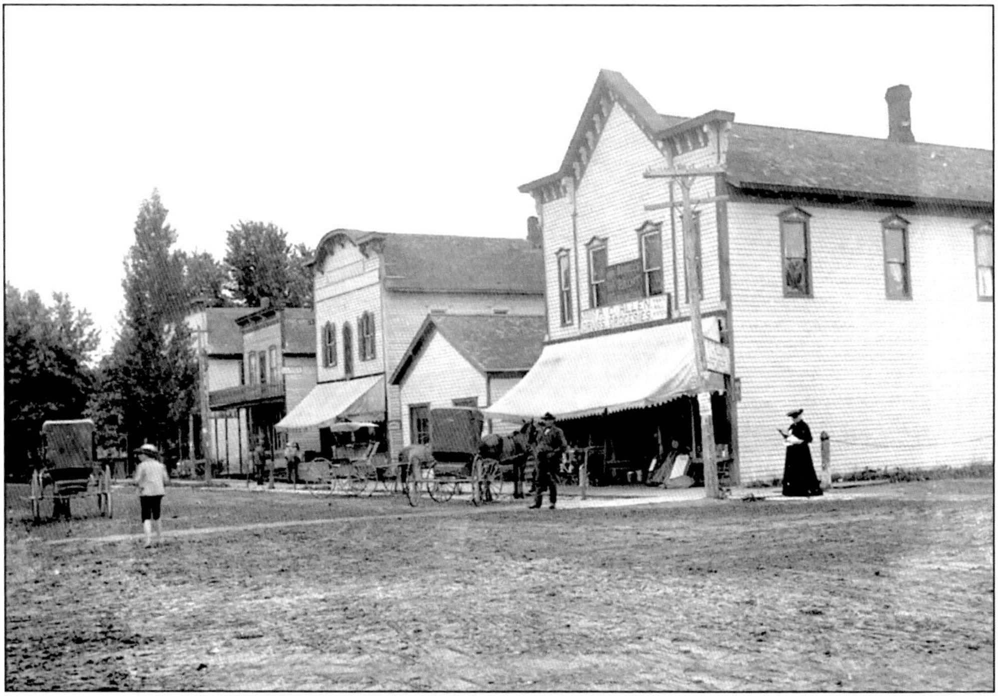

This photograph, featured on the book cover, shows the business section of State Street from Beckwith Street north. This was taken in the 1940s and shows the location of the Township Library.

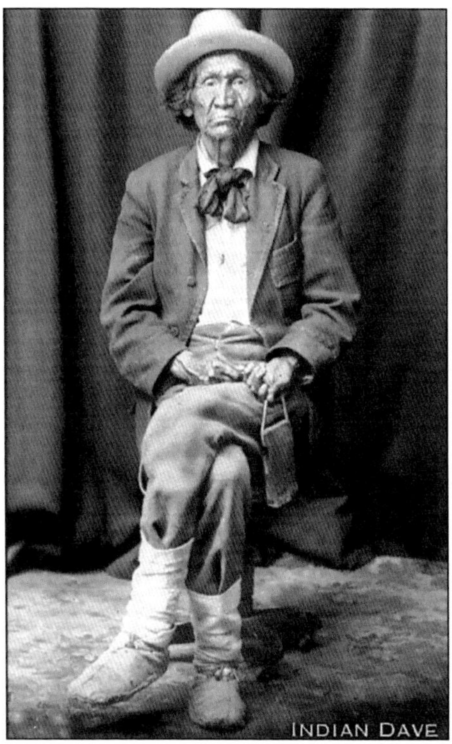


Indians were a large part of the population in Millington's early days. This photo shows Indian Dave, a great friend of the people. He lived in the area until his death at the age of 106.

IMAGES
*of America*

# THE MILLINGTON-ARBELA AREA 1854–2004

Millington-Arbela Historical Society

ARCADIA
PUBLISHING

;BN 978-0-7385-3225-7

ublished by Arcadia Publishing
'harleston, South Carolina

rinted in the United States of America

ibrary of Congress Catalog Card Number: 2003114307

or all general information contact Arcadia Publishing at:
elephone 843-853-2070
ax 843-853-0044
-mail sales@arcadiapublishing.com
or customer service and orders:
oll-Free 1-888-313-2665

'isit us on the Internet at www.arcadiapublishing.com

*This book is dedicated to the memory of Beverly Chapin and Rosemarie McPherson vho had the foresight to organize our society. With their leadership and hard work we were able to publish this book for you.*

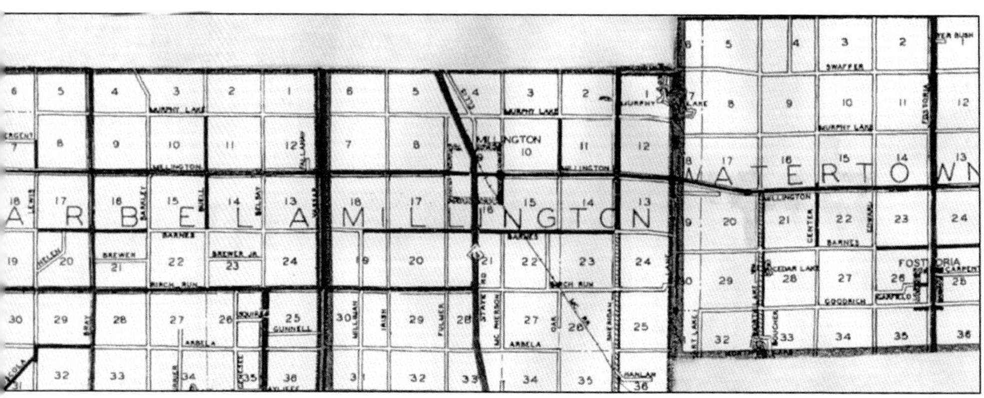


n the early days, townships consisted of Millington, with Watertown as part of it, and Arbela. 'he region is in the lower portion of Tuscola County.

# Contents

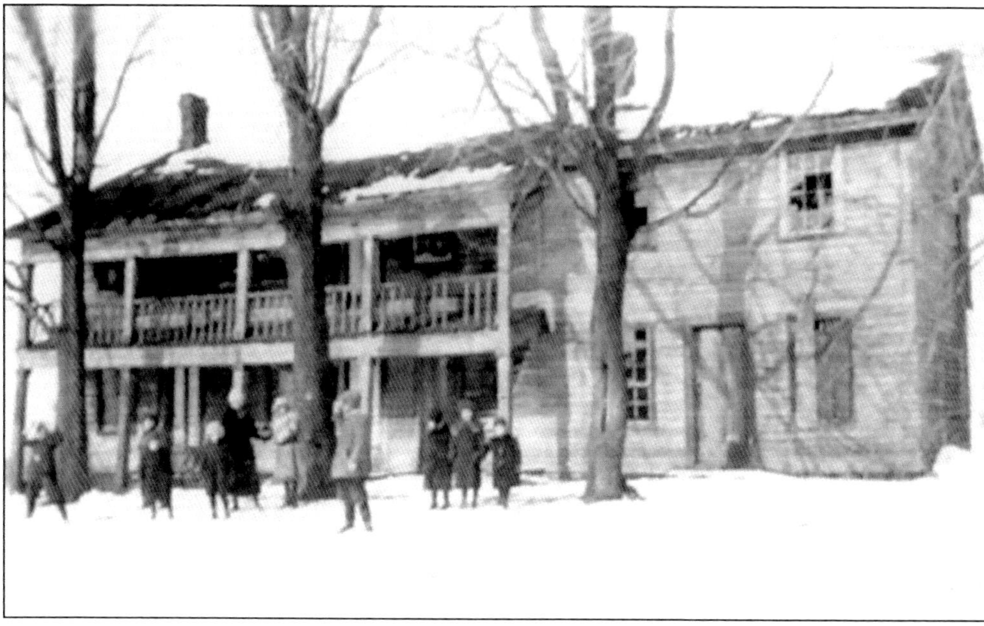

Lodging places were a very valuable asset in the communities because of the time needed to traverse the poor roads and trails between towns. The Pinegrove Inn in Arbela and the Millington House in Millington are examples of these conveniences.

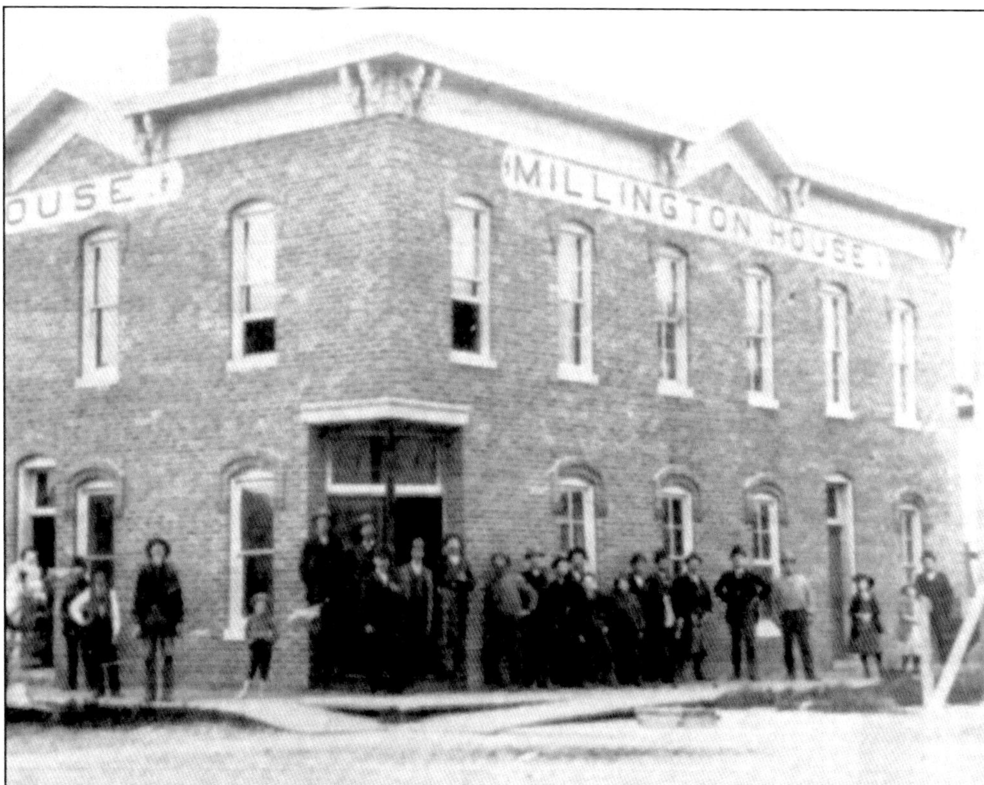

# INTRODUCTION

The first settlers to the Millington area came to a heavily forested region consisting of huge hardwood and pine trees. It was known as 10 North Range 8 East as surveyed by Joseph Fletcher in 1822.

The township was organized in 1855 by a special act of the legislature and included the present township of Watertown. This involved a change in county lines because the previous line dividing Lapeer and Tuscola counties was placed so as to cut the present towns of Millington, Watertown, and Richmond through the center. The separate township of Watertown was organized in 1857.

Edwin C. Brainard moved his family to Section 6 on December 24, 1850, and was the only resident for three years. His daughter, Elmira, born February 24, 1852, was the first white child born in Millington. The next settler, Homer Beach, came from Brighton in 1853. Shortly thereafter, Marcus Titsworth and Alfred Fox arrived, but Mr. Fox died soon afterward. Alfred Foster came from Ohio in 1854, and Amos Worthington came from Oakland County in the same year. Settlers from Groveland, Oakland County, included: Reuben Henry, the Dewitt family (a father and his sons Antony, Christopher, and Dingman, and a daughter, Cornelia), and Amariah P. Ireland. Jay Rice came from Hamburg, Livingston County, in 1854. Bernard Beals came from Ann Arbor. Charles Miller, Charles Webster, Calvin Crippen, Scott Van Norwick, Simpson Bentley, Ira Patterson, Nathan Newcomb, and a Mr. Knickerbocker all came to the township in 1855; the last seven settled in the southwest part of the township, Fractional District 1. Andrew Hanking settled in Section 7 in the southwest corner; Jacob Mack settled on the southwest quarter of Section 18. George Anthony from Vassar settled on the southeast quarter of Section 9. William Pool, George and Charles Anthony, Walter Richardson, and Cortez Gordon all came from Vassar and settled near each other. In 1855, Moses Farnum and John G. Smith each settled new land; Farnum took Section 24 and Smith took Section 25. They were joined there by Joshua Perkins.

The first township meeting was held in April of 1855 at the log home of Amos Wolverton on Section 16, one mile south of the village. Amos Wolverton was elected Supervisor, Jay Rice was elected Clerk, and H. Pattison became Treasurer.

The village was platted in 1860 as Lanesville. That plat and name was abandoned in 1872 when another survey and platting was made in the name of Millington, which it had unofficially adopted in 1866. The 1872 platting was done by Samuel Atwood, Joel Beckwith, and D.N. Blocher, with Mr. Blocher as the principal owner. The township took its name from the Millington Creek which was so named on the original government survey plat. That survey was made in 1822 and the reason for naming the creek Millington will probably never be known.

The town of Arbela lies in the southwest corner of the county, with the county lines as its western and southern boundaries, and with Millington on the east and Tuscola on the north. The actual and active settlement of Arbela dates to 1850, though Milton Whitney had at that time been a resident for several years. Whitney's entry of land in Section 5 dates to December 10, 1845.

In November of 1849, Simeon Newton and William Allen came from Livingston County on foot, to explore the northern wilds in search of a location. Having made a selection, they returned the following January, and Mr. Allen made an entry on the way in the northeast quarter of Section 17. They worked on this tract for two seasons, making shingles. These were sent out by the team that brought them supplies, and by teams passing in and out. This enterprise found them in debt of $9 by the end of the first year, not to mention the risk of starvation they had endured. But the second year found them $40 ahead, and at this point they turned their attention to farming.

In March of 1850, Mr. Newton built a log house in Section 16. That same month he sent for his family: a wife, two boys, and a girl. They began keeping a hotel, and the increasing traffic of lumbermen and settlers frequently gave them a full house. They brought in three cows, several young cattle, one and a half bushels of corn, a barrel of buckwheat, flour, and 50¢, with which to run a shingle camp, farm, and hotel. Mr. Newton said the hotel could not but pay, as by the time a traveler reached it he was so exhausted—by reason of the length and character of the road—that he could get no further. He must have thought of the promised land of rest long before he reached it, for within two miles there were 27 bends in the road which would hither and thither to escape the low places. And at best State Road, which was cut through in 1849, was but a place for a road. Mr. Newton was frequently asked to show newcomers suitable locations for homes and aided largely in settling the area. After Newton and Allen came Alanson Calkins, James Brophy, and others. Indeed, after the first settlers arrived, others came in rapidly. For several years, mail was obtained from Tuscola, but in 1858 or 1859 a mail route was opened and a post office established in the southwest part of town.

The first schoolhouse was built by Newton and Allen in 1853 or 1854, in Section 9, and school was taught by Mr. Hodges who boarded at Newton's. Among the first buildings was a road shanty belonging to Mr. Wilson, who had the contract of cutting out State Road, and which was occupied by Newton and Allen before their shanty was ready. In 1855, Methodist religion was brought to the area, with Elders Klump and Andrews being among the pioneers. In 1851 Hinckley and McLean built a sawmill on Section 32. Another mill followed, and in a short time the present village of Pine Grove grew to considerable prominence. A large amount of trade was done, hotel business was lively, and the roads were lined with teams, hauling the product of the mills to Saginaw and elsewhere.

Upon the opening of a mail route, a post office was established. Samuel Evans was appointed postmaster but did not serve. Nathan Hinckley of Pine Run was appointed next, and he put a deputy, Truman Curtis, in charge. The next postmaster was Roger R. Rathburn, who was succeeded by Clark Powell, and he by John Jacobs. The post office was relocated closer to town c. 1872, and H.H. Crosby served as postmaster at that time. He was succeeded by R.L. Merrick, and he by William Allen. The office was called Elva.

# *One*
# Centennial

In the year of 1954, Millington celebrated its centennial, having been organized 100 years earlier. The celebration included a parade, a pageant, and a visit by Governor G. Mennen Williams to crown the King, Queen, Prince, and Princess. Men were required to wear a beard and/or mustache and many wore period costumes. We commemorate this event with the following pictures.

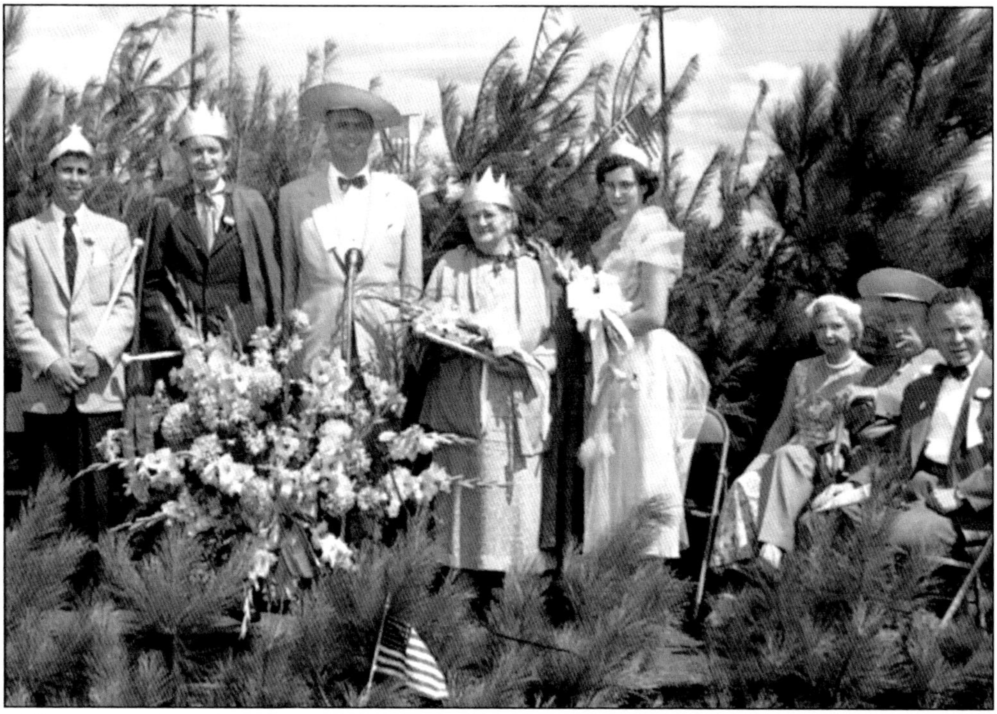

Millington celebrated its centennial by electing a King, Queen, Prince, and Princess. They had the honor of the presence of Governor G. Mennen (Soapy) Williams to officiate at their coronation.

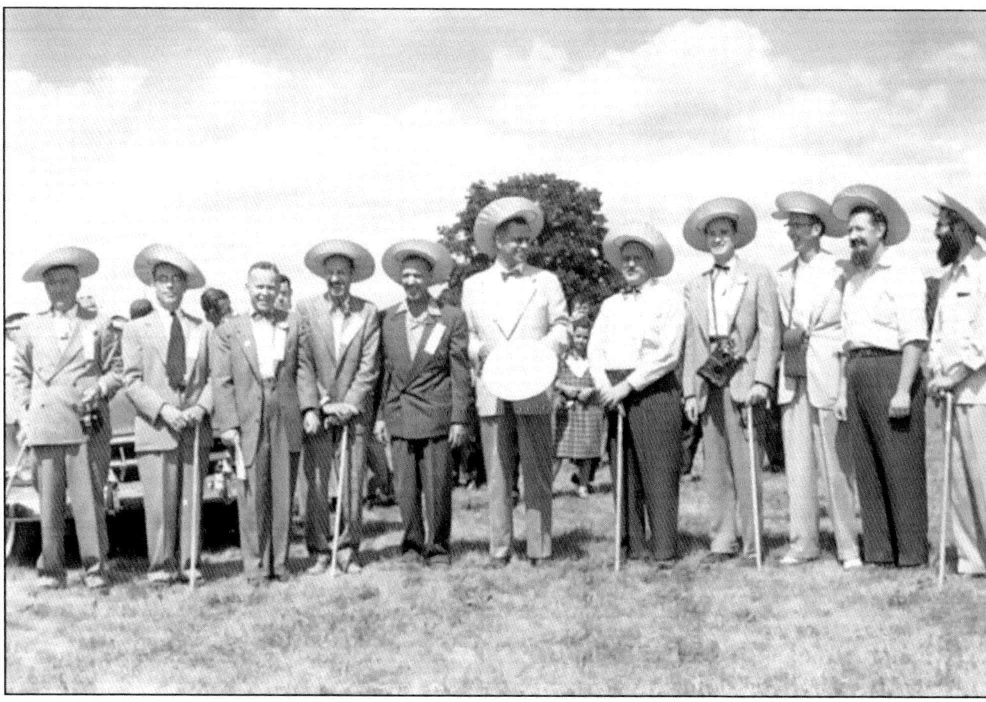

The men of Millington, in all their period costumes, were happy to pose with the Governor. Note the facial hair required of all participants.

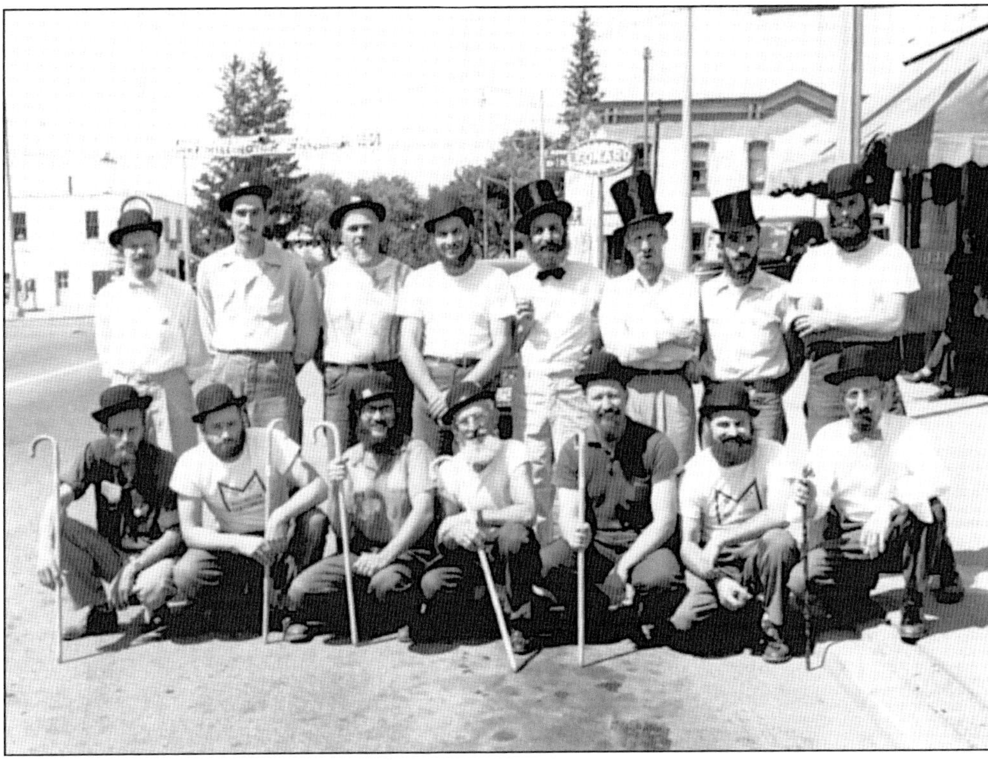

The men posed again in their period costumes.

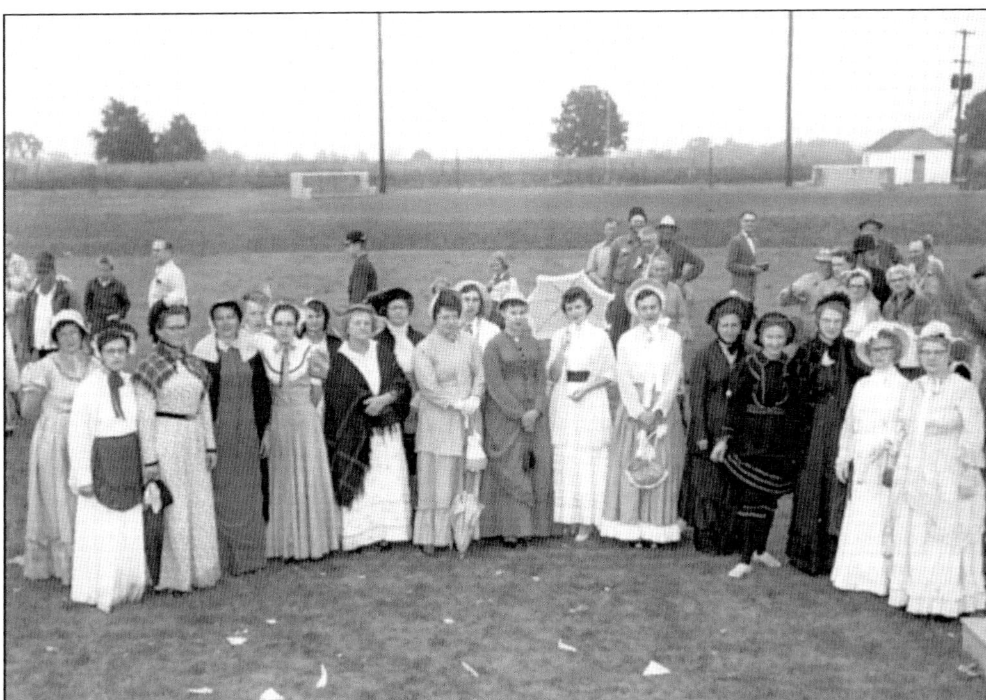

Not to be outdone by the men, the township ladies pose in their period costumes and hats.

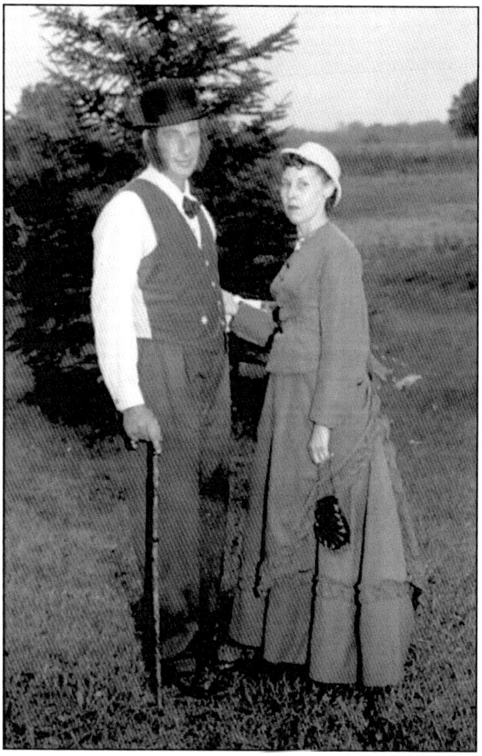 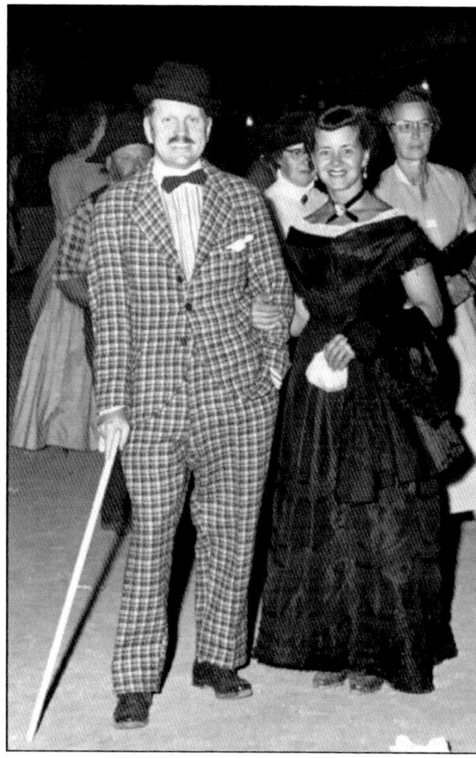

These couples show off their finery and are ready to attend the inauguration ball.

# *Two*

# AREA GROWTH

The village of Millington was incorporated on March 27, 1877. It originated in the business enterprise of Lane and Wolfe, who constructed a saw mill in 1859. In 1860, a village was platted under the name of Lanesville. This plat, however, was abandoned along with the name and in 1872 another platting and survey was made under the name of Millington. Many remember the more familiar name of "Podunk" which was never recorded. The first Village President was D.N. Blocher. One of his sons, Clarence Blocher, was a frequent visitor in Millington.

The first council members were I.T. Damon, M.M. Atwood, Anthony DeWitt, Jacob Hoover, and Arthur B. Gould. The village newspaper was called the *Millington Messenger* was established by Mr. Patterson. The name was changed later to the *Millington Retina*, *Millington Gazette*, *Millington Herald* and is now once again the *Millington Messenger*.

One of the oldest recorded farms is the Frank Rice farm, one mile south and two miles west of Millington. Thomas J. Rice obtained the land from the government in 1852. Other old farms are the E.E. Brainerd farm, the Marcus Titsworth farm, and the Sigelko farm. Other farms were purchased later and many are still occupied by members of the original families.

The hardships synonymous with pioneer living were the golden threads woven into the finished fabric of these great but humble early settlers, our ancestors.

When the road and the railroad were established from the south to Bay City, the village and the township began to grow rapidly. Interurban commerce was established and many new businesses evolved. We commemorate this growth with the following pictures from an earlier era.

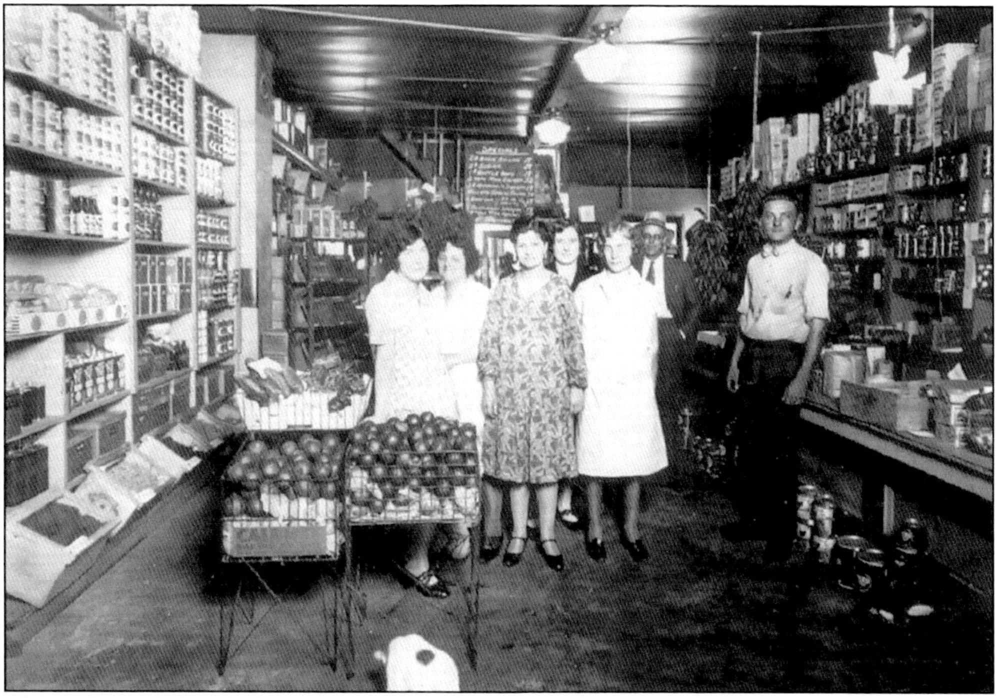

This is the interior of the Farm Bureau Store at State and Center Streets. Pictured from left to right are the following: Fern Fischaber, Ada Brandt, unidentified, Ruth Gray, Nilda Lennox, Bill Hanlin, and manager Bill Brandt.

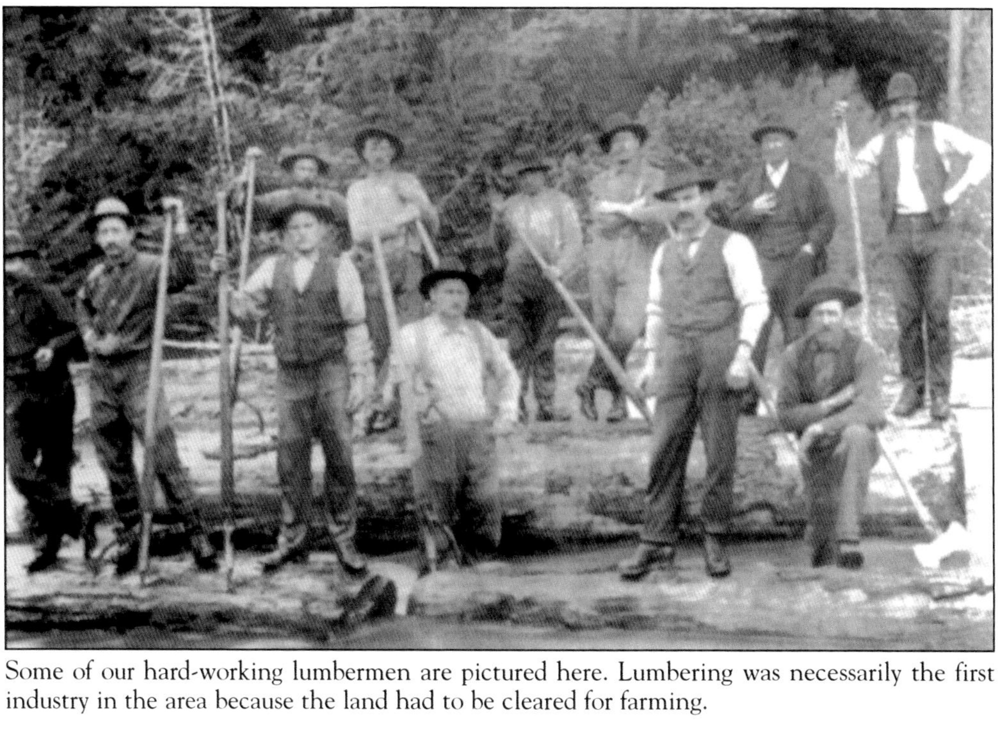

Some of our hard-working lumbermen are pictured here. Lumbering was necessarily the first industry in the area because the land had to be cleared for farming.

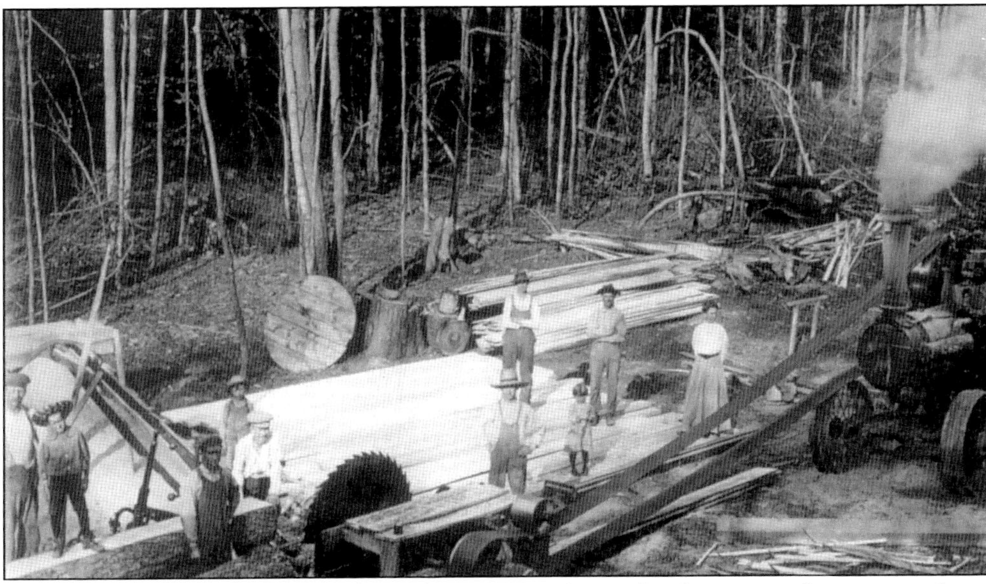

This is one of the many sawmills used to process the timber being cut. It was owned and operated by Otis Farnum (far left) and his wife, Lottie (far right).

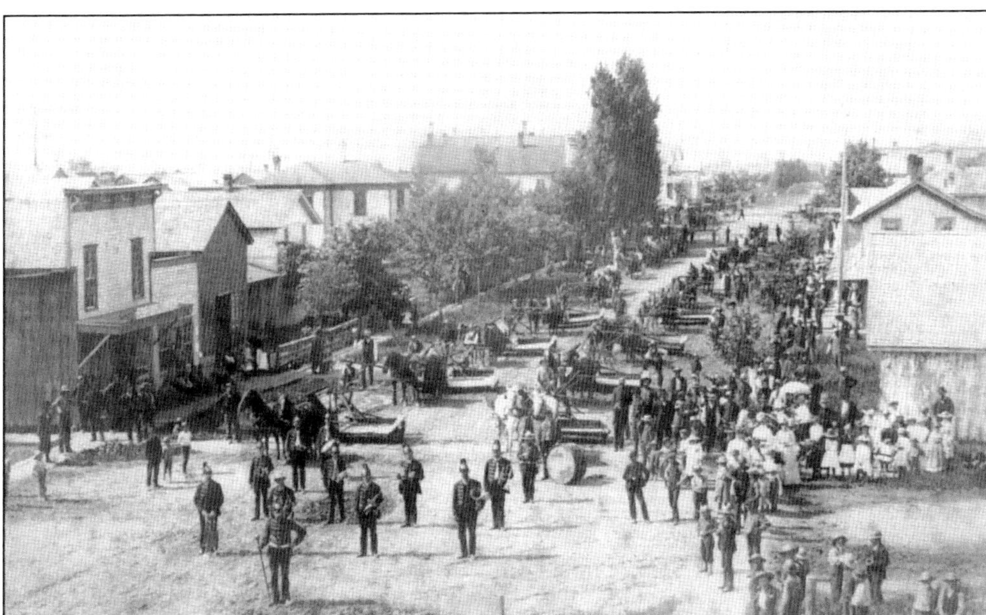

This photograph captures an early village parade, with band, celebrating the successful end to a summer's work.

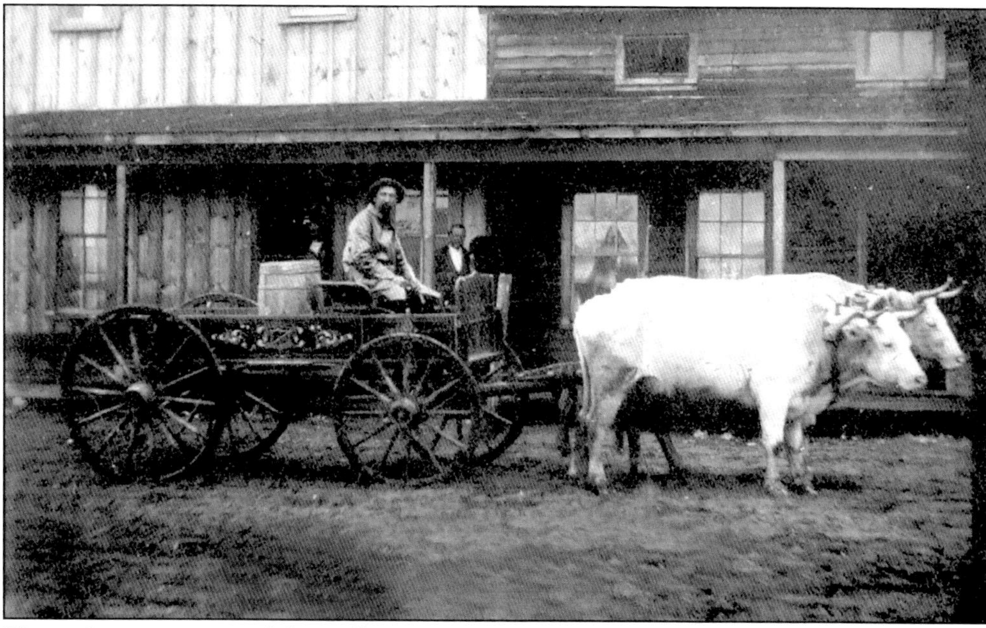

The earliest inception of the Millington Hotel also included a freight company. The photo shows one of the freight wagons driven by Jacob Staples and pulled by oxen.

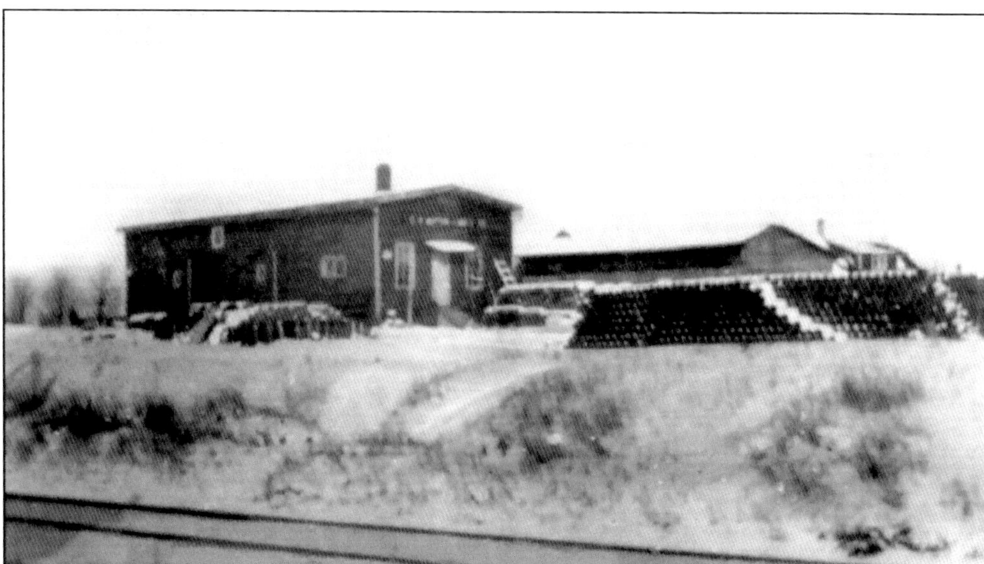

This 1920s photograph shows an early lumber company owned by C. Mutton. This is in the same area as the present Self-Serve Lumber.

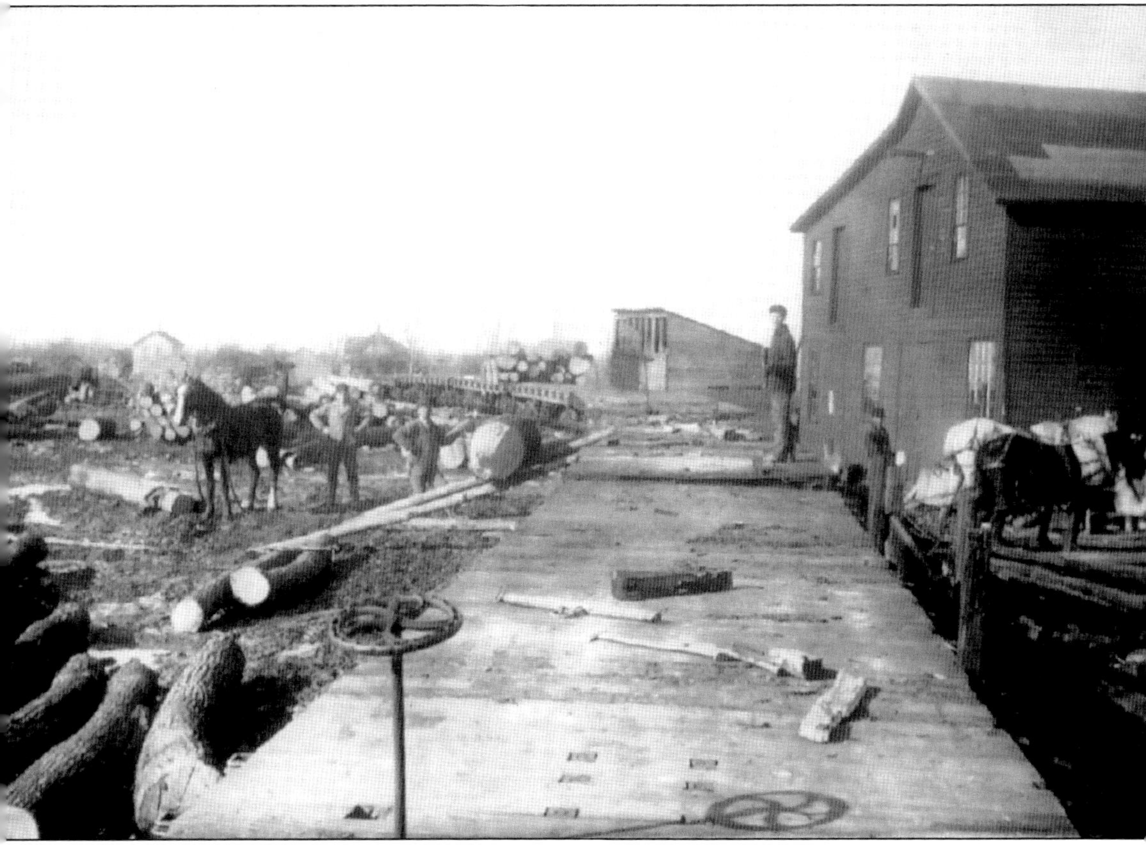

This is another early sawmill, the one owned by Roy Beach.

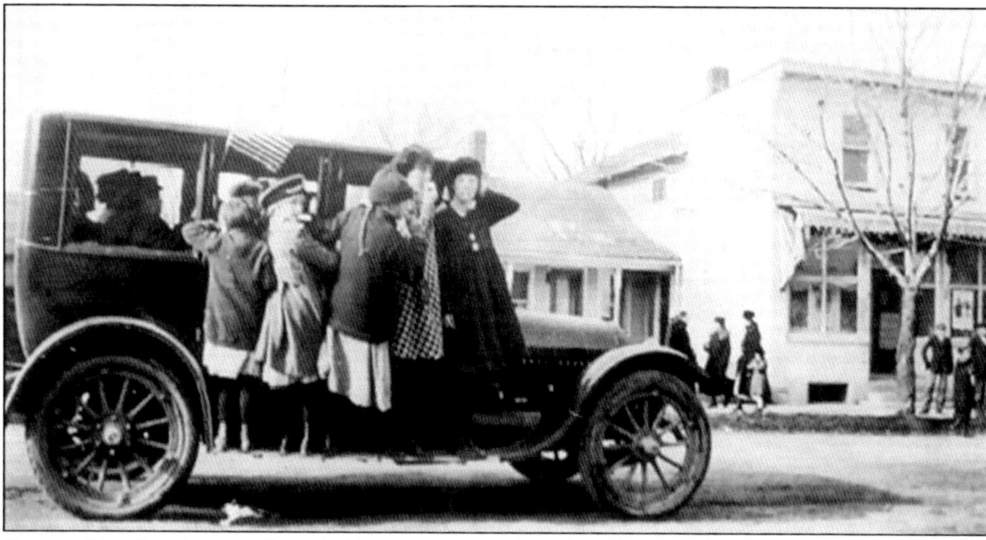

Some of the lovely township children are shown here celebrating the 1919 Armistice Day.

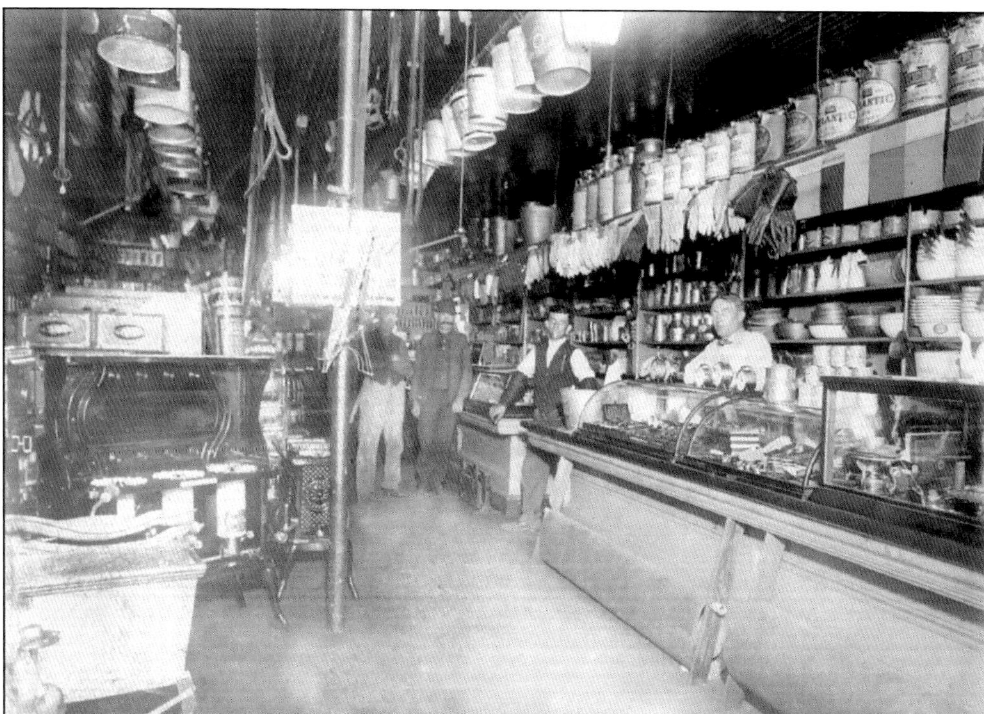

The photograph depicts Bird Hardware in 1912. Mr. Bird, the proprietor, is behind the counter at far right. The Bird family lived above the store for three years.

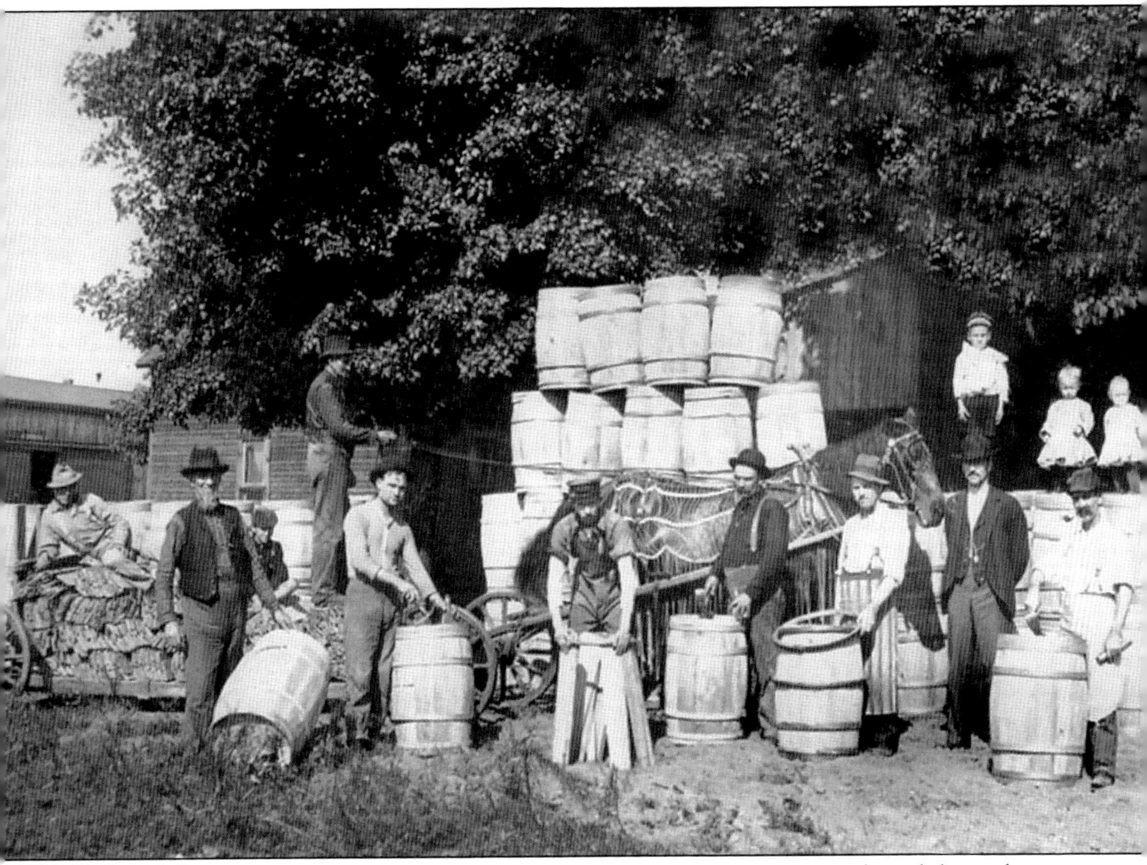

Another early business was the popular Allen Barrel Factory. Barrels were made and shipped to many destinations. The employees pictured here have paused to show off their wares.

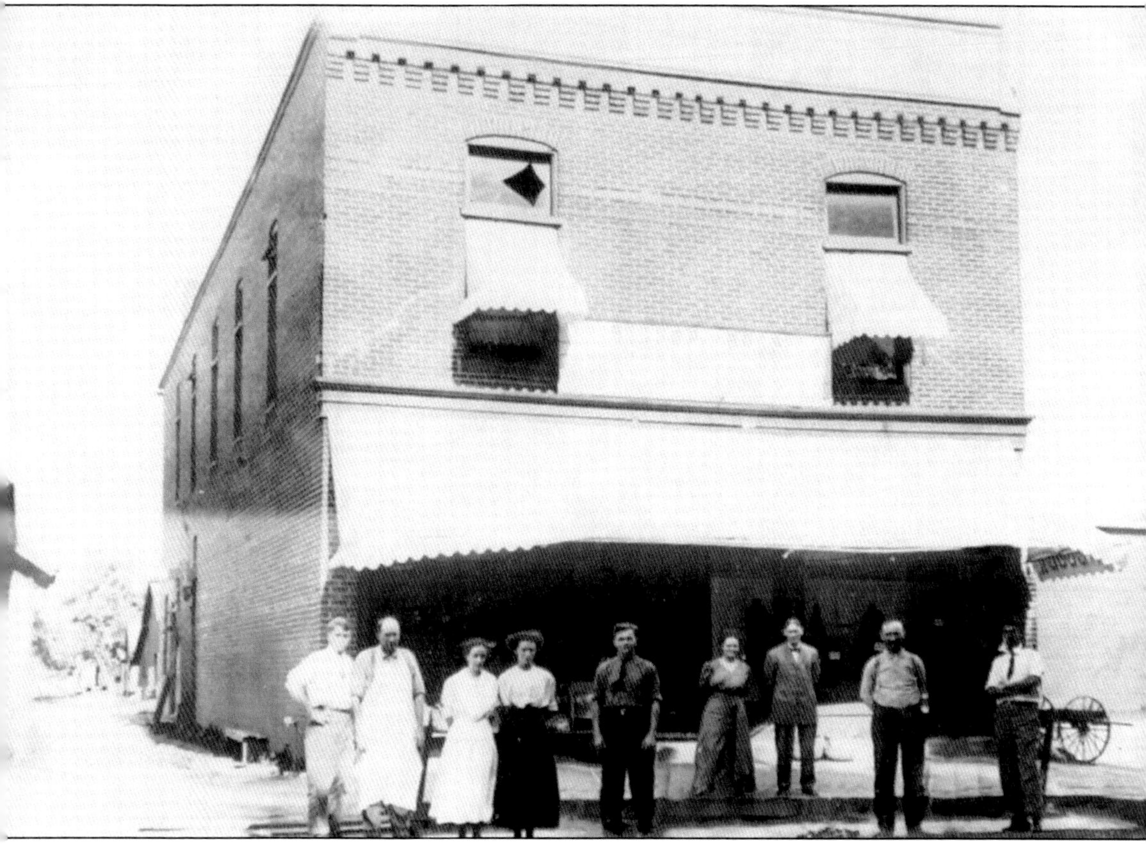

This was a variety store owned and operated by the Bishop brothers.

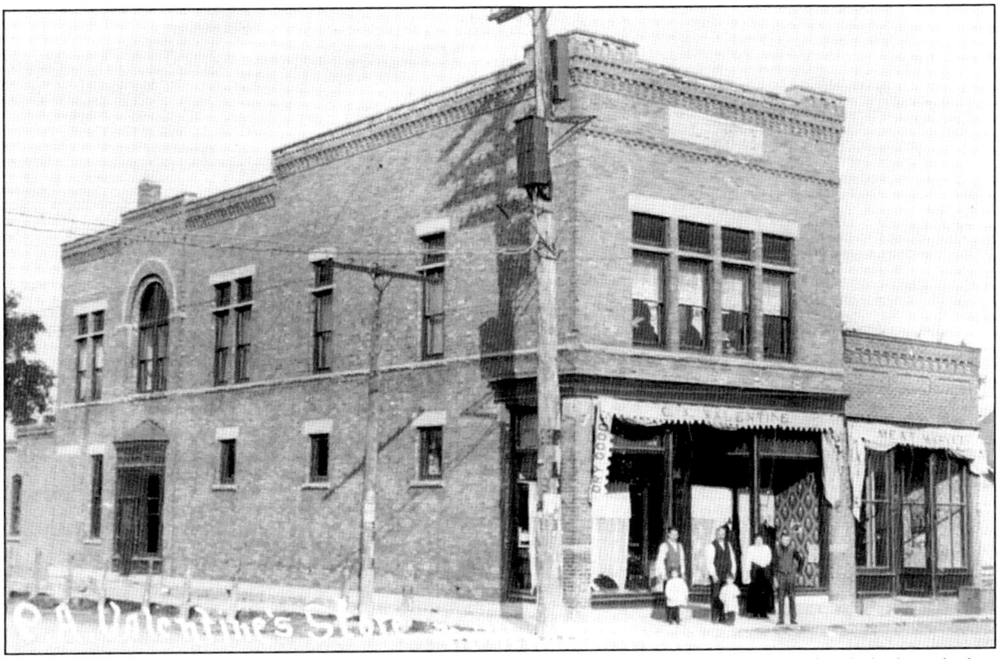


This variety store was owned by C.A. Valentine. He is shown second from the left, beside his son, Max, and two grandchildren. This building also contained the first telephone office in Millington. Note the telephone wires on the pole.

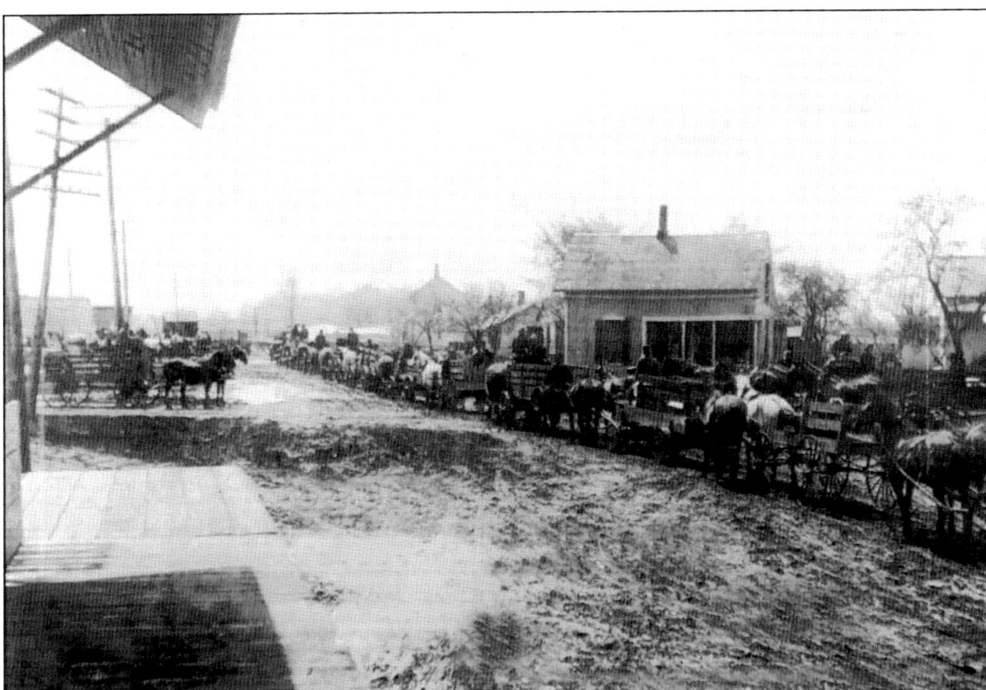

This photo shows stock day at the depot. In the early 20th century, most goods and livestock necessarily traveled by train.

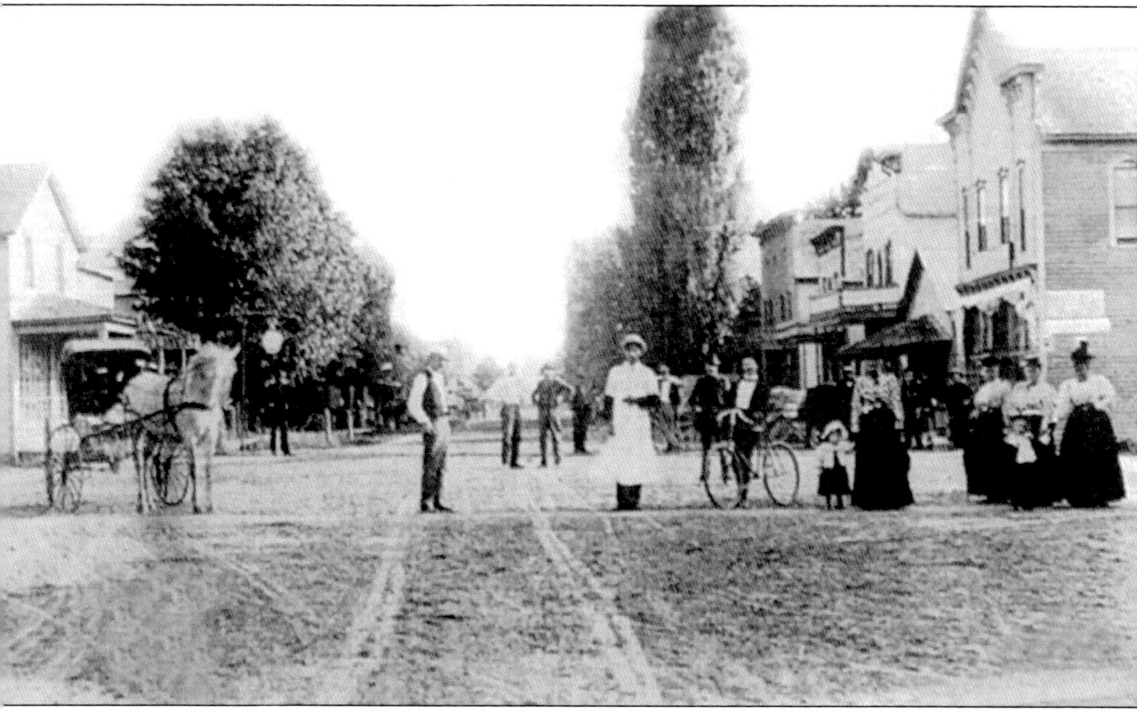

This is a view of the village looking south from State and Main Streets. Notice the lack of traffic.

# *Three*
# MILITARY

Although not officially a part of the United States until after the American Revolutionary War, thousands of soldiers from Michigan fought in the War of Independence and the War of 1812. Millington-Arbela has always answered the call to send sons and daughters.

The Civil War called and received over 96 men from the Millington-Arbela area. One of the earliest records documenting this was *Census of the State of Michigan: Soldiers, Sailors, and Marines*. Published in 1894, it shows that 26 men from the Village of Millington, 25 from Millington Township, and 45 from Arbela Township entered the Union Forces of the Civil War. Millington Township Cemetery records also show that one man, Jacob Thomas, fought with Ramsey's Company, U.S. Rifles in the War of 1812. After the close of the Civil War, many veterans from elsewhere in the country relocated and settled in Michigan.

Many of us knew and recall Millington and Arbela veterans who served in World War I. Accurate records have not been found naming all of these men, however, local cemetery records show that Orville B. Kitelinger served in both World War I and World War II.

World War II has been well-documented, with over 250 individual pictures and military records on file and open to display at the Millington-Arbela Historical Society and the Millington Township Library. The records have been collected and compiled by Ivan McPherson and Clayton Betzing, who decided to honor persons from the area who had been a part of our armed forces. Veterans were asked to loan a picture and their discharge papers. The picture was copied and as much of their military history was gained. This became part of books honoring all military personnel. To date, over 200 of these records have been compiled.

This is an example of the military records entered in our books at the museum. If your information, or that of a family member, is not found there, please contact the historical society to help complete our records. These books can be viewed at the Historical Museum or the Township Library. Names will be added as long as material is available.

Millington and Arbela will always remember the men and women who gave their lives in service.

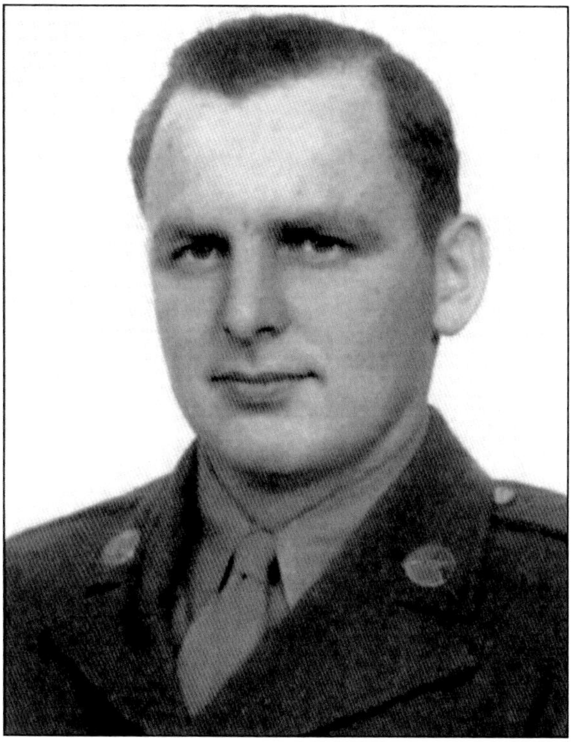

Mervin A. Cole was born June 19, 1921 in Arbela Township, where he resides to this very day. He married Violet M. Morley on October 14, 1938, and left for the service on August 17, 1944. He was sent to Camp Claiborne, Louisiana, where he trained in Engineering. He was then sent to Marion, Texas, where he underwent basic training for the Infantry. He became a member of the "Blue Infantrymen," which was the 310th Infantry. On March 7, 1945, his unit shipped out to Europe, and arrived in England March 18, 1945, and went on to Germany where the Blue Infantrymen fought in the Rhineland area. Cole was awarded EAME Theater with two Battle Stars, a Good Conduct Medal, and a Victory Medal. He was honorably discharged March 2, 1946 from Camp Atterbury, Indiana, returning to the Millington area to his wife and children. He retired after working 41 years in Frankenmuth at Universal Houdalille, and is a father, grandfather, and great-grandfather.

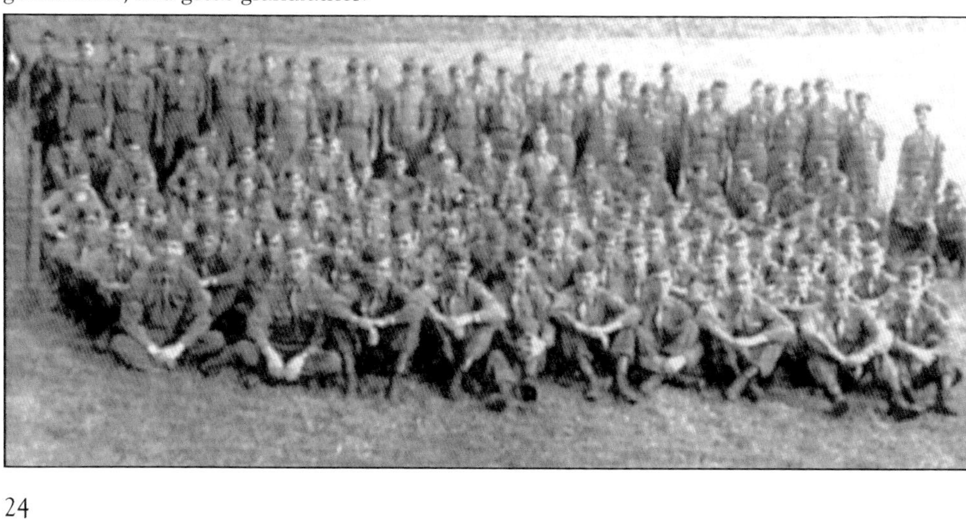

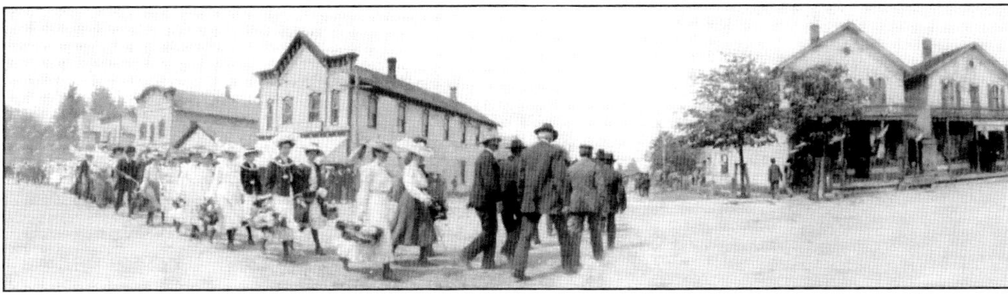

Shown here are our Civil War veterans at various events in Millington. Many of these men are buried in the Millington Township Cemetery. In the above picture, a group of residents march down the present-day M-15 and turn west on Millington Road. The photograph dates to c. 1890s. Below left, Civil War veterans pose for a picture. Below right, the Millington GAR gathers for Decoration Day in 1907.

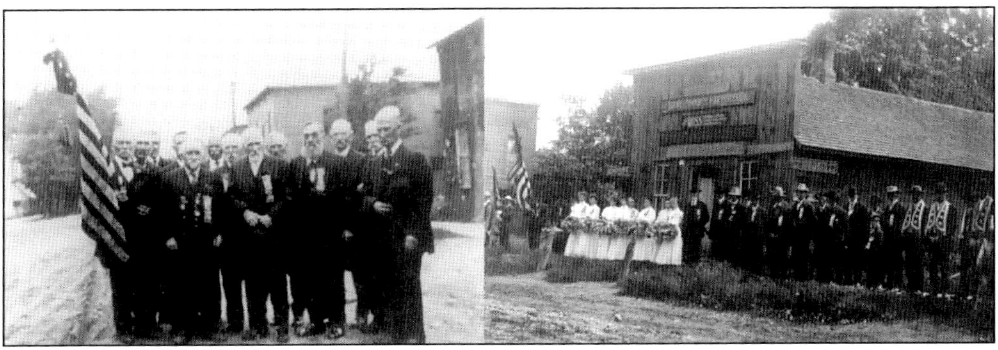

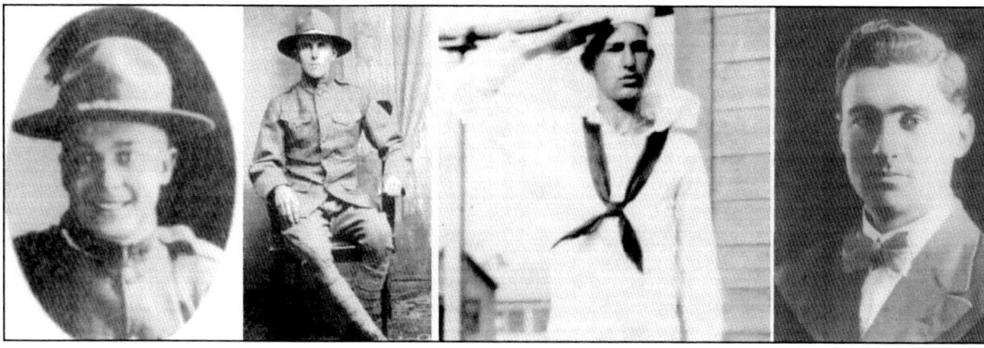

Pictured here are the Millington and Arbela men who sacrificed their lives while in service. Those who died in World War I are pictured above, from left to right: Raymond L. Allen, Ray W. Henderson, Guy Graham, and Lee F. McComb. Those who died in World War II are pictured below, from left to right: (top row) Paul R. Farnum, Nave A. Fuleihan Jr., Vernon Harvey, Raymond Higgins, and Carl J. Koshaba; (bottom row) James Lange, Roger M. Parker, Thomas Shroyer, Robert Sigelko, and Lee E. Starr.

Three Millington men were at Pearl Harbor on December 7, 1941: William "Bill" McPherson was aboard the battleship U.S.S. *California*; James Schultz was aboard the battleship U.S.S. *West Virginia*; and Max Losure was stationed at the Air Base. All three men survived the attack and served until the end of the war. The Millington area had six men from one family who served in World War II. The Gleason brothers—Francis, George, Stuart, Carl, Kenneth, and Harold—all returned home after the war. Three Millington men were prisoners of war in World War II. Roger M. Parker died in the Batan Death March in the Philippines. Lt. John Staples and Edgar Gilchrist both returned home safely as the war ended.

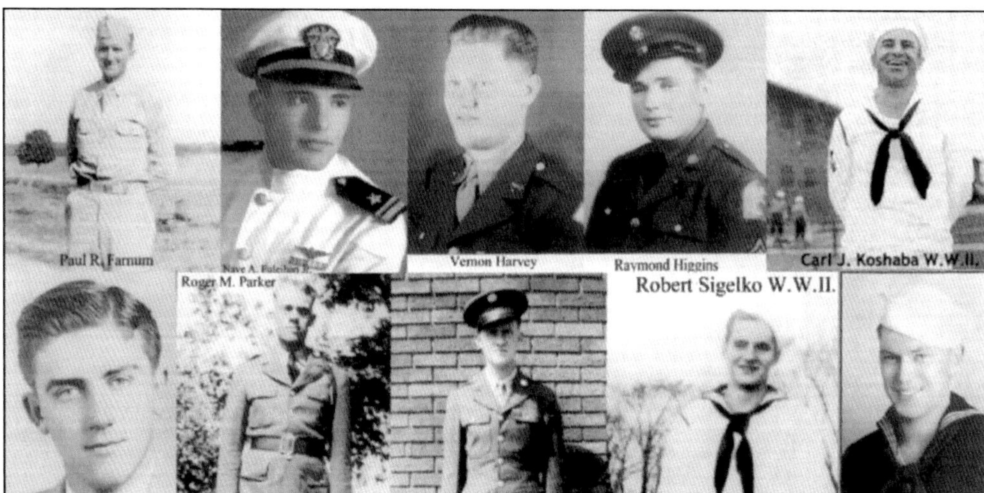

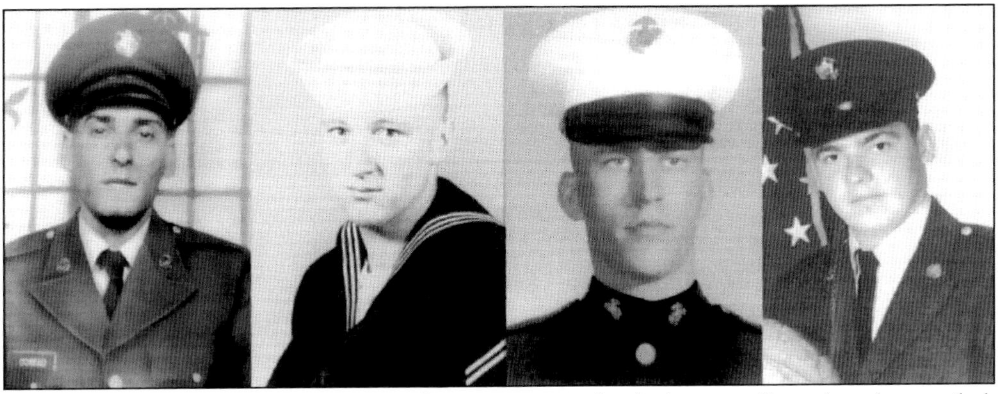

Our records of the wars in Korea and Vietnam are slowly being collected and compiled. Millington lost four young men in Vietnam. They are pictured here, from left to right, as follows: Andrew Charles Conrad Jr., Richard James Wager, Walter Martin Keene, and Donald A. Hall. The American Legion Post No. 164 is named after three of these young men. It is called the Conrad-Wager-Keene Post. In the coming years we will continue to compile the records of the brave men and women who have served and continue to serve their country, giving them the honor they so deserve.

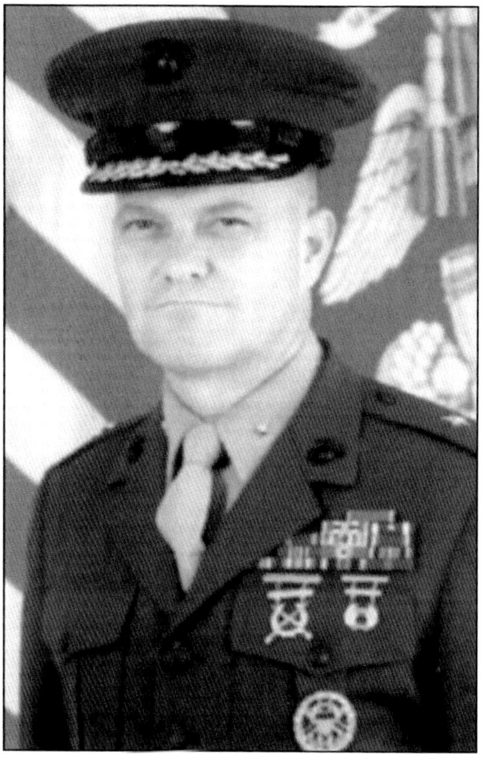 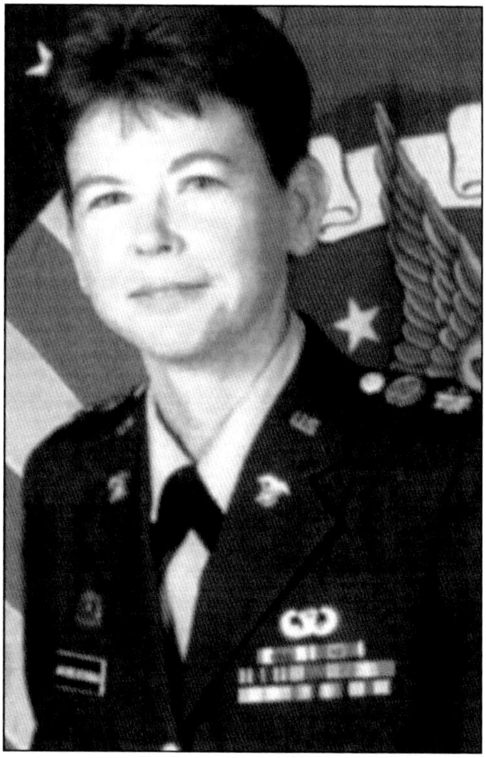

Special honors are hereby given to two exceptional people who graduated from Millington High School and went on to serve their country. They are: Brigadier General U.S. Marine Corps Michael R. Lehnert, active, who graduated with the Millington High School class of 1969; and Lieutenant Colonel U.S. Army Rhonda Jakubik-Workman, who graduated with the Millington High School class of 1973 and is now retired from the military.

# *Four*

# CHURCHES

From the earliest days of Millington, churches have formed the cornerstone of the community. The first organized church in the township was the Free Will Baptist Church, later called First Baptist Church, which formed on August 28, 1857. It was organized by Rev. Charles B. Mills at the residence of Amos Wolverton. The Native Americans who were present and participated in the service were an interesting part of this first church. Before the erection of the first church on Center Street, the meetings were usually held at the old school. In 1877, plans were made for the erection of a place of worship; this building was completed and first used in March of 1880. Changes were made throughout the years, and 100 years later in March of 1980, part of the congregation decided to break ties with the American Baptist Church and relocated to 4009 E. Millington under the leadership of Pastor Ron Scott. The others chose to remain in the original church, which is now called Millington Baptist Church. They have Pastor James Sheldrake as their leader.

The Methodist Church was organized in 1864. Previously, circuit riders went from place to place, usually on horseback, preaching. One of the first was Henry Carlson, who was supposed to receive $301 annually but actually received $76.71. In 1872, a lot was donated for a church. The cornerstone was laid on June 7, 1875. Services were first held on August 4, 1876. Prior to this, services were held in the log schoolhouse on the Lavone Titsworth farm, in the lumber camps, and in private homes. The old church, after being used for 24 years, was sold to the Macabees for $175. The new church was built and dedicated in 1899. The church continued to grow and mature, sending quite a number of its people into the ministry. In 1968, because of the unification of the EUB and Methodist churches, the name was changed to the United Methodist Church. Under the leadership of several fine pastors, the congregation continued to grow. The decision was made to relocate, and a beautiful new church was constructed and opened one mile south of Millington on August 12, 1979, with plenty of growing space. The current leader is Pastor Drew Hart.

The first Lutheran services were held in 1874 by Rev. J. Karres of Hadley after a small band of Lutherans arrived in the Millington area. Later, services were held in an old schoolhouse. In 1897, the group agreed to buy land for a future church building. Organizational meetings were held and the name St. Paul's was selected. After further planning, a church was built and dedicated on August 21, 1898, under its first resident pastor, Rev. G.M. Zucker. Several pastors served during the early years. On May 16, 1937, Pastor Hugo Ferber began a long and fruitful ministry. The original church was expanded and modernized. The day school was enlarged and ultimately consolidated into a new school at the site of the church. During his 34 years of ministry, the church and school continued to grow under Pastor Ferber's leadership, and in time included a complete new sanctuary complex and additional educational facilities. The current leaders are Pastor James Bruner and Pastor Tim Bickel. Elaine (Petzold) Bickel, a Millington native, is the school principal.

The Church of the Nazarene dates its beginnings to 1919 when some tent meetings were held. The meetings resulted in 30 charter members who organized the present church. For several years the congregation worshipped in buildings that were available to be rented. In 1939, the church began at its present location. People gave enthusiastically and attendance grew. The building was altered and enlarged several times. The church continues to thrive and grow and is now under the leadership of Pastor Ed Kile.

In the year 1879, the church at Watertown was erected and dedicated. It was served by the Millington pastor for many years. In about 1952, the church building was badly damaged by fire. After standing vacant for several years, Rev. Hollings from Saginaw sold his life insurance policy to help rebuild and restore the church to make it usable again. With the new congregation's hard work and dedication, they ended up with a new building. The church was called Pilgrim Holiness for a number of years, and later became Watertown Center Bible Church. It is presently very active and grows under the leadership of Pastor Bert Hilborn.

The Arbela United Methodist Church first met in area homes in the late 1800s, then in the Arbela Township Hall. In 1900, Rev. B. Allen dedicated the original church building. This building later burned and only the pulpit and Bible were saved. A new church, the Methodist Episcopal Church, was built at the cost of $2,314.21. It was on a charge with Tuscola with Rev. H.A. Hudgins as pastor, and became the center of community events. In the 1950s, Arbela joined with Millington, as Tuscola wanted to be a community church on its own. The Arbela church almost closed in the 1960s, but was then chosen "Church of the Year" and managed to add new members, remodel, and redecorate, including the addition of bathrooms and a well. In January of 1996, the Arbela church became the "independent" of sister churches when the Millington church chose to support a full-time pastor. They continue to grow and their leader is Herb Wheelock.

West Forest United Methodist Church was first organized in 1885 on the Otisville circuit. From 1925 to 1933 it was on the Millington circuit. It is currently on the Otter Lake circuit and is known for miles around for the delicious Buffalo Bar-B-Ques, originally begun in 1979 by farmer Sherwood Smith. Smith donated a buffalo as a means of restoring and supporting their little country church. They serve hundred of meals each year around the first Saturday in September. The current pastor is Bill McKown.

The first service of the Mennonite Gospel Mission was held in August of 1938. The work progressed as Bibles and Bible story books were distributed during the visitation week. In the early 1940s, Orrie Kauffman from Pigeon was charged with the work and drove from Pigeon for services in a schoolhouse. A new meeting house was built in 1950 with nine members at that time. Emery Helmuth was called from Minnesota in 1972. When he retired in 1991, Tom Berlin was installed as pastor. He passed away suddenly while vacationing in Montana on July 7, 2000. Roger Hazen was called from Nebraska and is the current pastor.

In 1991, God was speaking to Brian and Sharon Pfeiffer about planting a "Full Gospel" church in Millington. After looking at various options for a meeting place, it was determined that this church would be started as a "home fellowship" in their house at 4785 West Main Street. In August of 1991, Sharon and Brian were licensed as Ministers of the Gospel by Gospel Crusade, Inc. of Bradenton, Florida. They applied for and received Articles of Incorporation from the State of Michigan on March 11, 1992. The church is an independent, Full Gospel (Pentecostal) church. A large stone was placed in their front yard as a symbol of the cornerstone of their faith, Jesus Christ. It is now called Cornerstone Full Gospel Fellowship. That stone remains to this day.

The Elkhorn Church of God began as a small country church on the corner of Vassar and Swaffer Road with about 25 members. After remodeling and renovating their little church, it burned. The congregation rented, and then bought the old Methodist church, which the United Methodists vacated when they moved to a new church building in 1979. The Elkhorn Church of God continued to grow, outgrew their space, and met in the school for a time while they built a complete new complex on Barnes Road one mile south of town. They continued to grow and now have one of the largest congregations in Millington under the leadership of Pastor Mike Cottrell.

Community Baptist Church was organized in the 1960s. They began by building a small church, which has undergone many additions since. Their congregation of about 130 come from a wide area. They have a bus ministry and are helping to support 31 missionaries. Their leader is Pastor James Wertz.

The First Baptist Church was originally located on Center Street. The church (inset), broke away in 1990 and moved to 4009 E. Millington Road.

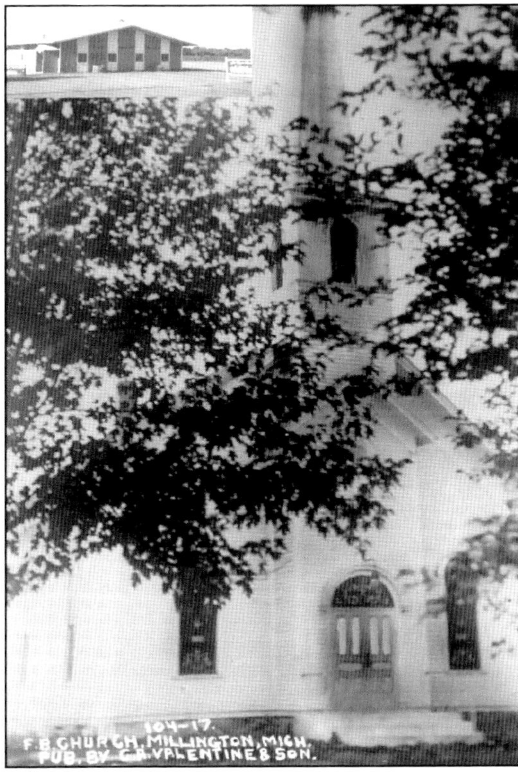


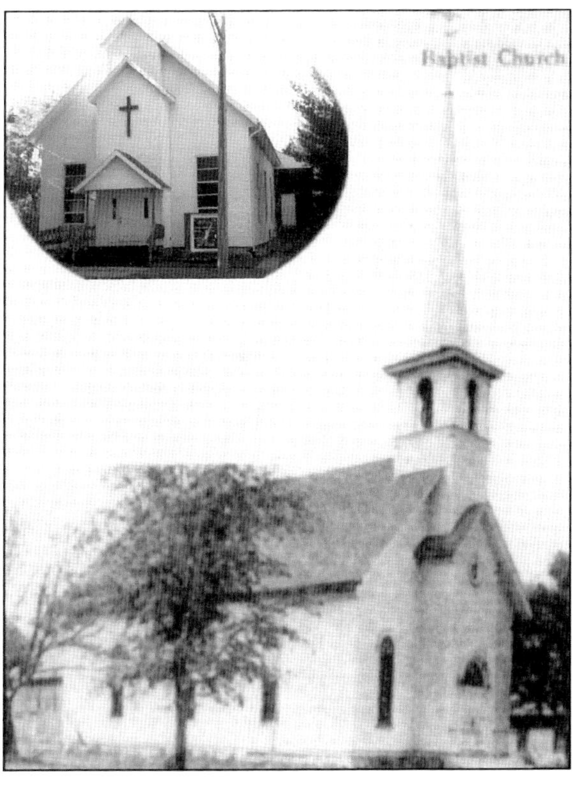


This is Millington Baptist Church, located on Center Street just east of State Street.

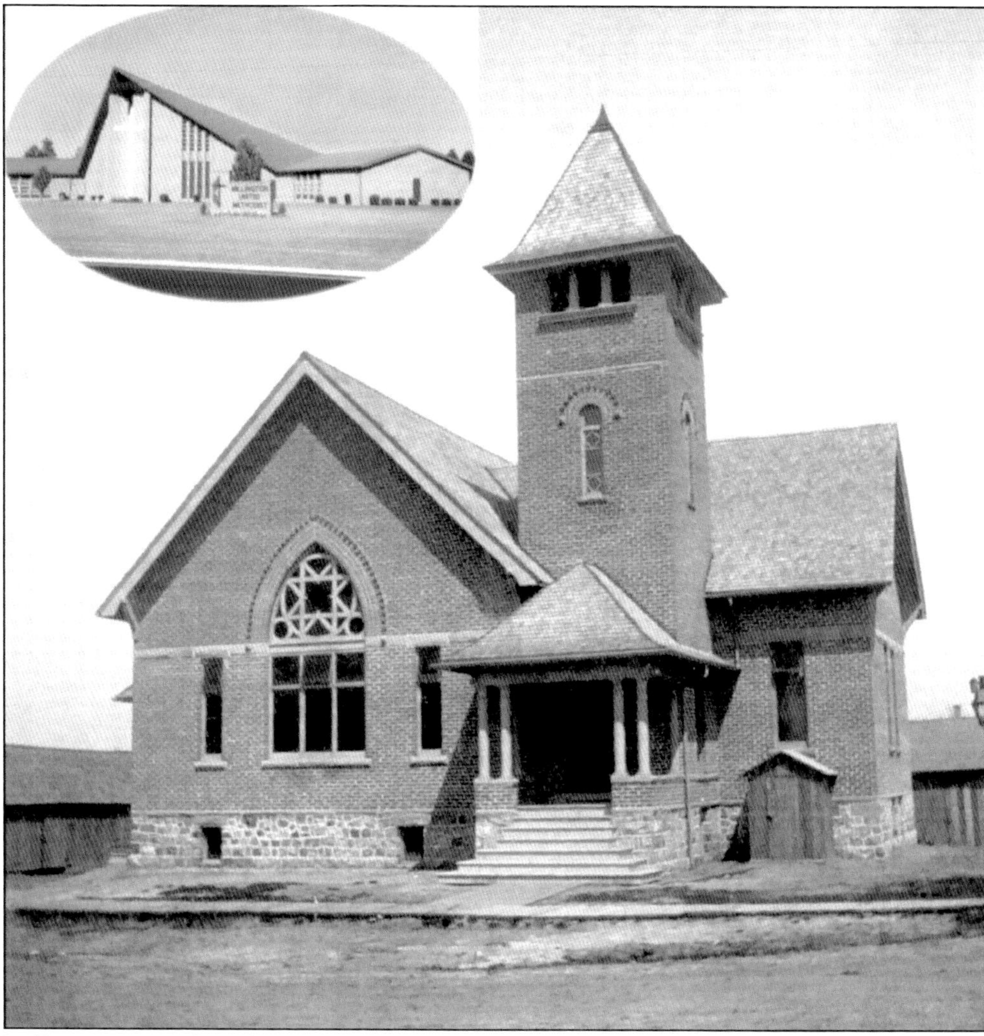

Millington United Methodist Church was originally located at Main and Blocher Streets. It is now located at the corner of M-15 and Barnes Road.

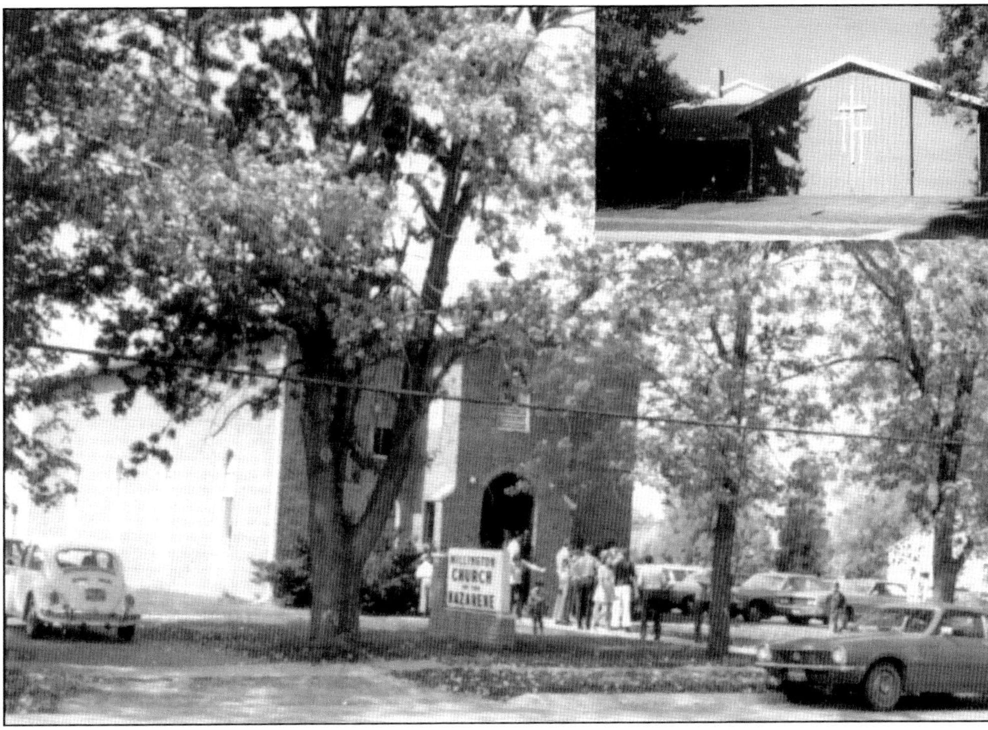


Pictured here is Millington Church of the Nazarene located on South State Street.

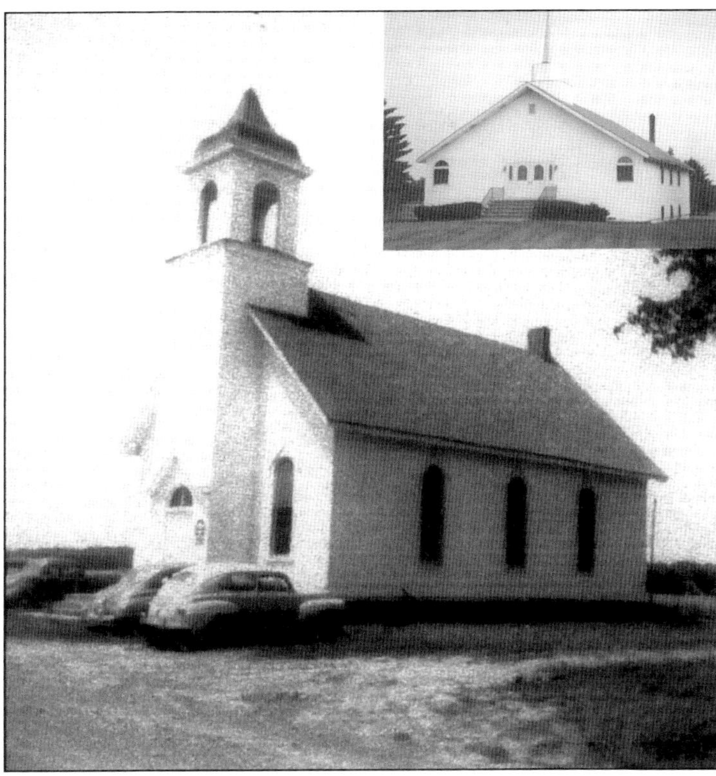

This is Watertown Center Bible Church, located on Millington Road at Center Road.

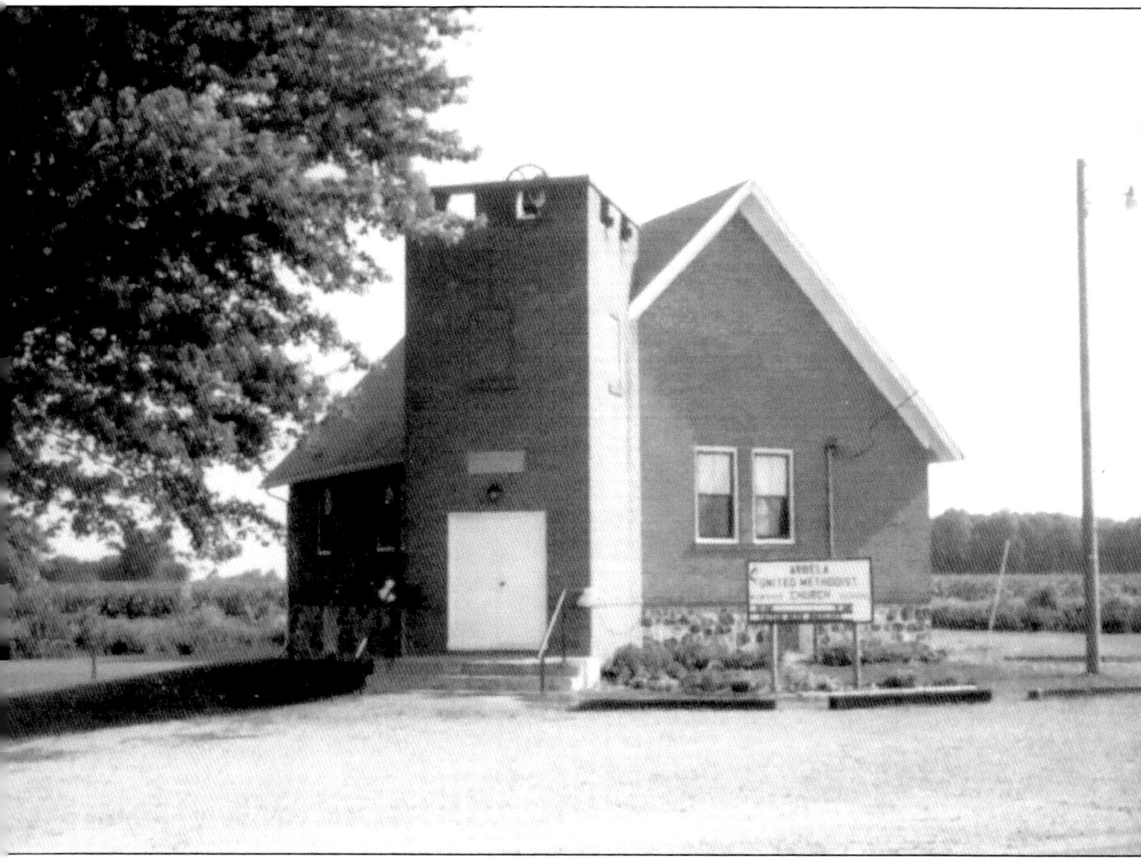


Arbela United Methodist Church is located at the corner of Barnes and Barkley Roads.

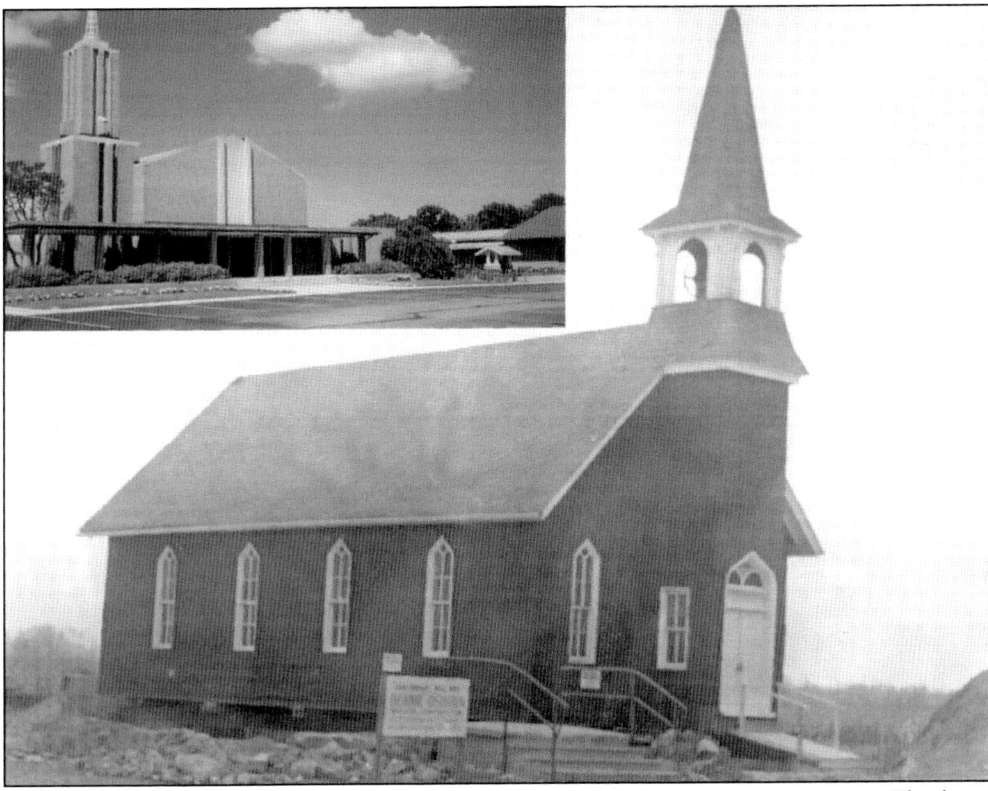

St. Paul's Lutheran Church is shown here at his location on West Center Street. The latest church is shown in inset.

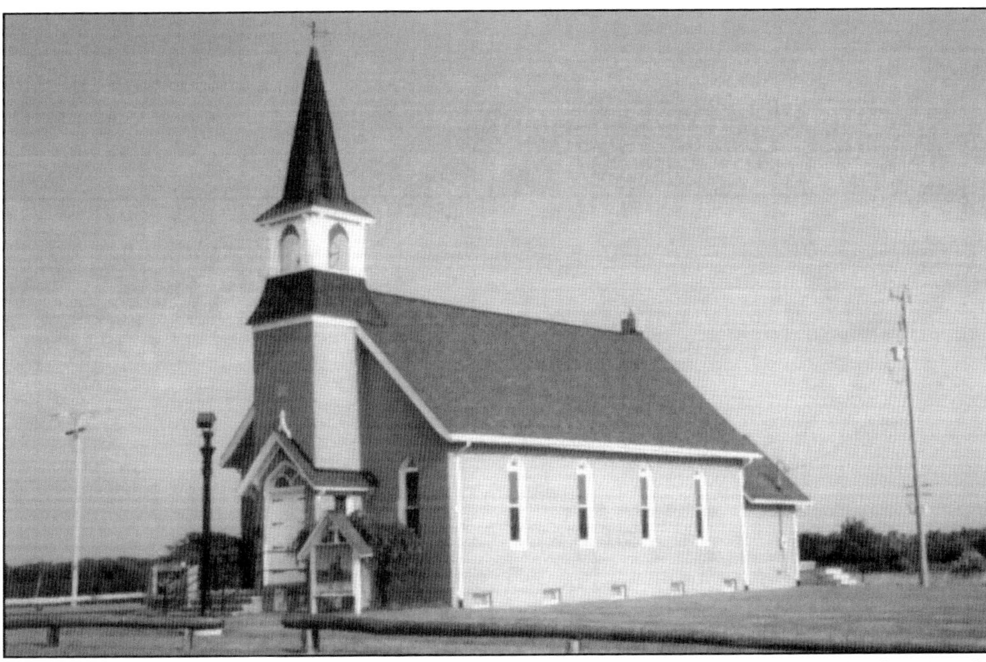

This is West Forest United Methodist Church, located on Farrand Road west of Belsay Road.

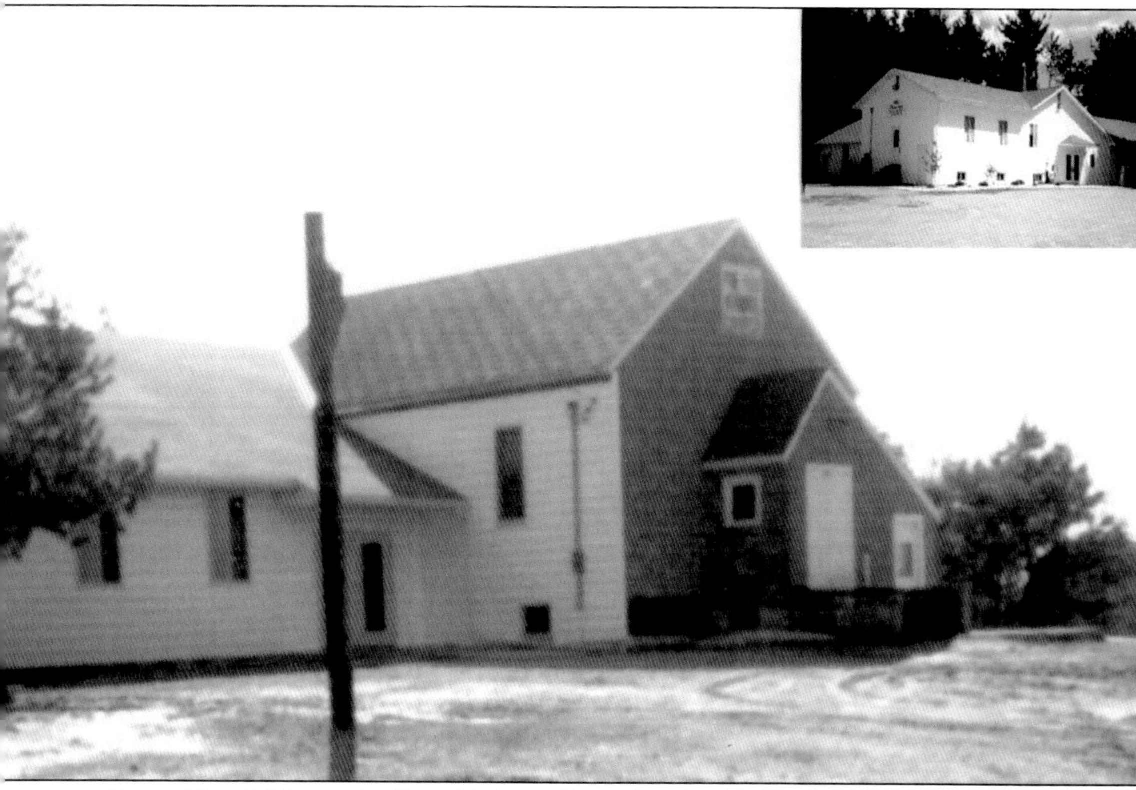

Pictured here is Mennonite Gospel Mission, located on Swaffer Road east of M-15. The current church is shown in inset.

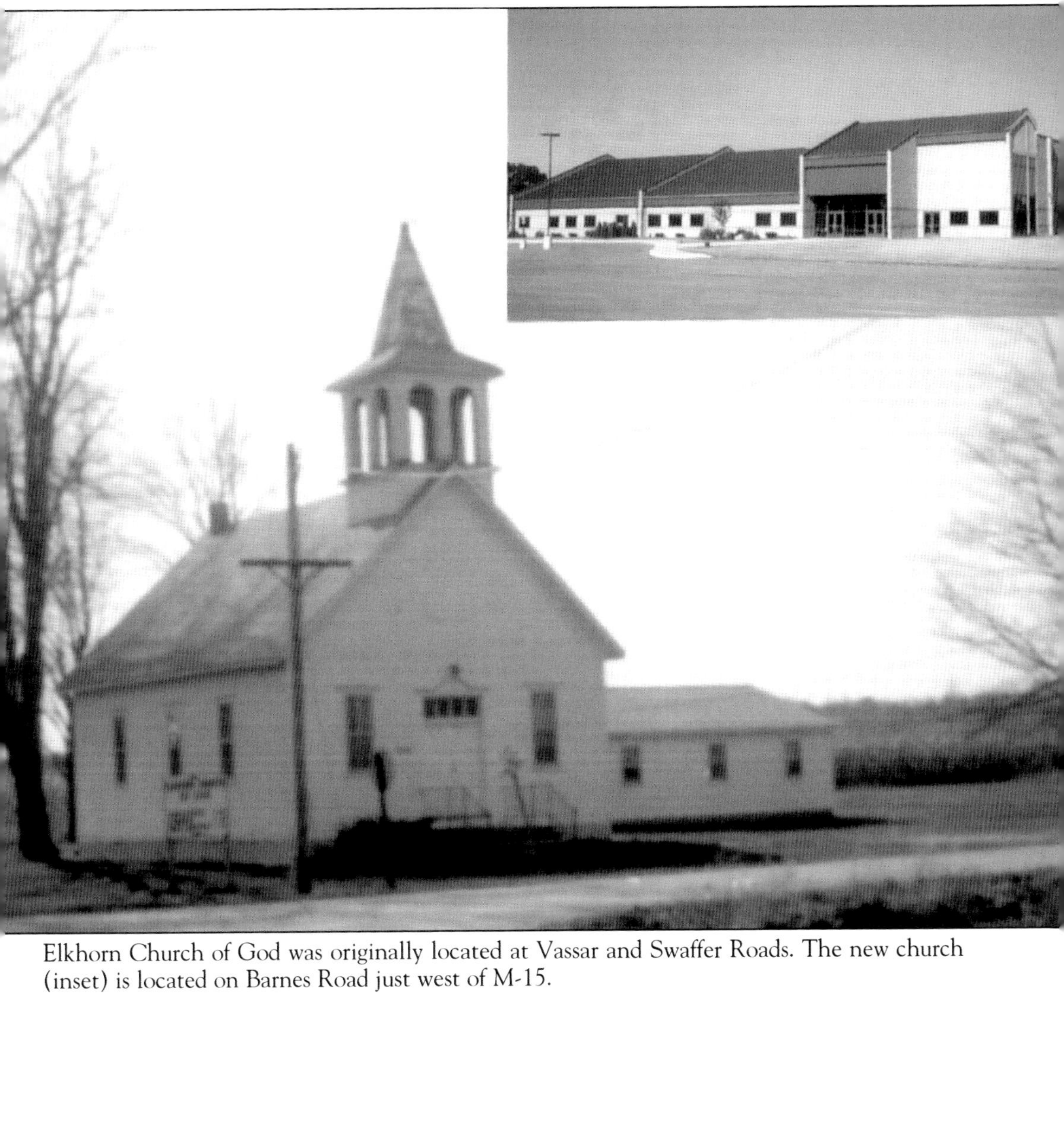

Elkhorn Church of God was originally located at Vassar and Swaffer Roads. The new church (inset) is located on Barnes Road just west of M-15.

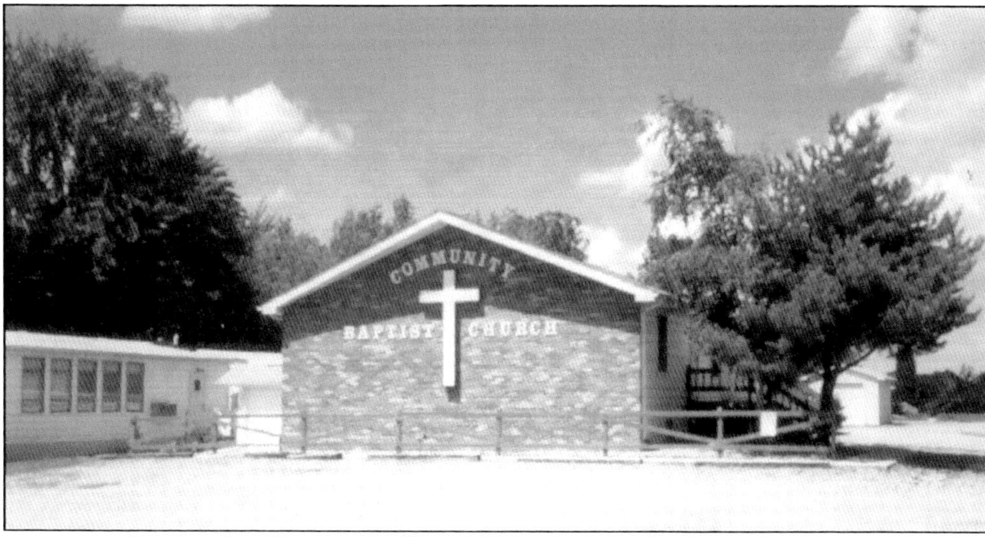

Community Baptist Church is pictured here. It is located on Birch Run road west of Belsay Road.

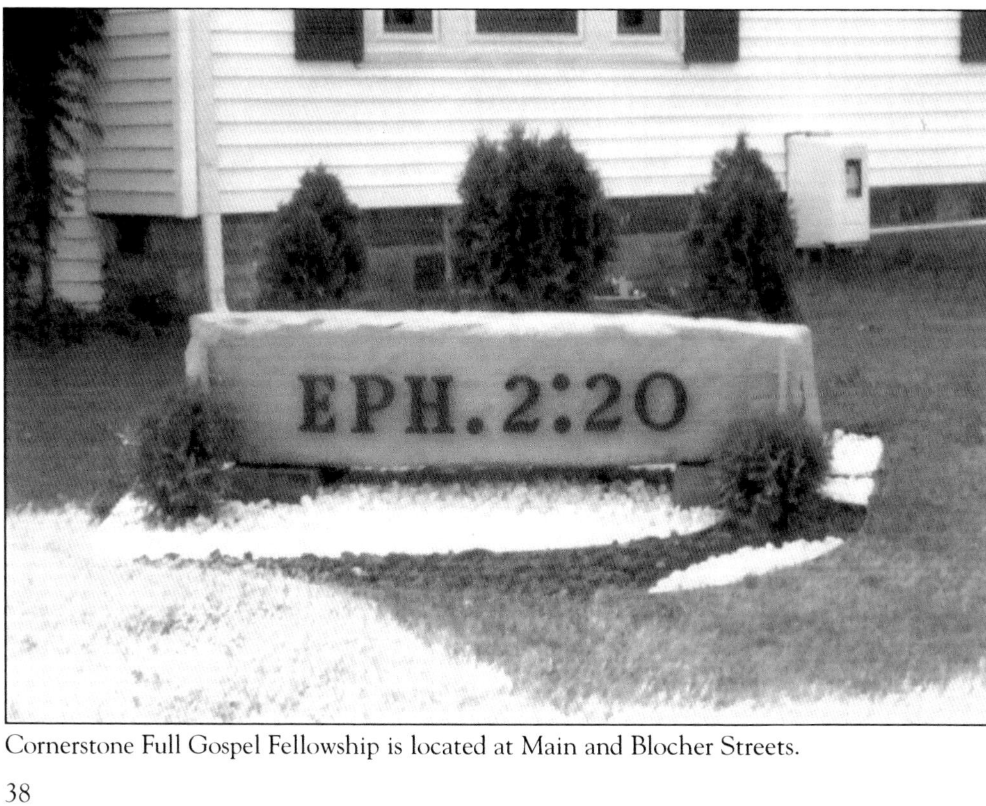

Cornerstone Full Gospel Fellowship is located at Main and Blocher Streets.

# *Five*

# SCHOOLS

The little one-room country schools were the foundation of our life in early America. They dotted the countryside, being placed strategically so that no child was required to walk more than two and one-half miles by state law. In the Millington-Arbela area there wee 20 little country schools. There were not many people from our early rural community who were not a part of a one-room country school with one teacher teaching eight or nine grades. Some schools were so small that they had eight to 12 students, and some had over 50. The average was between 25 and 35.

Not only was the school a place of learning, but the hub of the community. Many of our early churches had their beginnings in country schools. All social events were held there as well.

Many of the buildings were quite primitive. They operated many years before electricity or running water. Most had a little building in a back corner of the school. How exciting it was when chemical toilets were installed in the cloak rooms, although this provided less space for lunches and coats. The front of each schoolroom was quite similar with large pictures of George Washington and Abraham Lincoln on either side of a Regulator clock. (They were not Democrats or Republicans—just good Americans!) There were blackboards across the front and some part way down the sides of the room. A large set of maps was mounted above the chalkboard and ABCs in script across the front. Penmanship was important!

After morning openings, including the salute to the flag, the teachers would call up each class starting with the youngest. There was no time wasted between classes. As she dismissed a class, she would say with a "teacherly" tone of voice, "Next class, rise and pass." And so it went until recess which lasted 15 minutes. Then the same process was repeated for arithmetic, which lasted until noon. After the first three grades were dismissed at 2:30, there was more time for the older grades whose classes were sometimes combined to conserve time. The older students had been studying more or less and on their own until this point in the day, but time never dragged. There was a lot of ground to cover in an hour and 15 minutes. Then school was over for the day and most students had to hurry home to do chores, carry in wood and water, and sometimes do homework—and hurry to bed to repeat the process the next day.

Some schools had what they called "Potato Digging Vacation" if enough families had enough potatoes to be dug and needed their children's help. Then school was over for the day and most students had to hurry home to do chores, carry in wood and water, and sometimes do homework—and hurry to bed to repeat the process the next day.

Columbus Day was honored somewhat, as all students learned that Columbus sailed the ocean blue in 1492 and discovered America on October 12 of that year.

Some schools had what they called "Potato Digging Vacation" if enough families had enough potatoes to be dug and needed their children's help. If there were not enough farmers who needed their children's help, school remained in session, but the children who were needed received excused absences. Virginia Jensen remembers hearing the school bell ring across the fields and feeling smug that she didn't have to be there. She doesn't remember making up any work, either, but it wasn't all fun. Picking up potatoes was back-breaking work and by the time the potatoes were all harvested the children were ready to go back to school. They felt good about being able to share in this important family event and see how proud the fathers were when all the potatoes were stored clear up to the rafters in the basement under each house.

Halloween was a big event in most schools. Every student came up with some sort of costume, all homemade—never bought—except for maybe a mask. Most costumes came from rummaging through Mom's rag bag and old clothes. Some moms helped design the costumes, but most kids were on their own. Mothers had enough to do around the farm. Classes were held until noon on Halloween, then after a hurried lunch, everyone dressed in their costumes and paraded in front of the pleased and amused teacher whose job it was to identify each student. They felt pretty good about stumping the teacher. Then games of all sorts were played, and finally, the goodies—fudge, candy of all kinds, and popcorn were passed out, sometimes cider and donuts if apples happened to be available in the neighborhood.

Christmas season was the biggest, most important time of the school year. Soon after Thanksgiving, the teacher began giving out parts for plays, recitations for the little folks, and songs for different groups. As it got nearer to Christmas, more time was spent on practicing and less on classes. Then, the week before Christmas, some fathers brought some long boards and made a makeshift stage in front of the school. They also strung strong wires across the room and some shorter wires at right angles to create dressing rooms. The teacher asked each family who could lend a large white sheet to be used as a stage curtain. After much practice and hard work, the big night arrived. The whole community came and squeezed into all the seats and the program began. Each parent and grandparent listened intently as each child, large or small, carried out what they had worked so long and hard for. After singing "Up on the Housetop," "Jingle Bells," "Joy to the World," and many others, and just as applause filled the room at the end of another successful Christmas program, bells could be heard out in the entryway. Excitement spread as Santa Claus entered with a jolly Ho Ho Ho. He had a sack of candy for every child in his big pack and a "Merry Christmas" for everyone.

Lincoln and Washington's birthdays were properly observed, not by a day off, but by the teacher or some of the students studying up on these great men and giving some sort of interesting report to the students.

Sometimes Valentine's Day was celebrated by inviting all the parents for a potluck lunch. Sometimes the events were only attended by students, but they were always fun with lots of treats, candy, and valentines, of course. Not long after Valentine's Day, Easter break was sometimes observed by a half day off to commemorate Good Friday.

The Tuscola County School Commissioner, Ben McComb, served from 1914 until his retirement on January 1, 1949. A few times a year, he would just slip into a seat in the back of the classroom. He often went unnoticed for a few minutes. Then someone would see him and motion to the teacher if she had not already seen him. Within a few minutes, the teacher would introduce him to the students and ask him if he would like to say a few words. He always shared a few words of wisdom, then went on his way to the next school. McComb is remembered as a grand old gentleman highly revered and respected in the whole county, and born in the Millington community.

Everyone walked to school every day no matter how cold or how deep the snow, and often the school was so cold when they arrived that the students were allowed to leave on their coats and snow pants. (Girls didn't wear long pants in those days—only long stockings with their long underwear.) Ink often froze in the bottles and inkwells, and this was before ballpoint pens, so it was back to the pencils until the ink thawed out.

After a long hard winter, everyone welcomed spring and warm weather. Often there was a woods near enough to the school that the teacher would allow anyone who wished to go pick wildflowers during the noon hour. The teacher often went, too, and the woods smelled fresh and clean after the long winter. Softball became a popular activity again for both boys and girls. The older students sometimes invited a neighboring school over for a game and vice versa.

Even when it neared the end of the school year, there was no let up in learning. Classes were held every day with much reviewing, and the teacher stressed the importance of trying to remember what had been learned all year.

Then came the big day called "The Last Day of School." All the desks had been cleaned out and everything was put in order for the summer. Before the parents arrived, the teacher passed out all the report cards, which had been filled out stating that the student had competed the current grade and had been promoted to the next grade. There were always some cheers and excited claims of, "I passed, I passed"—and always a few moans and sighs and "I didn't think I would." When parents arrived they had picnic baskets full of delicious farm-prepared food. After a bountiful meal and lots of happy conversation, someone suggested it was time for the annual ballgame in which kids played against parents. Too soon, the game was over, the picnic baskets re-packed, and everything was put in order for another year. And none too soon. Farmers had already begun the spring work and were anxiously awaiting school to be let out, as they needed all the help they could get from the kids. The kids were just as anxious to be free from school until school rolled around the next fall.

Gradually, as electricity spread across the nation, living conditions improved. Electric lights and indoor plumbing were added to schools and homes. Life became easier on farms and in rural areas. About this time, someone got the bright idea for school consolidation. Roads improved, school buses were introduced, town schools were remodeled, added to, and rebuilt so that by the 1950s and 1960s, the country schools had completely disappeared from our lives. Some schools were made into homes, some used by farmers for storing hay, and some were just left to the elements to disappear. Progress? I wonder!

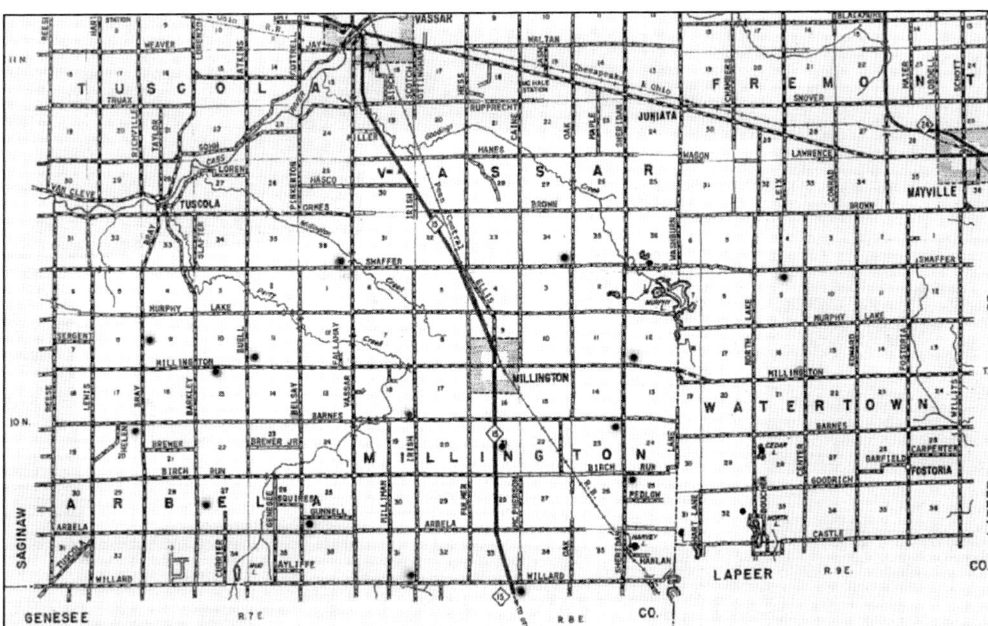


The dots on this map show the locations of early schools in the Millington-Arbela area.

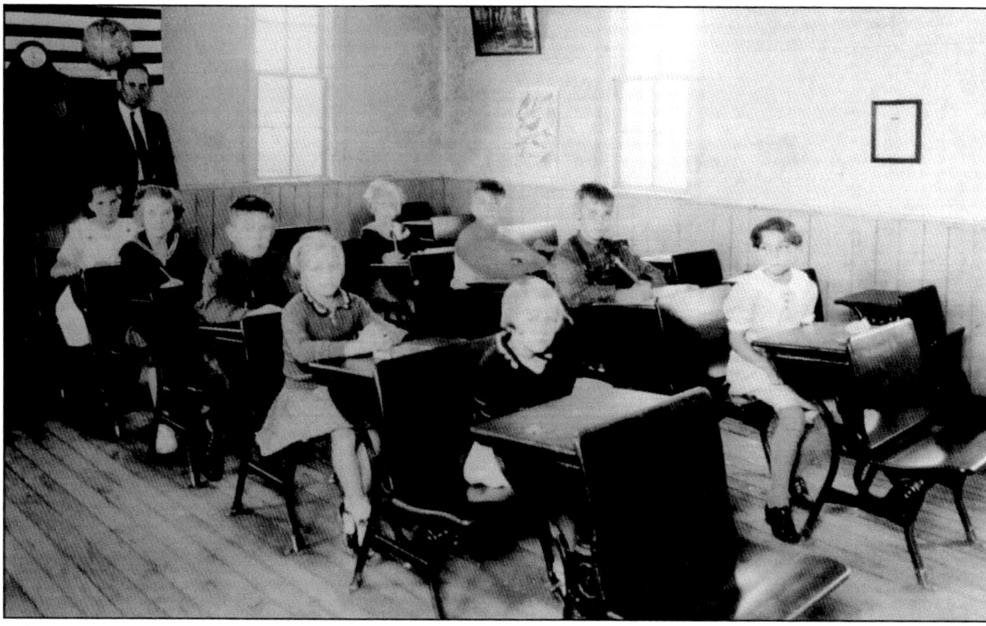

The Case School, also known as Lakeview School, was located at Sheridan and Birch Run Roads. Pictured from left to right are as follows: (top row) Mr. Parish (teacher), Mary Husted, Norma Osborn, Ted Draper (son of Jacob), Myrna Parish, and Elizabeth Parish; (bottom row) Gerine Parish, Max Osborn, Harold Draper (son of Clarence), and Martha Husted.

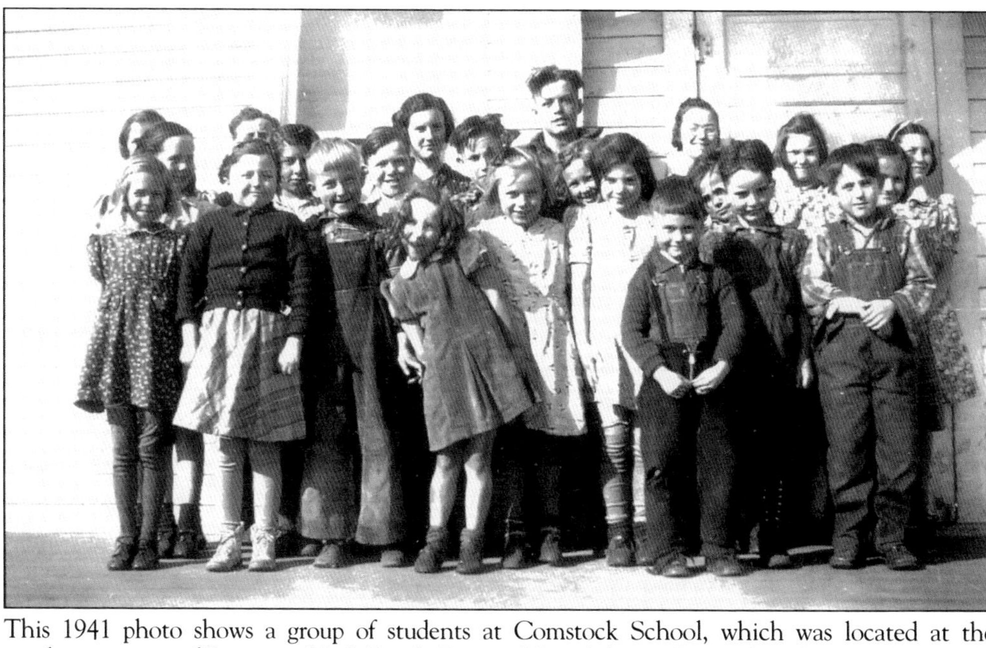

This 1941 photo shows a group of students at Comstock School, which was located at the northwest corner of Barnes and Irish Roads. Pictured from left to right are the following: (back row) Duane Mitchell, Lela Kurpsel, Ben Roberts, Vera Kurpsel, Florence Green, and Ruth Daenzer; (middle row) Roberta Mitchell, Joyce Proctor, L.J. Winiarski, Jerry Foley, Ardath Smith, Joyce Green, and Edna Kurpsel; (front row) Peggy Sherman, Joyce Wilson, Jarrett Smith, Mary Winiarski, Niola Kitelinger, Clarence Daenzeer, Ray Green, Gordon Foley, and Lillian Green.

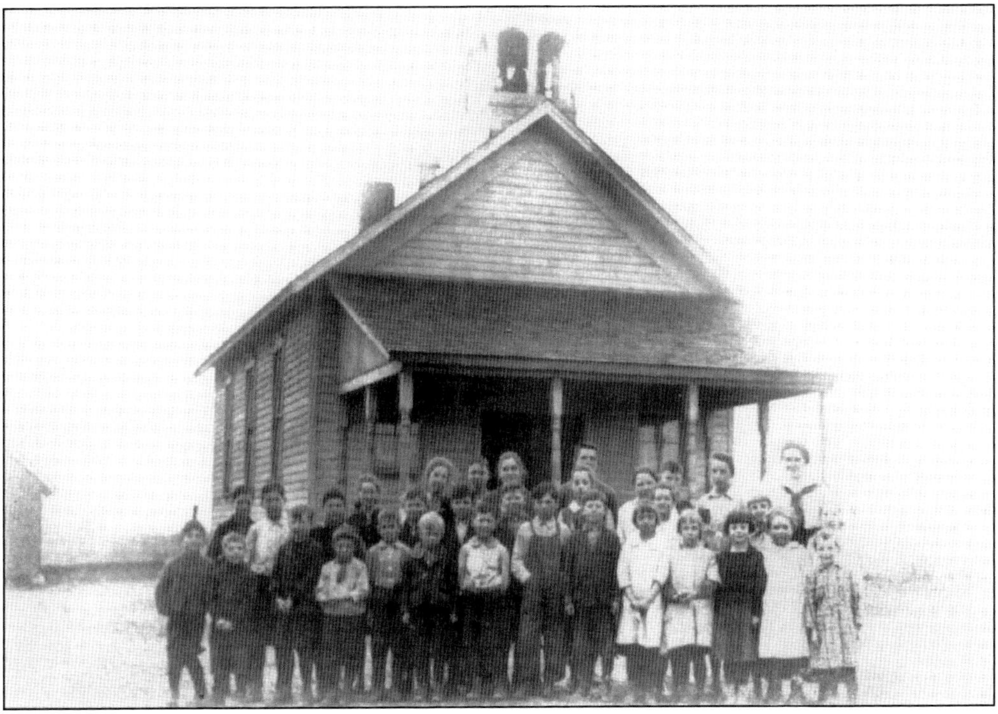

The Delmar School was located four miles south of Millington on the south side of Willard Road, east of M-15.

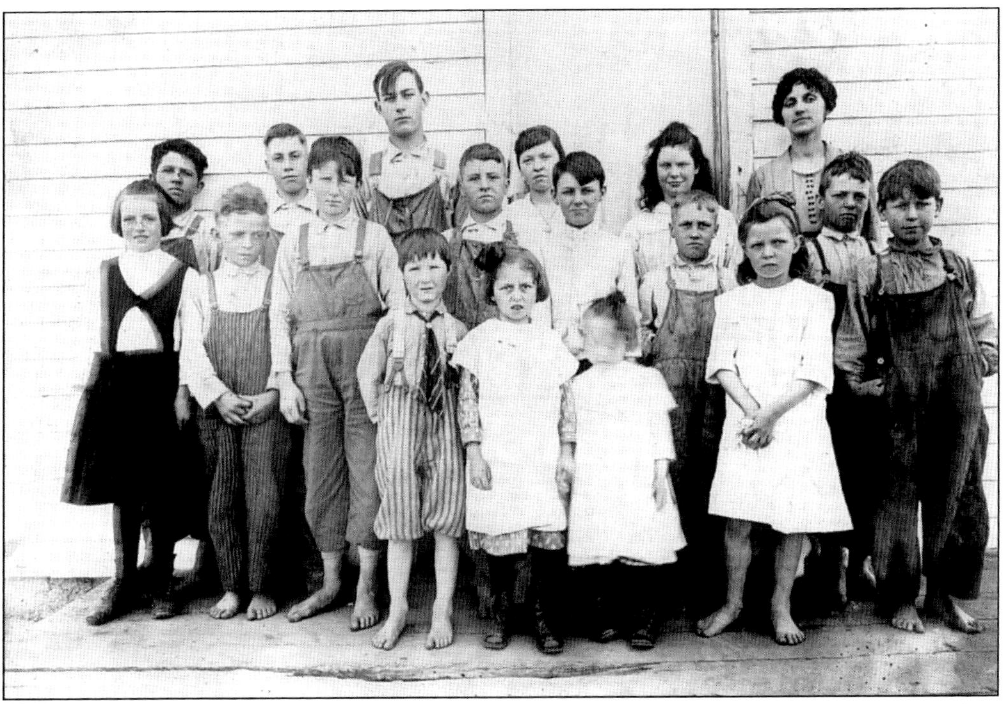

The Dimond School, which may also have been known as the Hub School, was located at Barnes and Bray Roads.

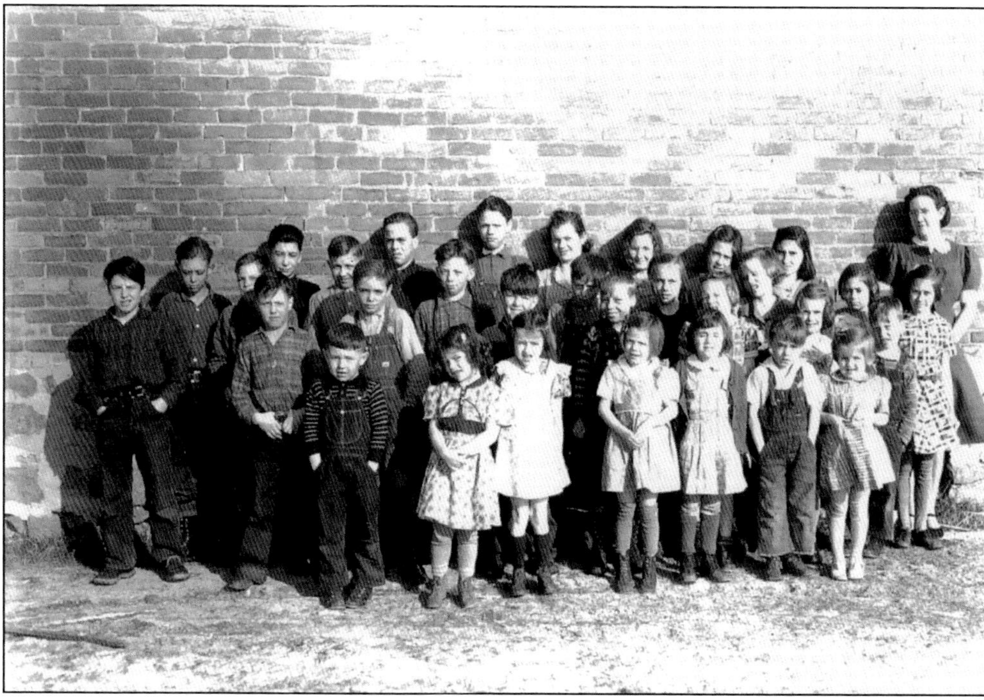

This is a March 1941 photograph of students at the Duncan School, which was located on Swaffer Road between North Lake and Center Roads.

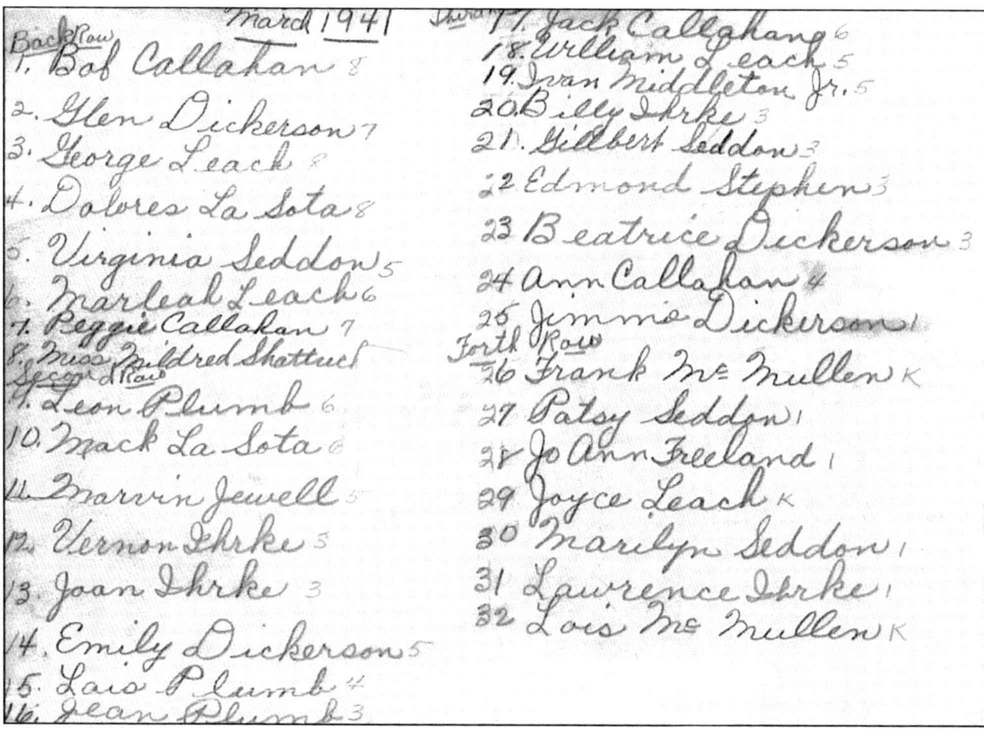

March 1941

Back Row
1. Bob Callahan 8
2. Glen Dickerson 7
3. George Leach 8
4. Dolores La Sota 8
5. Virginia Seddon 5
6. Marleah Leach 6
7. Peggie Callahan 7
8. Miss Mildred Shattuck

Second Row
9. Leon Plumb 6
10. Mack La Sota 6
11. Marvin Jewell 5
12. Vernon Ihrke 5
13. Joan Ihrke 3
14. Emily Dickerson 5
15. Lois Plumb 4
16. Jean Plumb 3

Third
17. Jack Callahan 6
18. William Leach 5
19. Ivan Middleton Jr. 5
20. Billy Ihrke 3
21. Gilbert Seddon 3
22. Edmond Stephen 3
23. Beatrice Dickerson 3
24. Ann Callahan 4
25. Jimmie Dickerson 1

Forth Row
26. Frank McMullen K
27. Patsy Seddon 1
28. Jo Ann Freeland 1
29. Joyce Leach K
30. Marilyn Seddon 1
31. Lawrence Ihrke 1
32. Lois McMullen K

This is a listing of the names on the Duncan School students in the picture at the top of the page.

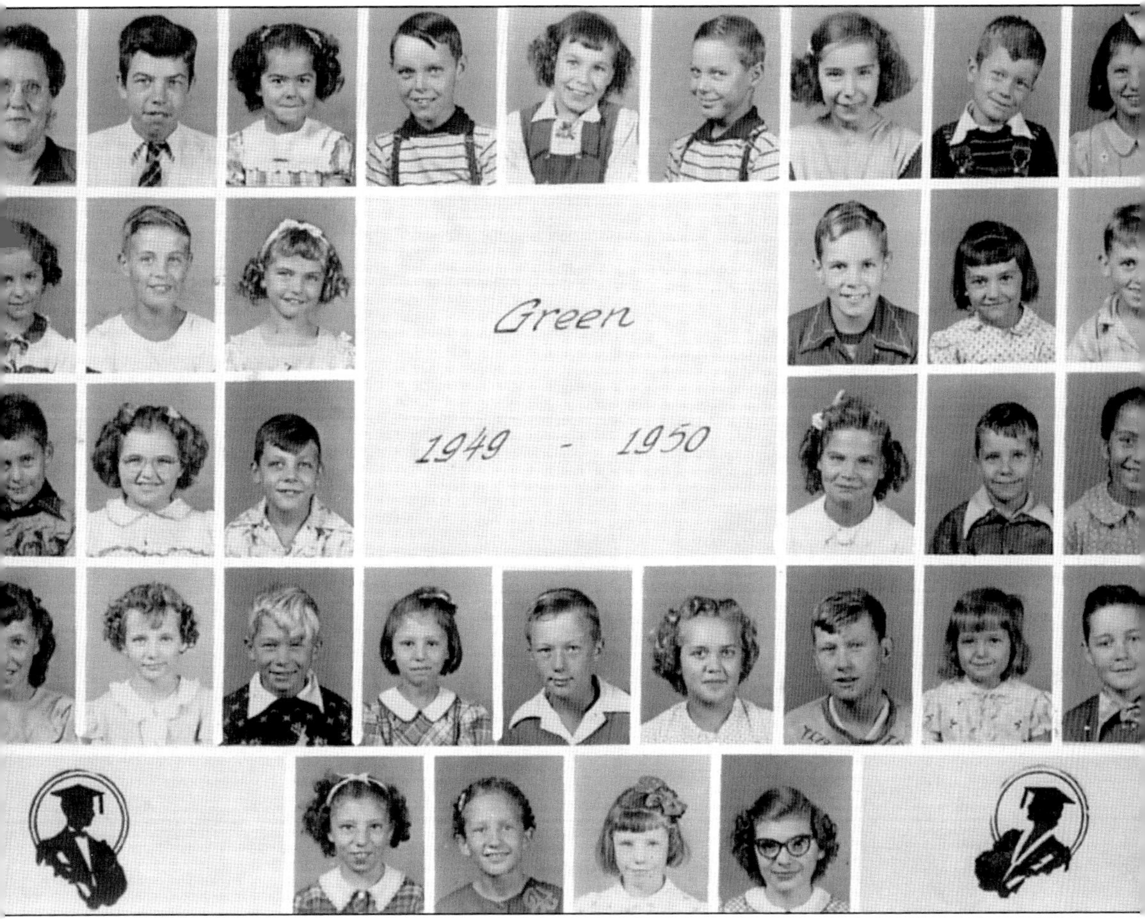


This class picture includes all of the students of the Green School for the 1949–1950 academic year. The Green School was located at the southwest corner of Barnes and Sheridan Roads. These students are identified, from left to right, as follows: (back row) ? Ward, Jr. Ward, J. Koch, Robert Fall, unidentified, Rolland Fall, ? Green, ? Martin, and ? Ward; (second row) ? Koch, Chester Cain, ? Cain, unidentified, Kay Harry, and Jerry Taylor; (third row) Ken Jensen, M. Baxter, Elden Engler, ? Cain, Bernie Osborn, and unidentified; (front row) unidentified, Judy Osborn, C. Schnettler, ? Ward, Bob Schnettler, Coral Baxter, unidentified, unidentified, and Marcus Jensen; (fifth row) ? Ward, ? Mallick, Betty Ward, and Estella Mae Engler.

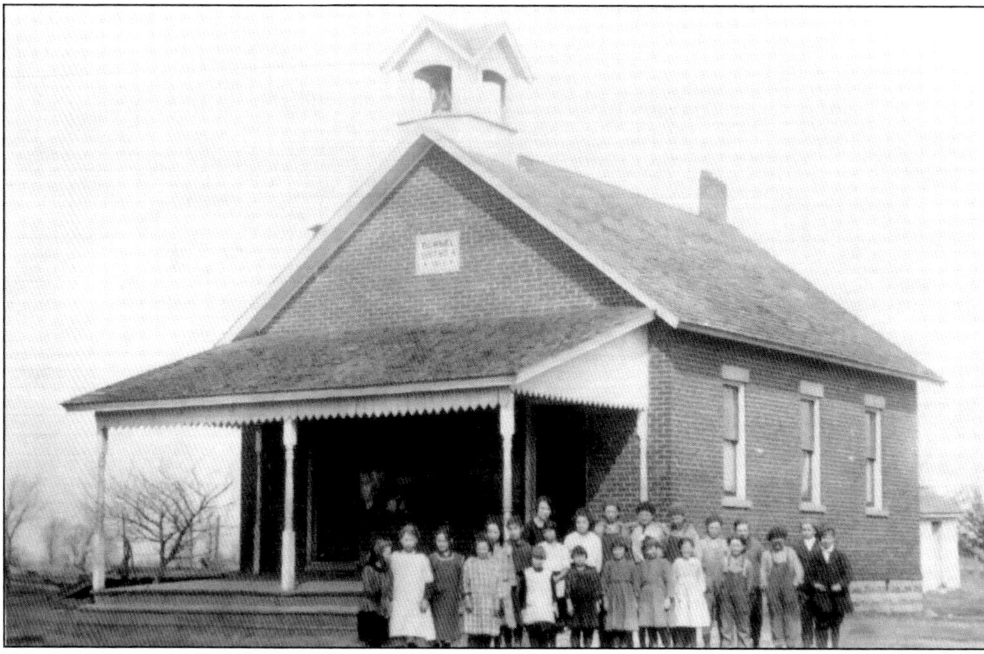

This is the Gunnell School, which was located at Arbela and Belsay Roads.

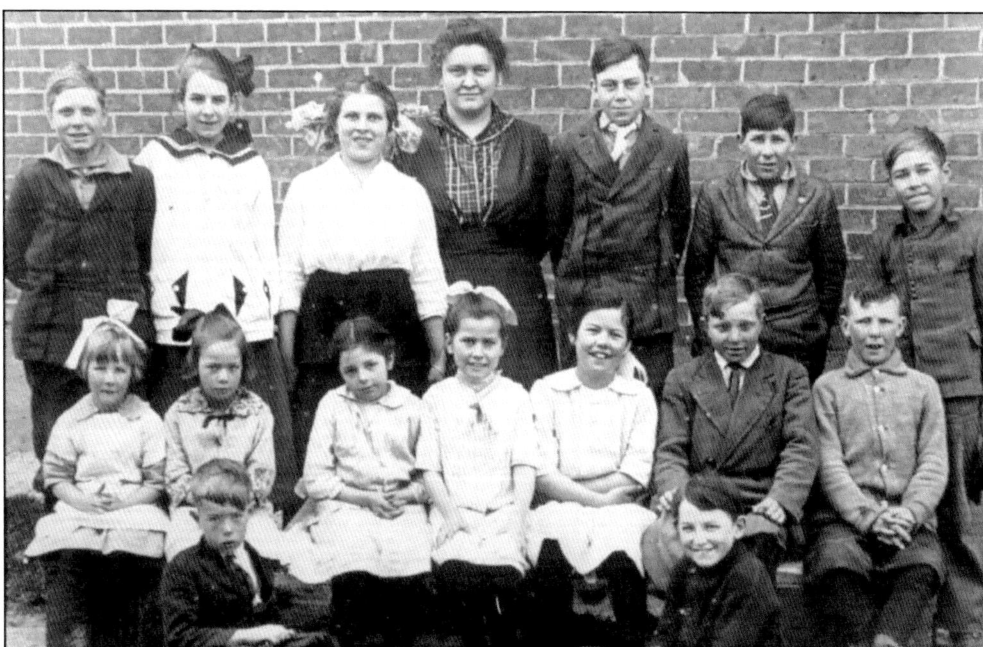

The Hopkins School was located at the northwest corner of Willard and Irish Roads.

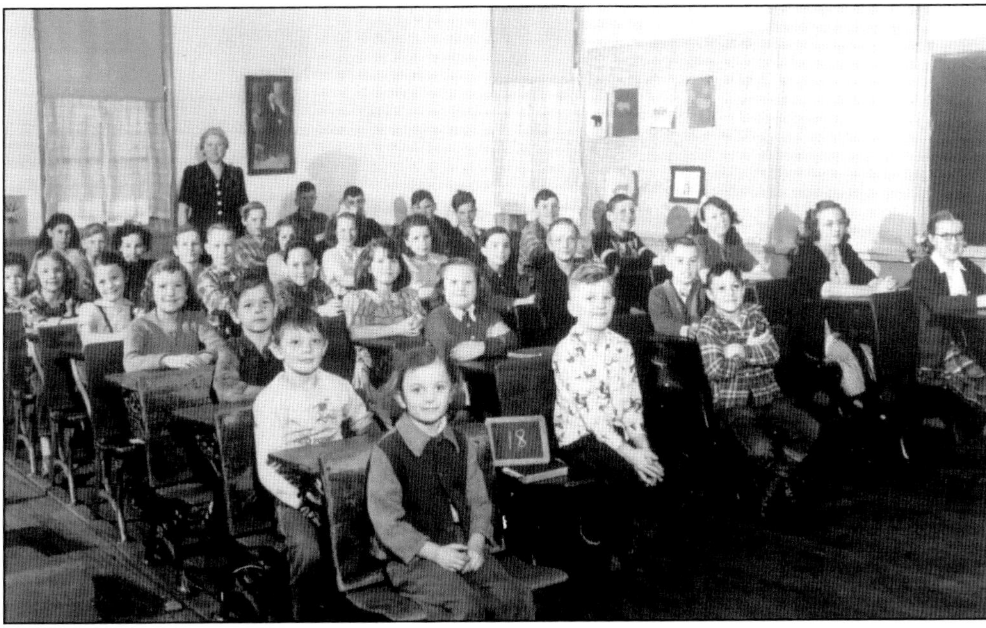

The Hinckley School, also known as the Pinegrove School, was located at the intersection of Lewis and Tuscola Roads in Arbela Township. This undated photograph shows the students of Mrs. Mary LaDuc, from left to right: (first row) Norman Matel, Jim Hitsman, Don Ratza, Charles, Taylor, Bill Loomis, Glen Connor, Helen Greer, Marlene Parker, and Lois Murphy; (second row) Harold Hanson, Marlene Riley, Hazel Greer, Charlotte Taylor, Carolyn Hitsman, Jacob Schlomer, and Dennis Loomis; (third row) ? Neeley, Gerald Greer, Barbara Kent, Pat Bogner, Larry Kirkey, Lyle Loomis, ? Taylor, Shirley Loomis, and Robert Schlomer; (fourth row) William Bone, Sandy Howe, Constance Hitsman, Patty Howe, ? Taylor, Zed Loomis, and Barbara Hitsman.

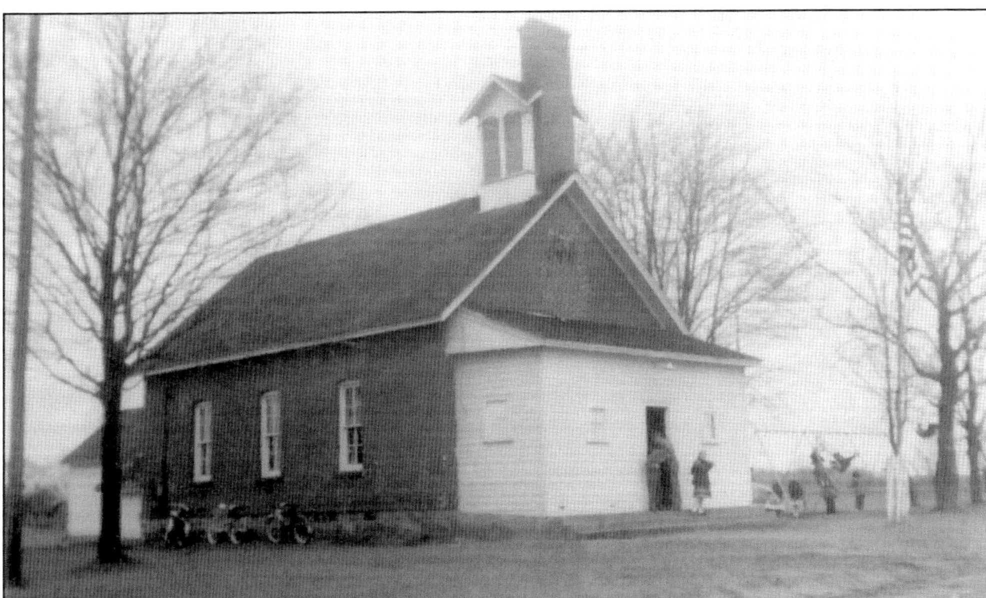

At the Elkhorn School, at West Swaffer and Vassar Roads, students enjoy themselves on the swing set before or after school. Note the three bicycles along the side of the schoolhouse.

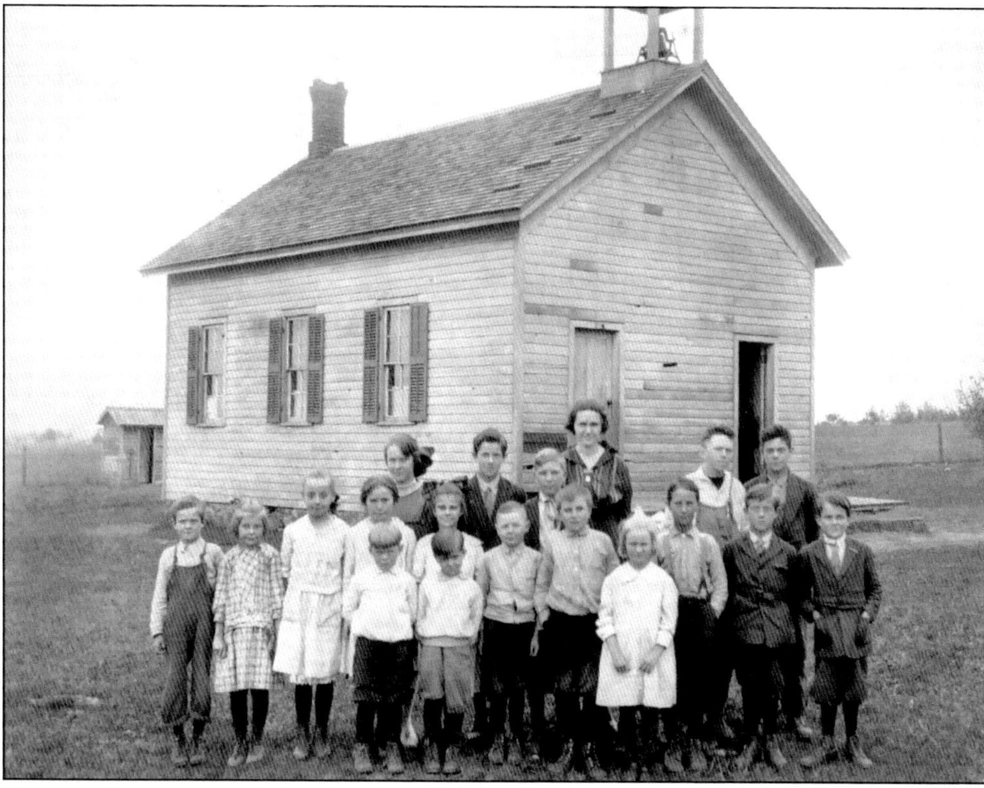

These students attended the Murphy School, which was located at the northeast corner of Sheridan and Millington Roads.

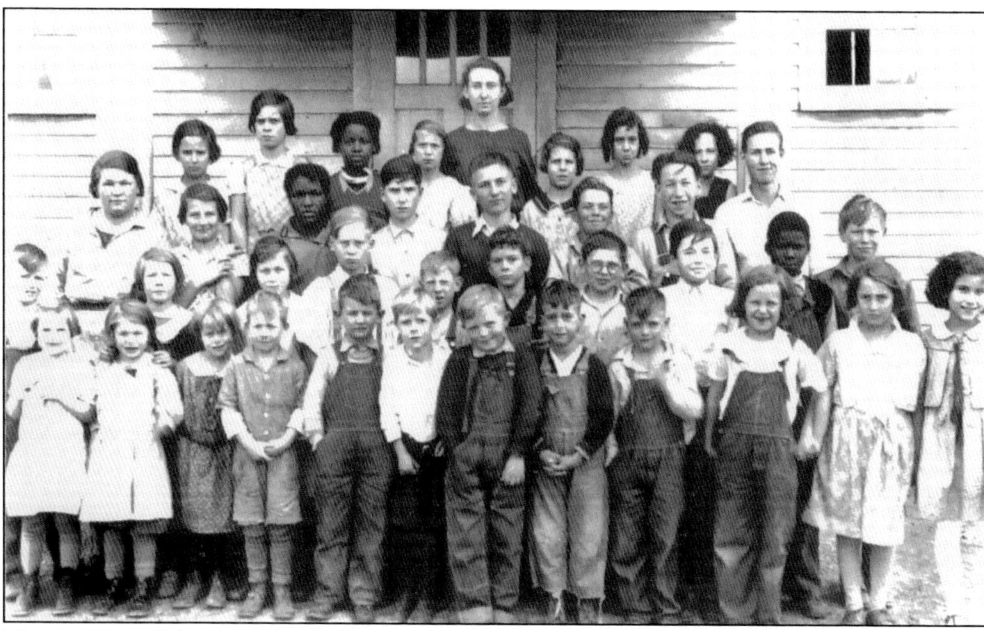

The Pinkham School was located on Barkley Road between Birch Run and Arbela Roads. This photograph dates back to 1934.

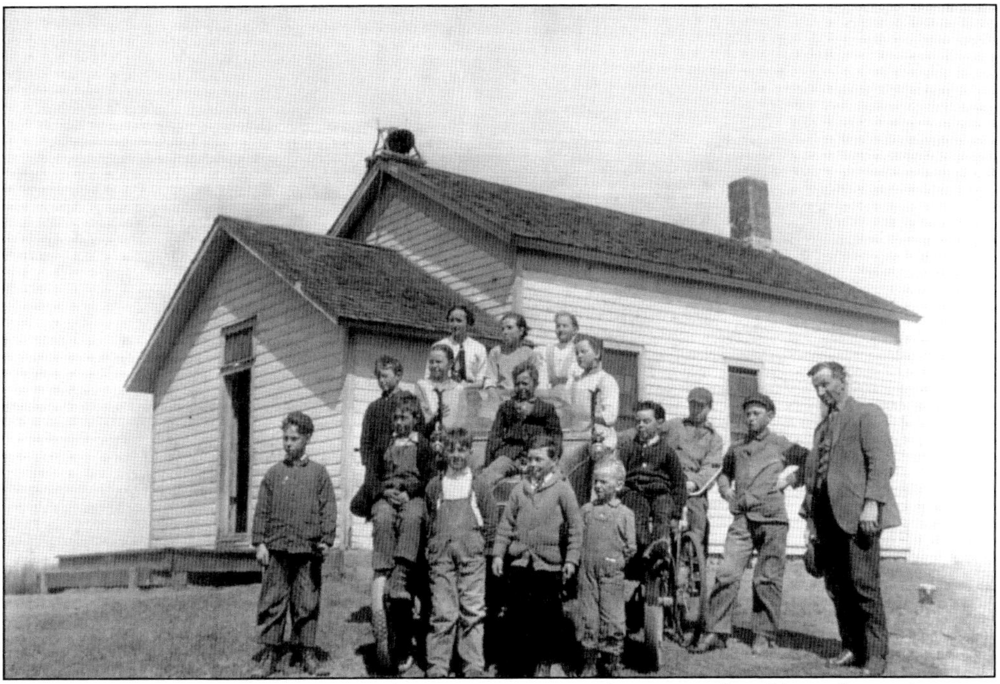

The Popple School was located at Belsay and Barnes Roads. Notice the old car the students are standing around and on.

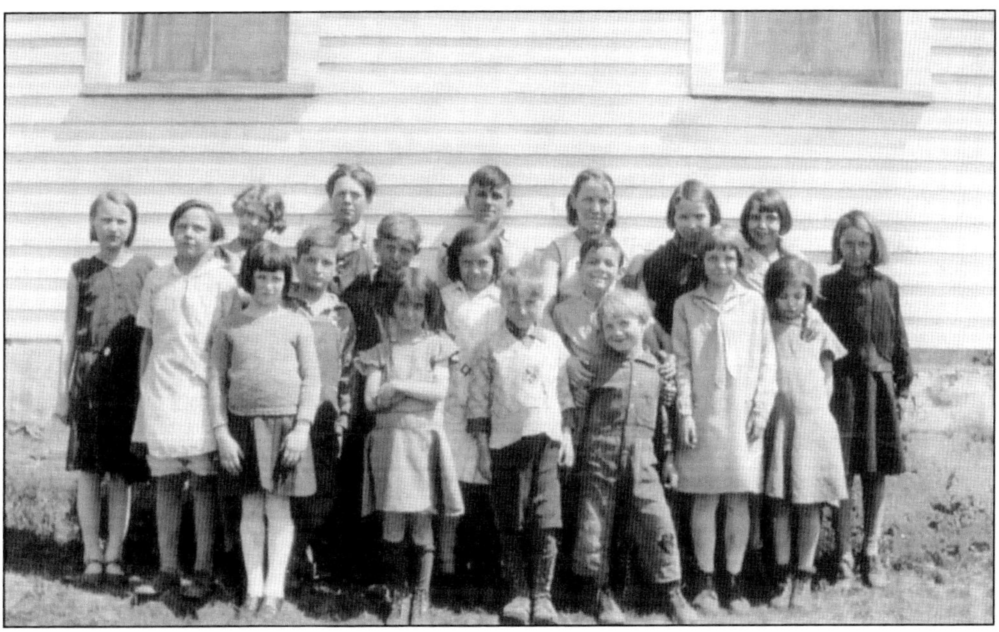

The Rohrer School was located at Swaffer and Oak Roads.

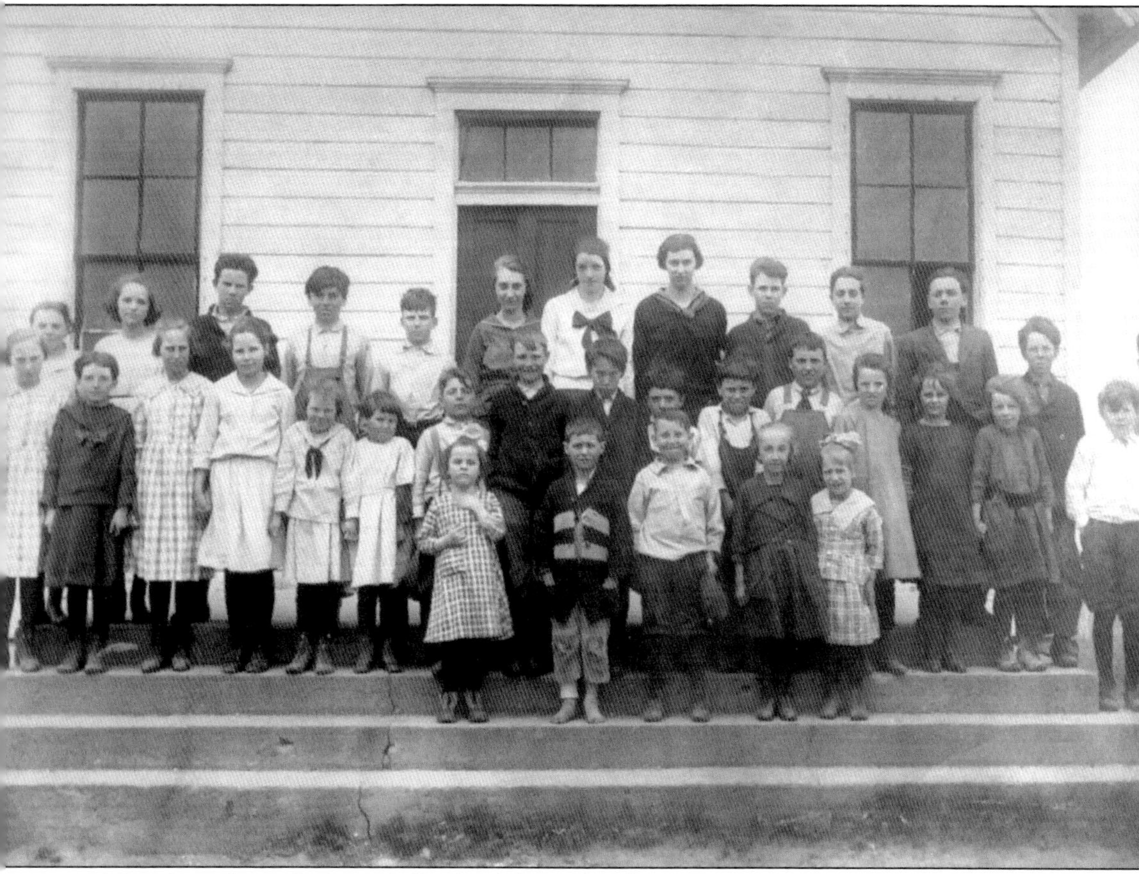

This photo shows the Springhill School, located at the corner of North Lake and Goodrich Roads. The students are identified as follows: (back row) Ethel McKnight, Ruth Rextrew, ? McKnight, Charles Lumsden, Clarence Gilchrist, Hazel Belnap, Beatrice Black, Hazel Johnson (teacher), Kenneth Gilchrist, Francis Richardson, Walter McKnight, and Albert Lumsden; (middle and front rows) Maud Stratton, Elaine Black, Myra Stratton, Susie McLaren, Thelma Batrow, Marguerite Johnson, Glen Wellington, Harold Belnap, Clifford Lumsden, ? McKnight, ? McKnight, Ward Lindsay, Evelyn Lindsay, Erma Lindsay, Eileen Batrow, James McLaren, and Harry Wing.

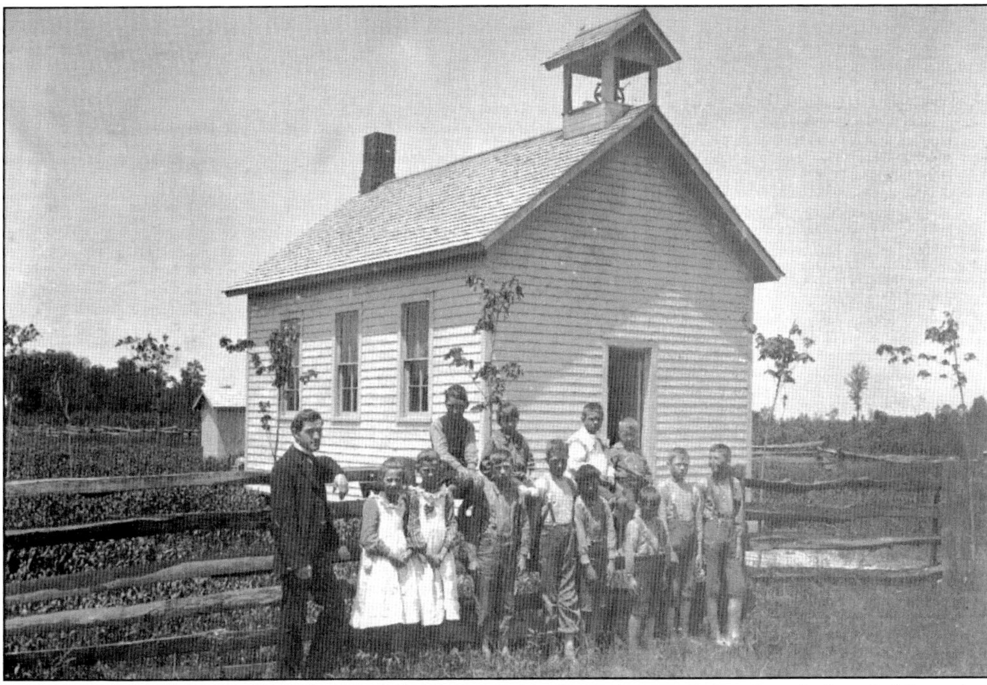

Pastor Wuggazer is shown in front of the first St. Paul's Lutheran School with the children that attended the first classes taught there. The school was located one-half mile north of Millington Road on the west side of Buell Lake Road in Arbela Township.

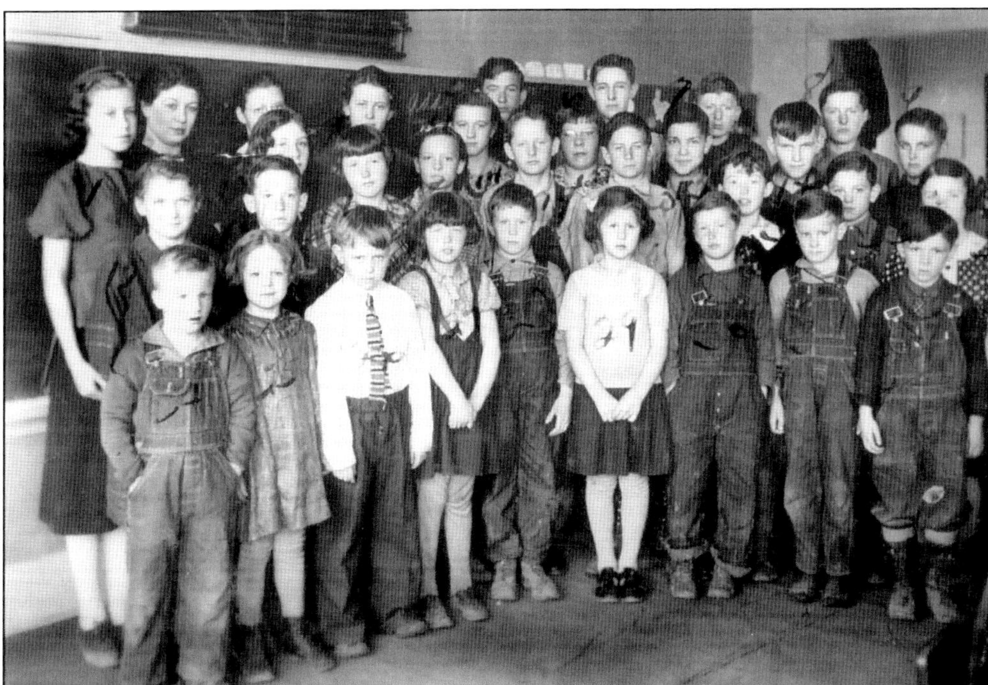

The Watertown Center School was located at the northwest corner of Millington and Center Roads.

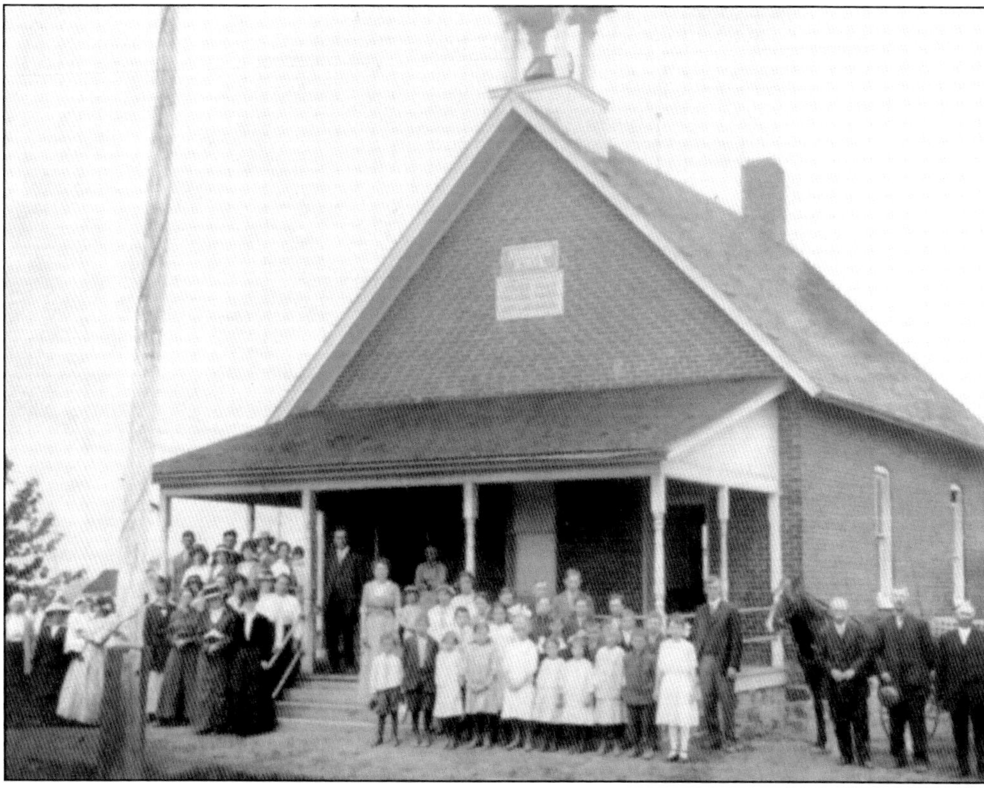

The State Road School was located on the east side of M-15 (State Road) between Barnes and Birch Run Roads. The photo above shows students at State Road School in 1940. The above image depicts a formal gathering of families wearing their Sunday best.

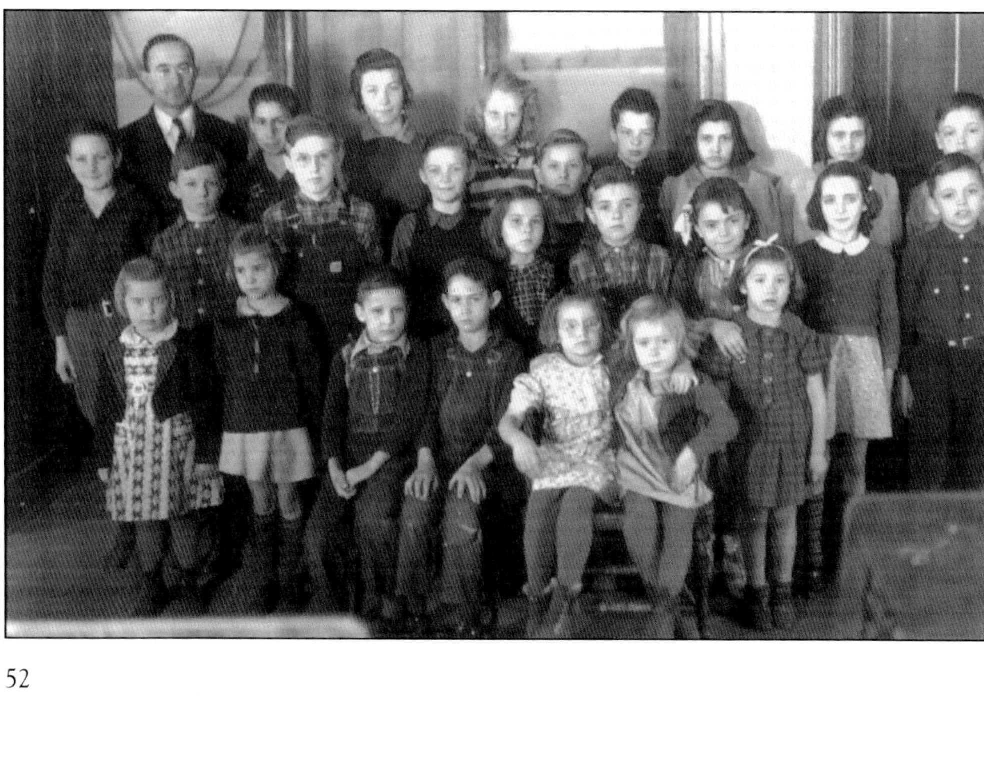

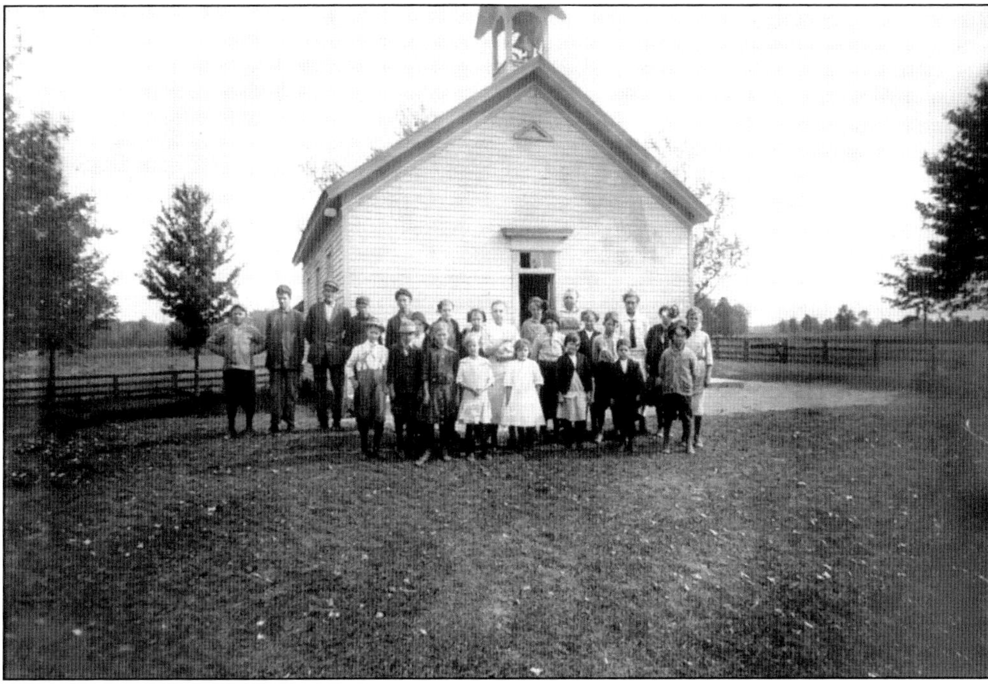

The Whitney School was located on Bray Road, one-half mile north of Millington Road.

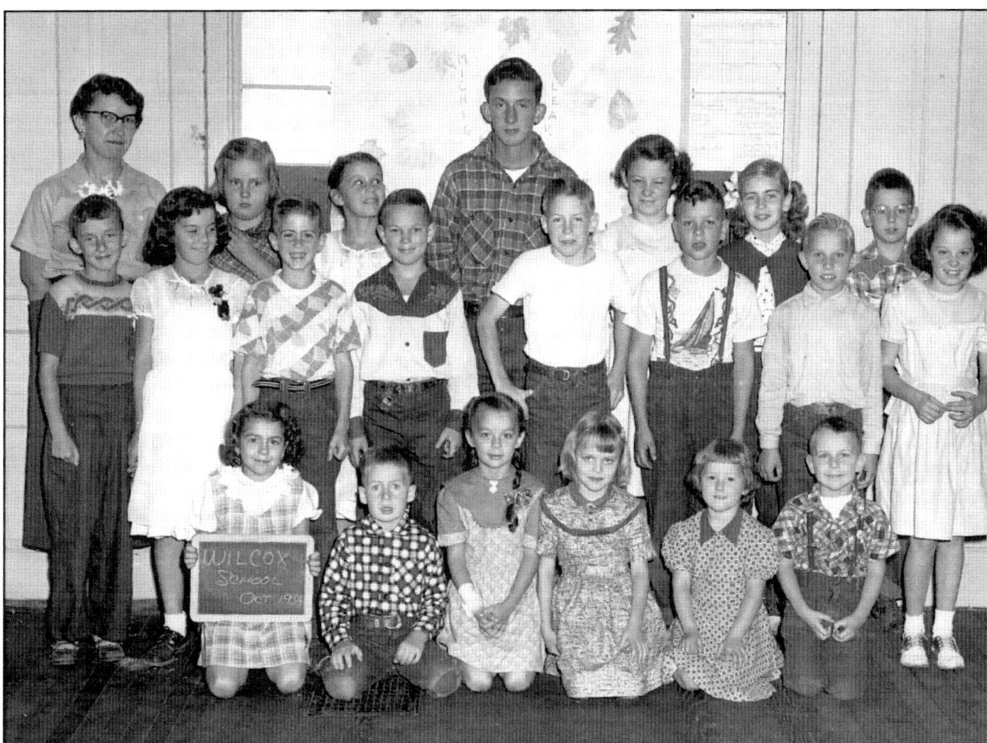


The Wilcox School was located on Millington Road between Buell and Barkley. These are the students who attended Wilcox School in October of 1954.

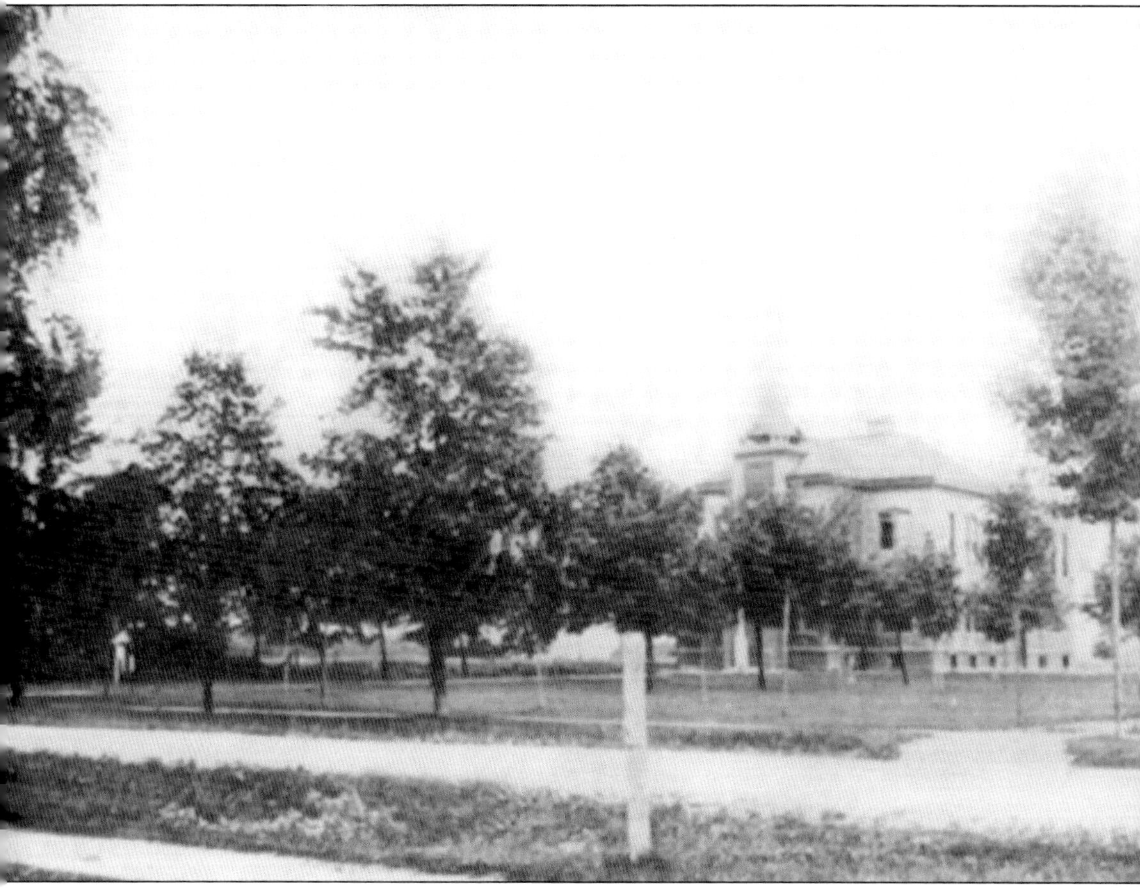

This photo shows Millington High School in 1912.

# *Six*

# Doctors

The early doctors were the backbone of the community. They were on call day or night and had to travel by buggy or on horseback. Many people owe their lives to these dedicated and knowledgeable people who would not be swayed from their duties. These family doctors treated patients, operated when necessary and developed medicines that we should have around today. The following are these medical men with as much history and background as could be found. Dr. John McPherson is the first doctor recorded who lived and worked in Millington, serving from 1863–1867. He is buried in the Millington Cemetery.

Dr. Russel Black indicated in his Medical Practitioner's Sworn Statement that he lived and practiced in Watrousville between 1853 and 1884. The statement was registered with the clerk in Caro in 1884. He took trips to Fairgrove, Quanicassee, and perhaps Millington. He stated he had practiced in Michigan for 31 years. His family was from Broome County, New York. He arrived in Michigan via Ohio. He may have practiced in Akron between 1884 and 1891.

Dr. David Rogers appears to be the second early doctor living and working in Millington, serving from 1870 to 1910. His assistant, Javes Hallwood, is mentioned only one place, in Samuel Atwood's History and had no title by his name.

In the Tuscola County Atlas for 1875, Dr. S.R. Harris is listed as a medical practitioner in Millington. Also for 1875, Dr. C.F. Golden and Dr. W.C. Gorman appear on a list given to Millington Township Library, with no accompanying information.

In March of 1876, Dr. Henry Bishop arrived from New York and was well-known and appreciated in Millington for 54 years. He is remembered for his personal care for patients as well as his medical knowledge. He served until 1929.

Dr. Thomas Studgeon is registered in Caro as practicing medicine and surgery in Millington, beginning in 1886. He had previously practiced in Michigan for ten years, but the statement does not say where. He "belonged to the Electric College of Medicine."

From 1894 to 1927, Dr. Wynne C. Garvin practiced out of his home at 4778 Main Street. He was a founding member of the Masonic Lodge in Millington.

Before moving to Vassar, Dr. Arthur Sachs practiced in Millington from 1928 to 1932. He played the violin.

Dr. Duncan Salot began practicing medicine in Millington in 1931. He left in 1938 to set up an ear, nose, and throat practice in Lebanon, Kentucky. He died there in 1988.

Dr. Perry Stewart practiced in 1932, but no other information is available.

In 1936, a Dr. Blakely opened an office on Main Street, perhaps in the area of Worth's Market or the telephone office. He had one son.

Dr. J.A. Vatz came to Millington in 1936 as a graduate of the University of Michigan and Western Ontario Medical School. He did work at Women's Hospital in Flint, as well as in Pennsylvania. He sold his practice to Harry Berman and took a position at Pontiac State Hospital on June 1, 1939.

In 1938 Dr. Richard Flett came to Millington to replace Dr. Salot and practiced out of Dr.

Salot's office at 8530 State Street. Dr. Flett was a founding member of the Millington Rotary Club and was its second president.

In 1939 Dr. Harry Berman bought the practice of Dr. J.A. Vatz. He set up his office in the former bank building, now the Millington-Arbela Historical Museum. He moved his practice to Flint in 1951 and died there in 1978.

Dr. Brazier practiced at 8600 State Street in the 1950s. The historical society has talked to a few people who were treated by him, but no other information is available.

Dr. Michael S. Pezo, D.C., and Dr. Martha E. Pezo, D.C., set up a joint chiropractic practice in Millington in 1960. Their office was at the Henderson House on State Street before it was moved. In 1967, they built and moved to their residence/office at 8758 State Street.

Dr. Chapin began practicing at 8600 State Street in 1961. He moved to a newly built office at 9030 South State Road in 1973. From 1966 to 1978 he was the only M.D. in Millington, with the exception of 1973.

Dr. David Hahn may hold the record for the shortest practice in Millington. He set up his office in the upstairs of 8600 State Street in April of 1973 and left in July. He now practices with a group in Okemos, Michigan.

Dr. Hoat Vu came to Millington in 1975 and opened his office in the north half of the Millington Professional Building at 9030 South State. He now practices in Otisville.

Dr. Larry Cole began practicing in the Millington Professional Building for Bay Medical System in 1994.

## Veterinarians

Dr. Henry Ferstl, D.V.M., worked with his wife Jean in the Millington Veterinarian Clinic at 8761 State Street until his death in 1993. Dr. Ferstl's son Thomas came to work with his father for a while before his death. Thomas, a graduate of Michigan State, assumed responsibilities at the clinic in 1995.

## Dentists

Dr. G.S. Harris is listed in the Maps and Brooks Atlas as practicing dentistry in Millington in 1888. The next known dentist is Dr. Norman Carter. His name appears in the 1912 Millington High School Yearbook. His office was above the post office and was open on Wednesdays.

A Dr. Sinclair is listed as another early Millington dentist, but no additional information is available.

Dr. Henry Brunk, D.D.S., came to Millington after serving in World War I but did not practice in here because of war injuries. He was born in 1888 and died in 1957. Dr. Brunk was a founder of the Millington Rotary Club and served as its first president.

Dr. Charles Quinn, D.D.S., had a practice at the southwest corner of Main and Depot Streets until he retired.

Dr. Eugene Surmont D.D.S. has practiced dentistry in Millington since 1973. He practiced out of the upstairs office at 8600 State Street. When Dr. Chapin built his new offices, Dr. Surmont moved into the south suite at 9030 State Street.

Dr. Jack Martin, D.D.S., came to Millington from Flint. He started practicing in 1992 at 4729 East Main, and in June of 1995 he built a new office on Industrial Drive.

In 1984, Convenient Family Dentistry of America moved in the offices previously occupied by Dr. Quinn. Dr. Carl Schwartz is president and owner of the group, which has offices in nine locations, including Millington. The headquarters are located in Grand Blanc. The group later moved to the office previously occupied by Dr. Martin at 4729 East Main. The following dentists practiced with this group in Millington: Dr. Alec Schultz, Dr. Dan Burns, Dr. Bryan Thomas, and Dr. Timothy Glowniak.

The Convenient Family Dentistry of America organization has since moved from Millington and in July of 1996, Dr. Joseph Vella moved into these offices. He has been practicing dentistry since 1988 and lives with his family in Davison.

## Optometrists

In 1983, Dr. Fred L. Zehnder came to Millington to practice optometry at 4729 Main Street in the building that once housed Osborne Farm Equipment. The building was owned by the First of America Bank when Dr. Zehnder moved to this site. In 1984, Dr. Steven Bierlein joined the staff. On August 1, 1994, they purchased the building which was also occupied by Convenient Family Dentistry. The south suite of offices will soon house a St. Luke's-associated physician. Drs. Zehnder and Bierlein also have offices in Frankenmuth.

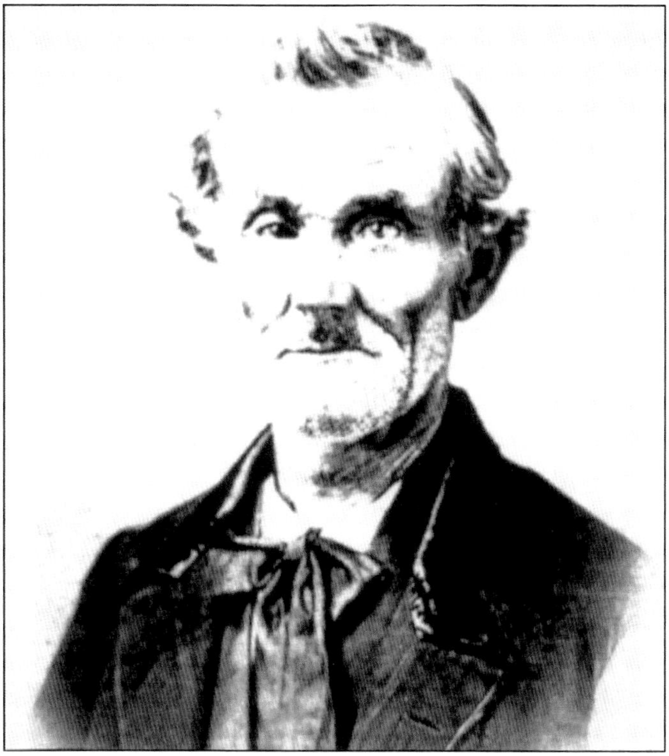

Dr. John McPherson, Millington's first doctor, practiced from 1863 to 1867.

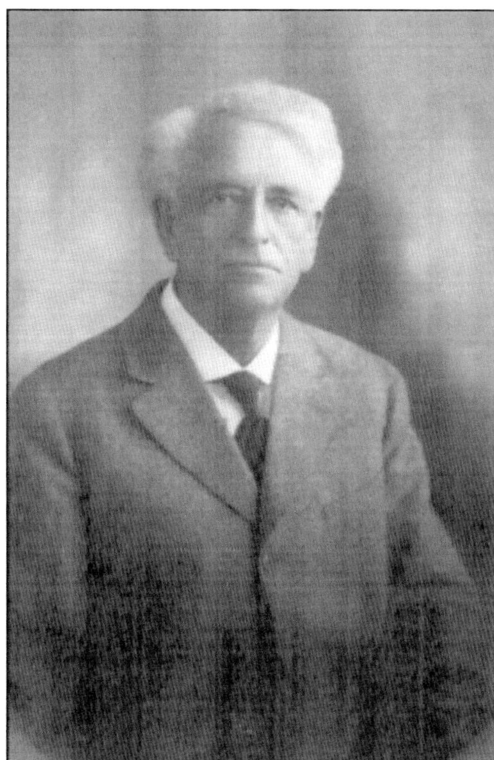

Dr. Henry Bishop, practiced in Millington for 54 years, from 1876 to 1929.

Dr. Wynne Garvin, practiced out of his home from 1894 to 1927.

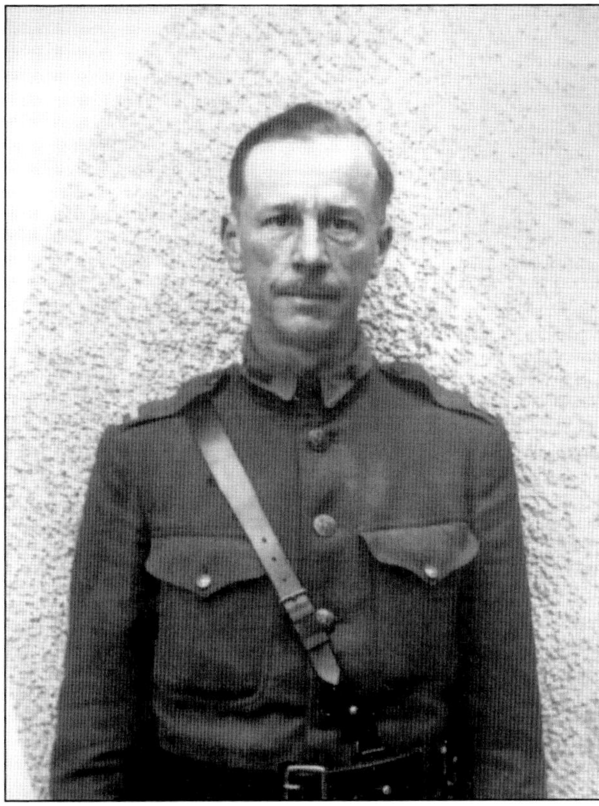

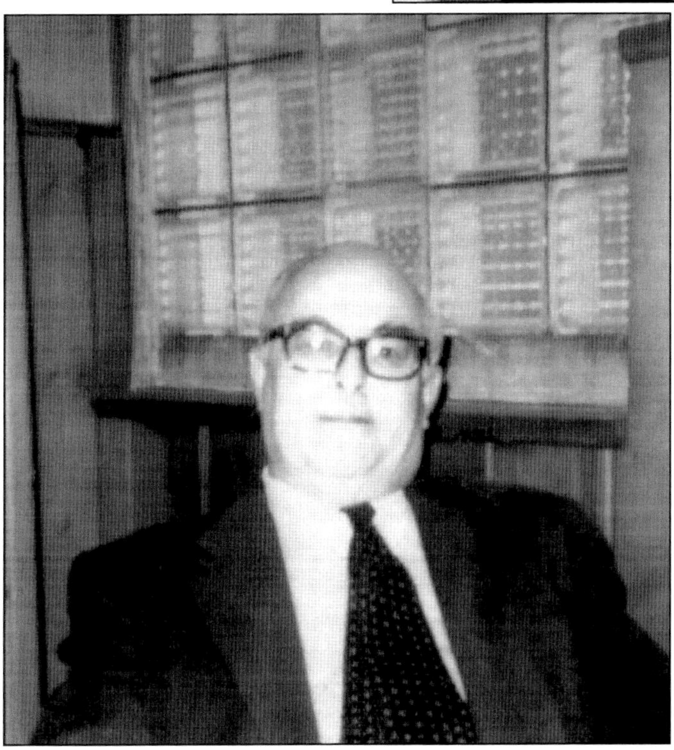

Dr. Harry Berman, practiced in Millington from 1939 to 1951.

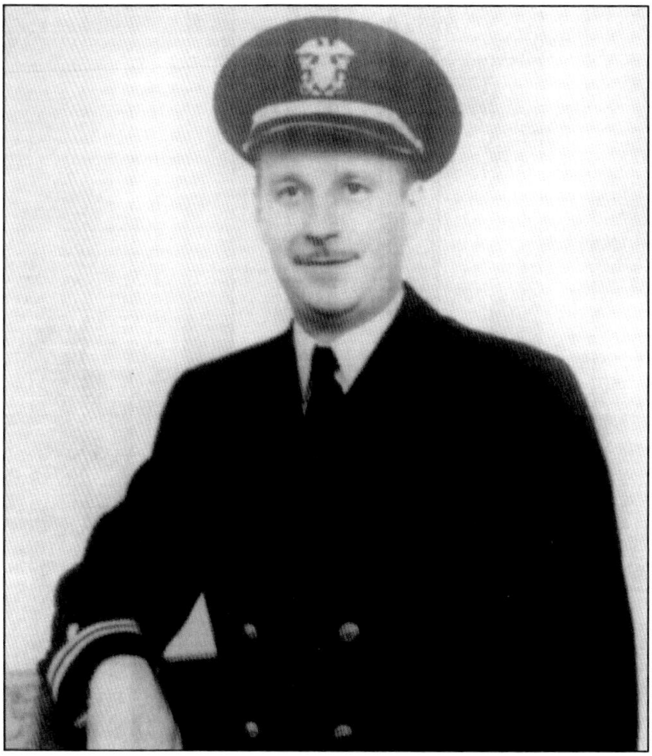

Dr. Richard Flett, practiced in Millington from 1938 to 1961.

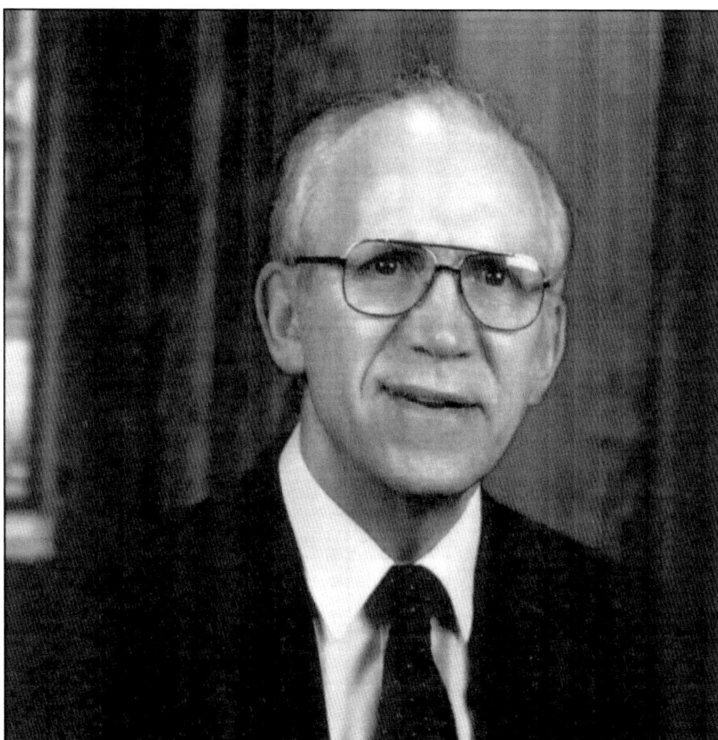

Dr. Maurice Chapin, began practice in 1961, retired in 1999, but still assists present medical personnel.

# *Seven*

# BUSINESSES

From the early 1850s, shortly after Edwin C. Brainerd became the first settler in Millington Township, Millington became a progressive, expanding village. First one and then two dams on the Millington Creek brought settlers and their families to the area. As Millington and the surrounding area grew, there became a need for grocery and hardware stores. There was also a need for good blacksmithing.

Slowed temporarily by the Civil War, Millington returned to normal immediately after the war ended, with a cemetery and better roads between the farm lands surrounding the town. Especially important was the Goodrich to Bay City Road that opened the town to other villages and communities. In 1873, the railroad was constructed through the village, bringing opportunities beyond all expectations. Now Millington residents had coal, building materials, and farm machinery delivered right to their doors. The railroad was also the means to ship out grains, potatoes, and livestock as well as lumber and pine shingles, which were abundant in the area.

In 1905, Samuel Atwood, a local Civil War veteran and businessman, published the following names of early businessmen who lived and operated in the village area:

Francis W. Brown
Beach and Gunn
Bishop and Vandermark
Moses Farnum
Roger Rathbun
O.P. Gold and Brother
M. Haws
Beach, Burnham and Co.
William Storms and Son
Greenough and Conlee
Clough and Forester
Huston and Valentine
Smith Botsford and Bough
Antony DeWitt
Edwin Sparrow and Brother
M. Bellemy
M. Flater
McPherson and Crippen
Bishop Brothers
A.C. Allen and Co.
Mr. Kollenburg
Mr. Lempke
C.A. Valentine and Son
William Baker
D.B. Helfrich
George Crow
Clinton E. Mosier
James Cypher
Archie Walterhouse
Peter Crowbar
McPherson and Tubbs
Mr. Yerden
Mr. McComber
Daniel McLean
W.S. Wing
Geo. Veitengruber.

Millington continued to expand before and after World War I. The Depression years of the 1920s and 1930s failed to slow the progress in the village. Wednesdays and Saturdays began at 7:00 a.m. and the stores remained open until midnight to serve the hundreds of shoppers and visitors who came to town. Automobiles parked in every conceivable parking place with a premium on spaces on State Street where people would sit in their cars and talk with neighbors and friends. Horses and buggies were parked on the side streets, tied to special steel posts. Farmers' wives traded cream and eggs for groceries and other needed items.

After World War II, better cars and improved highways allowed everyone to travel longer distances to work and to shop. Larger stores and shopping malls in Flint, Saginaw, and Bay City offered lower prices and a larger variety of groceries and clothing. Despite easier travel, there remained over 70 businesses in Millington to serve the area in the 1950s. They were:

Wards Gas Station
Millington Feed Co.
Geo. McIntyre Co.
Cobb's Standard
Harvey Eno's Rest.
Fern's Beauty Shop
Style Shop
Schumaker's Rest.
Kroger Store
Boyce Dalrymple
Charles Valentine
Hahn's Bakery
McPherson's Hardware
Swett's Barber Shop
Millington Hotel
Pure Oil Co.
Millington Block Co.
Jerry's Sandwiches
Quality Market
Arky's Garage
Hanlin Funeral Home
Avery Shoe Repair
Evergreen Nursery
Ed Wilkinson
*Millington Herald*
Cobb's Dairy Bar
Farm Bureau
McGinnis Sales
Fall's 5¢ to $5.00
A.H. Cobb Co.
Henderson's Drugs
Peggy's Shop
Red's Appliances

Conway's Rest. & Bar
Hall and Dean
Standard Oil
Millington Gas & Oil
Capitol Theater
Millington Lumber Co.
Beagle's Barber Shop
Ohman and Blossom
Osborn Sales
Gasper's Welding
H.P. Spender Print
Millington Telephone
Millington Mfg. Co.
M. and D. Beauty Shop
Geo. C. Garvin
Clark's Cleaners
Holmes Real Estate
C.K. Smith Signs
Millington Well Service
Millington Rec.
Dr. H. Ferstl
Dr. Berman
Dr. Flett
Dr. C. Quinn
Kennedy's Drugs
P.T. Chevrolet
Schwab's Garage
Frankenmuth State Bank
Sinclair Oil Co.
Millington Truck Body
Millington Photo Service
Millington Collision
May's Welding

At the time this book was published in 2004, the businesses in the Millington-Arbela area total over 225 names and companies. We have attempted to list the businesses within the village and those close to the Millington shopping area. Some may change or be added before our final printing time and we trust we have not omitted anyone in our listing:

Millington Chiropractic Center
D. Rock Photo Inc.
Country Shop
McPherson's Restaurant
Millington Hardware
Weber's Village Market
Colling's Barber Shop
Just off Main Salon
Millington Antique Depot
The Clutter Bug
DJ's Beauty Salon
Prime Time Tanning
Car Quest Auto Parts
J. McLoud Realty
Puff and Stuff Antiques
Dipzinski Basket Shop
Marathon Service Station
Gunnell, Inc.
Chocolates Galore
Mayville State Bank
Curly Cone
Kirby Sweepers
Amoco Service Station
Bo's Village Peddler
Kovacs Insurance Agency
Schwab's Insurance Agency
Jack Martin, D.D.S.
Millington Car Wash
Kaumagraph Corporation
Kaiser Engineering, Inc.
Dick's Auto Repair
Ramsey's Collision
Country Mouse Flowers
Valentine's Tax Service
Credit Auto Leasing, Inc.
Millington Inn
Millington Family Barbers
Worth's Laundromat
Millington Elevator and Supply
Dian's Beauty Salon
Prajuol Joshi, M.D.
Cardinal Cutz
Tax Affairs
TDS Telecom
Self Serve Lumber
Joseph A. Vella, D.D.S.
Millington Library
Millington Post Office
Century 21 Realty
Zehnder and Bierlein, O.D.
Dr. Larry Cole, O.D.
National City Bank
McKatm's Pub
Village Hallmark
Village Pharmacy
Millington Insurance Agency
Fairway Discount Store
Antique Mall Co-op
Millington Township Hall
Millington Fire Hall
Village Town Hall
Nelson's Auto Repair

M-15 Businesses beyond Village Limits:

Joseph Chevrolet
Jensen's Equipment
Pro-Tec Auto Repair
Rao Shidmar, M.D.
Loudon Steel
Cardinal Pizza
Automotive Machine
Artuso Cement Co.

This poem appeared in a 1929 issue of the *Millington Herald*. The author is unknown.

Millington lies in Michigan state
In Tuscola County, as I would relate
A nicer town for its age you'll not meet
And for water supply it can't be beat.

The first we see on the east side of the street
Is the Capitol Theater, whose shows can't be beat
You may search all over this broad land
But the Capitol's plays are simply grand.

Vernon Farnum next greets you with a smile
It's only true friendship that makes life worthwhile
Low and behold it's the Ford service station
Where is sold one of the best cars in the nation.

Then when you are tired and want a good sleep
Frank Ashley will a close vigil keep
He will put you in bed in snowy white
At the Millington House with food that is right.

Journeying eastward we find Avery the cobbler
Who mends boots and shoes
As he sits on his bench thinking what's the use
We are all growing old like a pair of these shoes.

C.E. Wright who next doth appear
Sells raisins, sugar, and syrup so clear
Beans, bacon, mustard and honey
So there's the place to spend your money.

The next we see is the Millington Bank
All built of iron and not of plank
The cash to you they will freely hand
If well secured by chattel or land.

Just take a step northward
From the Millington Bank
Now Bill Lowell's place can be seen
Where he specializes in poultry and cream.

After Bill you have visited just journey with me
The Cass City Grain Company now you see
Mr. Briggs greets you with a how do you do
Could we sell some hard coal, soft coal, or grain to you.

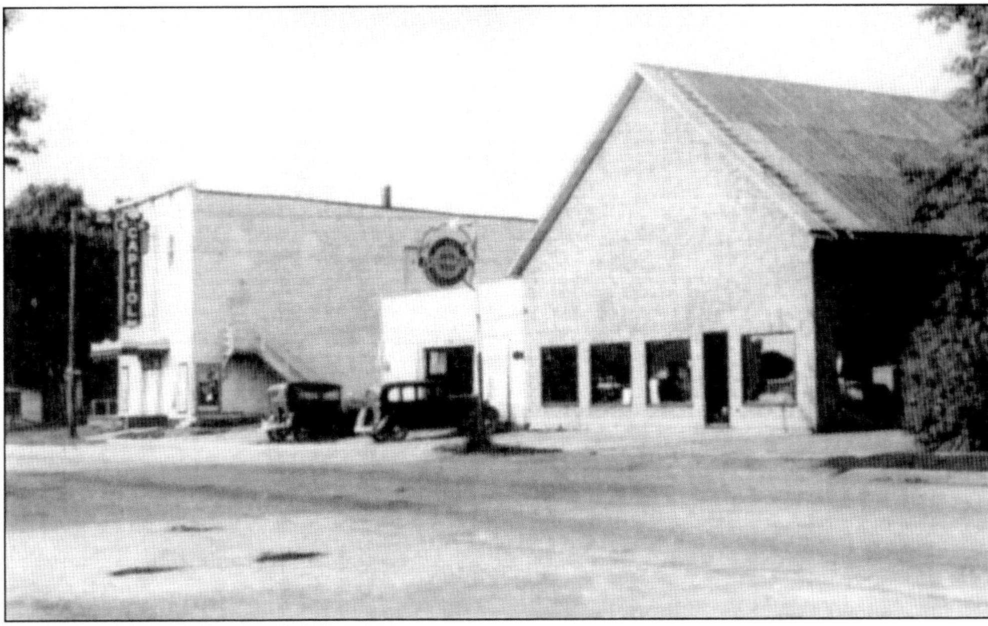


This old photo shows the Capitol Theater and an early Chevrolet dealership in Millington.

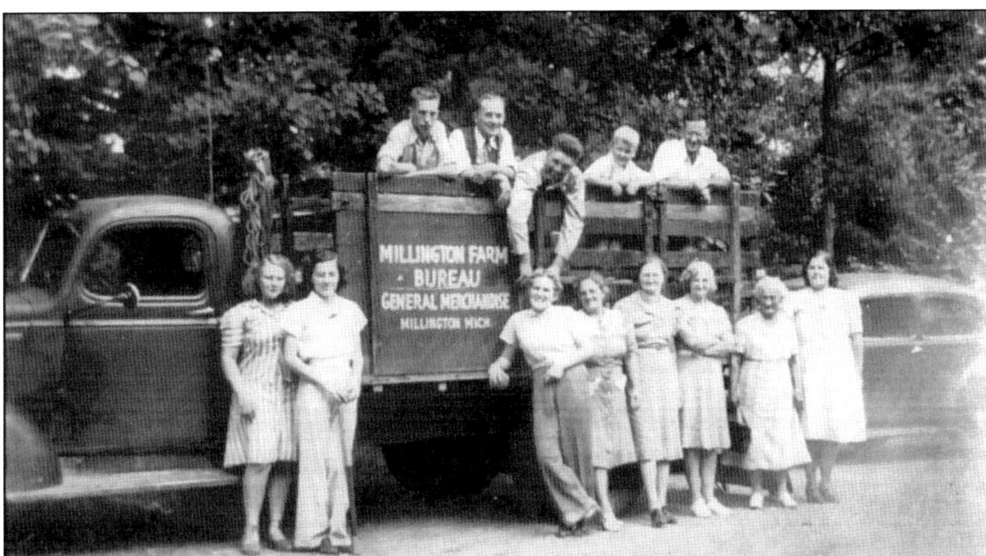


Workers at the popular Farm Bureau Store appear in this picture from the 1940s.

Now just turn and walk back to the south
On the street running east
You'll find Beagle's shop
Where you get shaves and haircuts with tonic on top.

Next, Alston Curriers will be found
Where notions, groceries, and goodies abound
Just step inside and try on a hat
There's one for you whether small or fat.

The telephone is next on our way
Where all calls are answered by night or day
No matter whether you call near or far away
You'll get the party and little you'll pay.

Bob Taylor you'll find on the run
If you have any blacksmithing you wish to be done
You'll find him on hand from sun to sun
And you'll say his work is never done.

Mr. Tom Gibson next you meet,
Who keeps coal and grain, everything in this line complete.
When spring comes and supplies you need,
The Millington Grain will supply you with all kinds of seed.

Across the track to the north we go
To Barber's Lumber Yard of which you all know,
When a house you are building just bear in mind
That better brick, cement, and lumber you'll not find.

Now back south across the street
The Helbing-Chase Company you will meet.
If your stoves and furnaces are smoking, there's the place to go
And get some Soot Destroyer of which you all know.

Then east and south the Millington Mill you'll find
Where farmers take their grists to grind.
Just wait, they will only a few minutes take
And from your grains they will flour make.

Now back west we go to the railroad depot,
Where Shaffer sells you a ticket to go
To any part of this big land of ours,
Mid-snows of the north or fair southern flowers.

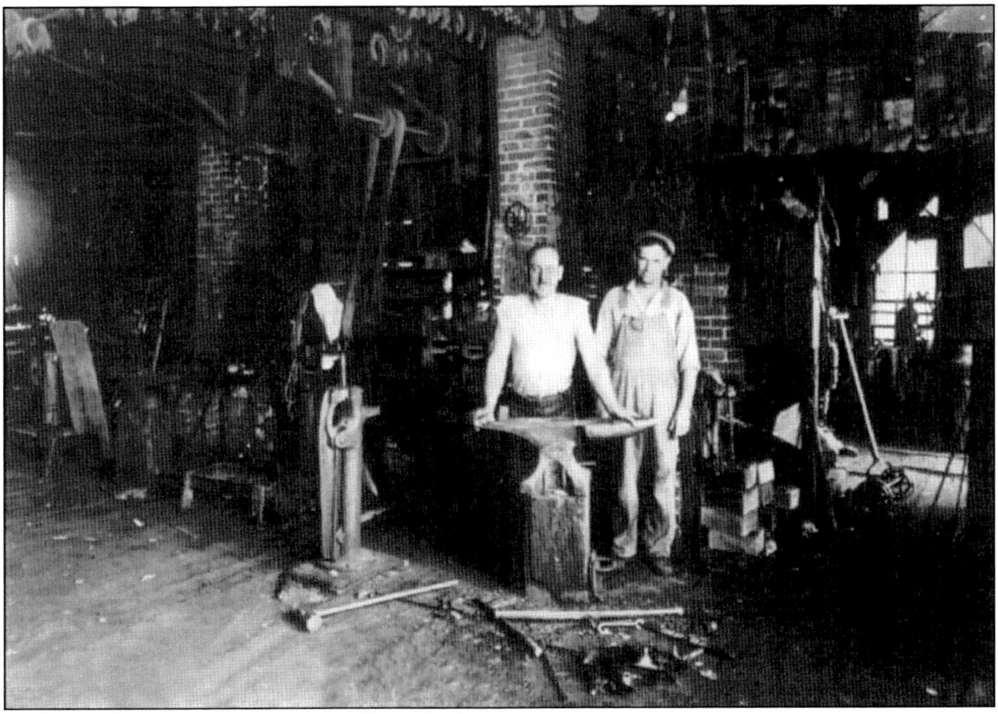

Bob Taylor is seen here in his blacksmith shop.

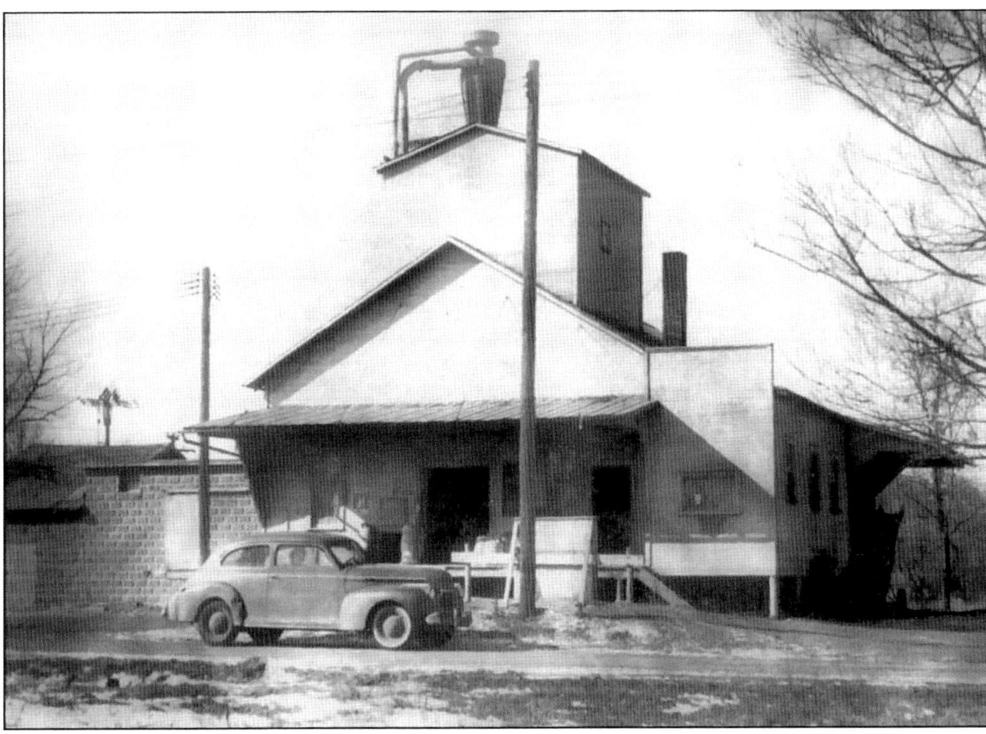

The Millington Grist Mill was operated by Alfred Fischaber and Herb Schleier.

Now back north and west journey with me
And Squires' Implement Shop we will see
Before we even get there, I will tell you now—
They sell everything from a hoe to a plow.

Right on the corner a filling station we see,
With Red Crown gas waiting for you and me.
Mr. Clare Bishop is the manager here,
For gas, people come from both far and near.

Right next door, plain in sight
Is the Whippet, Oakland, and Pontiac whose lights burn bright
Mr. Hall will be there to show you around
And three better cars cannot be found.

This is the Post Office where everyone sails
There to receive their letters and mails
In this same place upstairs is the office of Doc,
He will cure all your ills and you'll be solid as a rock.

Right here is McPherson's you can tell
Who keeps a big line of hardware to sell
From a big steel range down to a wagon jack
To a penny nail or a small carpet tack.

There's L.J., the barber, and he is no knave
Or Wilson, each will give you a good shave.
Their cups are all clean, and their brushes are too,
A good place to go if you need a shampoo.

After you get a shampoo, just step in the back
And Miss Brand will greet you and give you a marcell
After she fashions you with waves and curls
You may then go out in society's whirls.

For oils, paints, varnishes, linoleum and these
At Parker's Hardware you will surely be pleased
Oil stoves, cook stoves, ranges and such
You'll find there and the cost is not much.

Gerald Farnum, the Druggist, next we meet
With a line of powder, perfumes, and drugs complete
Books by all authors there abound
And the fact that they're interesting soon will be found.

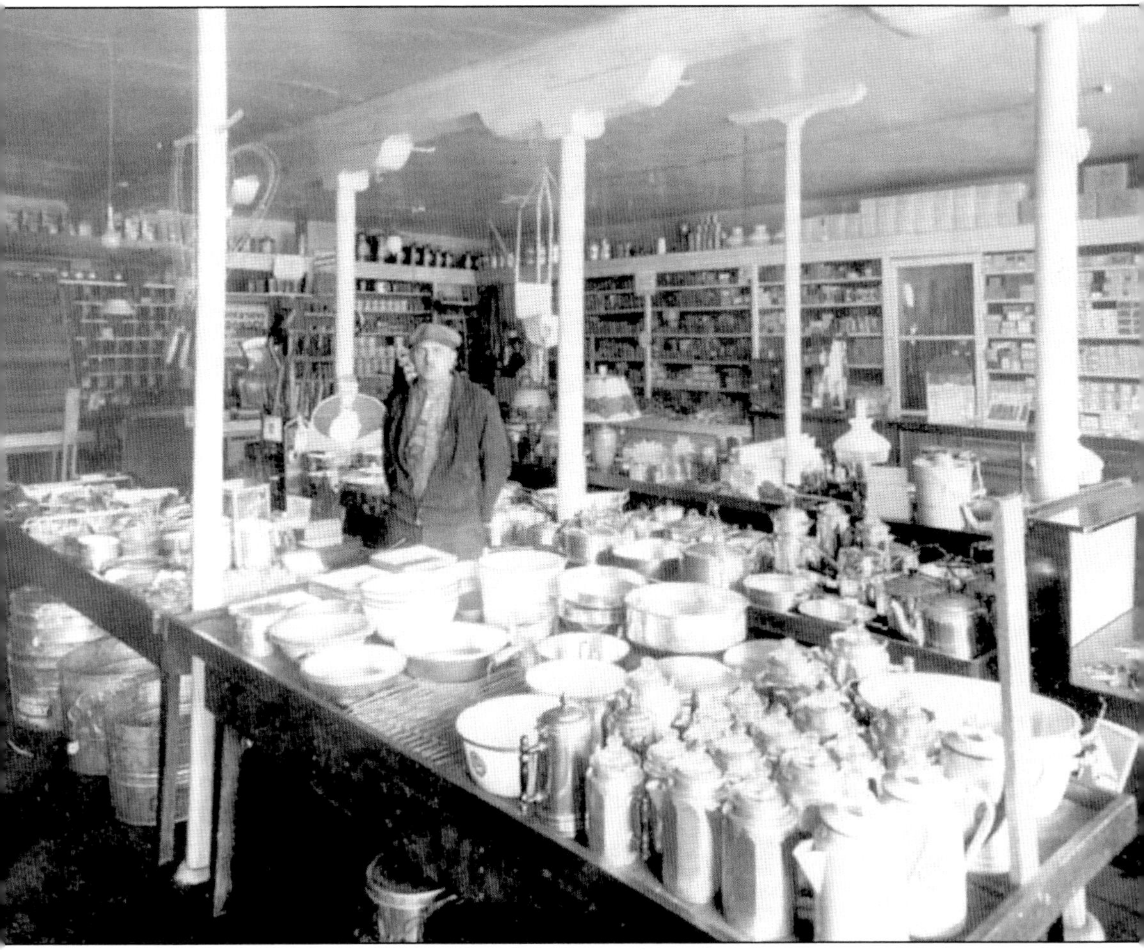

George McPherson is pictured in his hardware store in the 1930s.

Not much farther need you go
To the Millington Oil Co., where they sell Sun-o-co
All their many patrons they delight
With quality and prices that are right.

Conway's Restaurant you will find
Is a very, very good place to dine
The very best cooking and baking you will say
For such a meal you will freely pay.

Crossing the street to Nixon's repair and tire shop,
If you have any trouble, be sure to stop,
We will repair like very few can do
An old, old tire just like new!

Now let us stop to Meacham's Implement Shop
Silos, Windmills, machinery and these
He keeps a line that will more than please
If the weather be rainy or fair, he will always be there.

Back westward we go with a slow, even tread
As we pass by the home of the Millington dead.
We bow our heads and whisper a prayer
We know not how soon we, too, may be there.

And now that my rhymes are almost ended
I hope that I have no one offended
For I am sure no harm has been meant
As it was composed by a Millington resident!

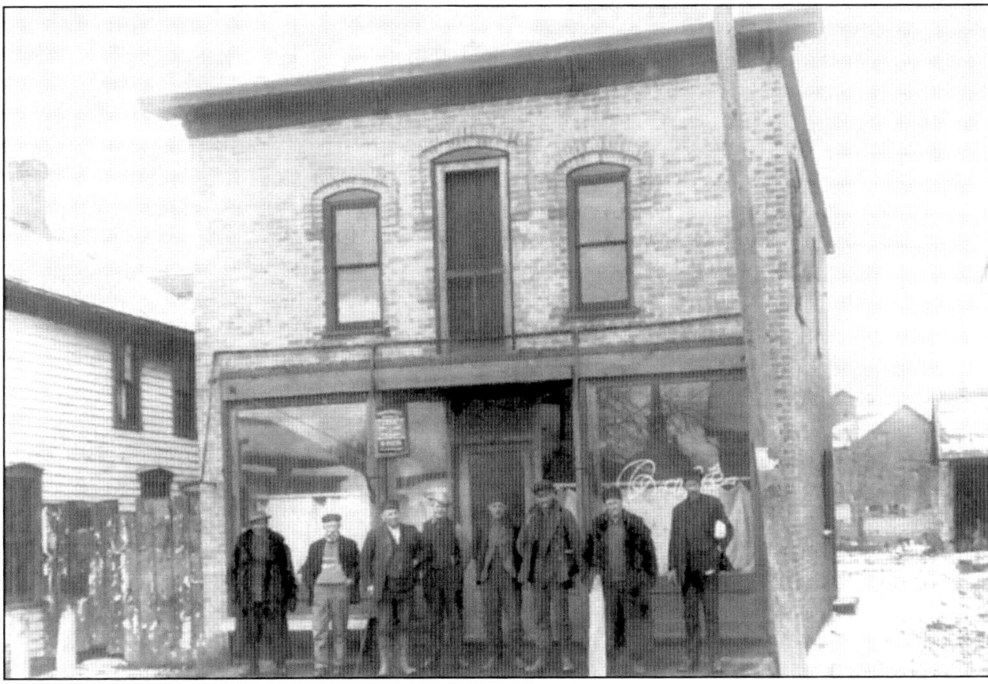

This café on East Main Street occupies the building that later became home to the telephone company. It is unknown who operated this café and when.

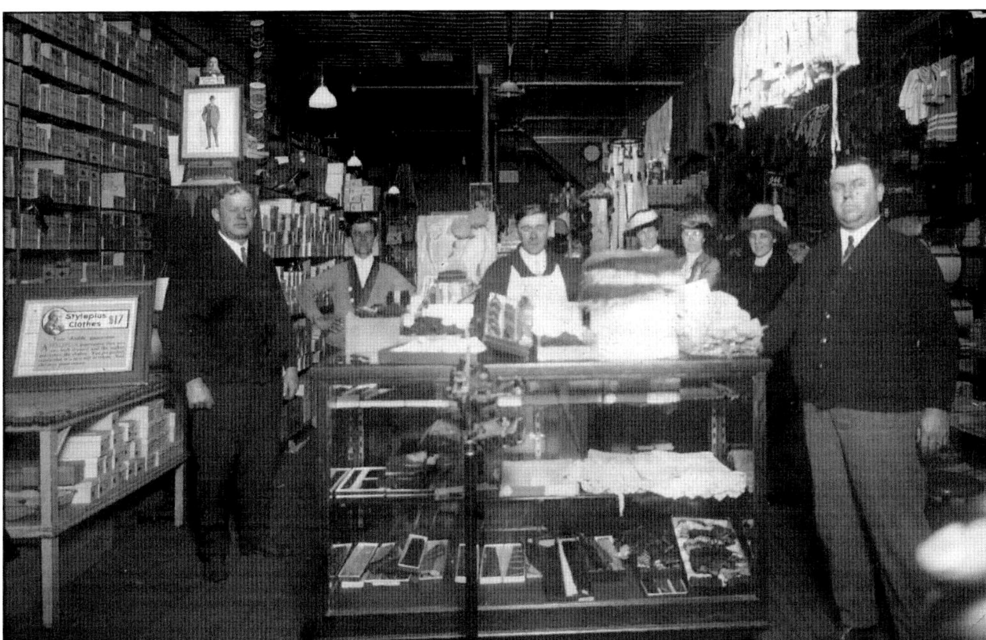


This old photo was printed on a postcard. It shows Alfred Fischaber's store in downtown Millington, which was called the People Store.

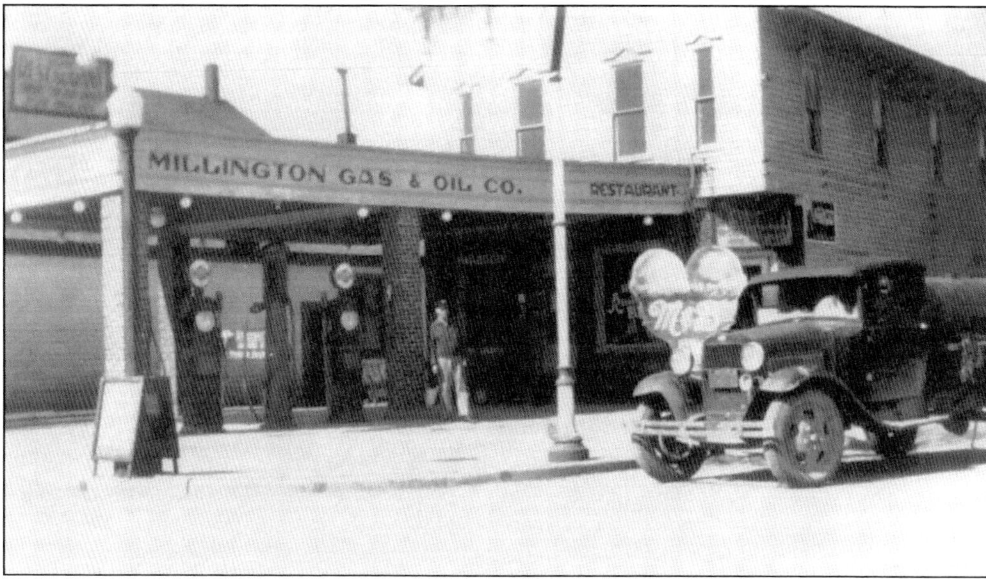


This photo shows the Millington Gas and Oil Company with Conway Restaurant in the corner. This building was built by the owners of the Millington Bank and leased to the oil company which was managed by Howell Haines.

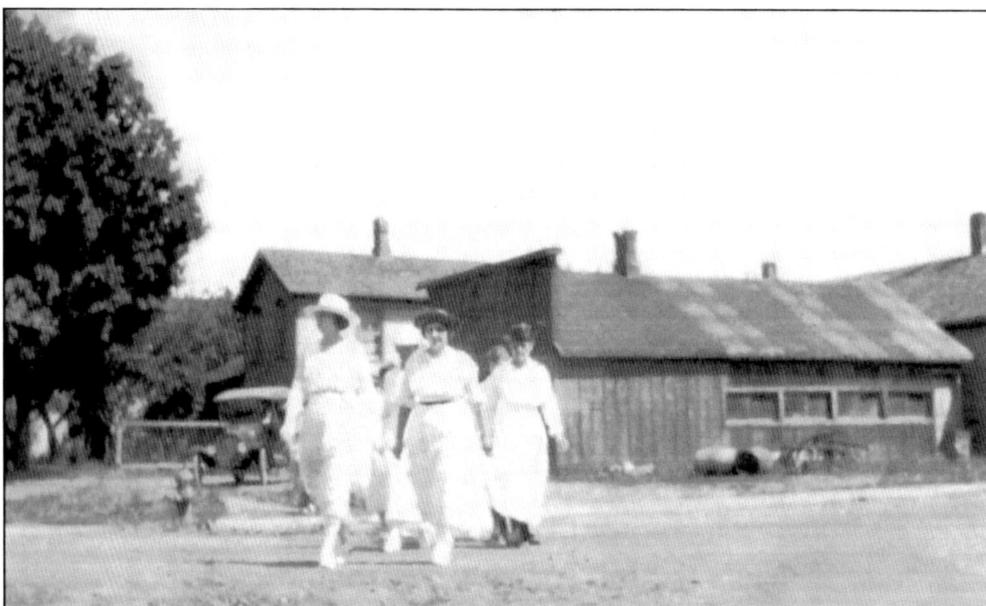

Ladies of Millington in the 1920s are pictured in their finery. Note the old car in the background and the storage building which was on the site of the current township parking lot at State and Center Streets.

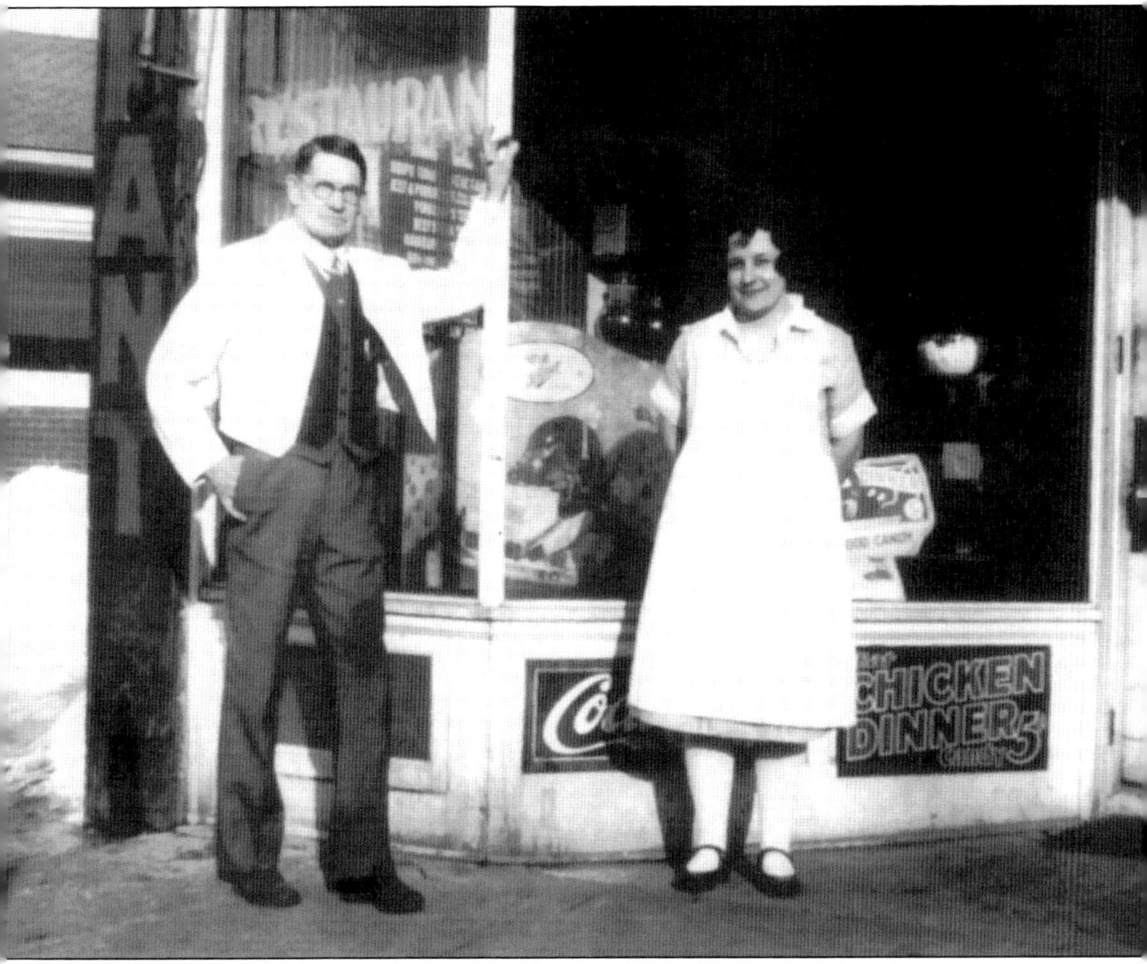


Cy Losure and his wife, Carrie, ran one of Millington's early bakeries with an excellent restaurant serving the finest of meals. The sign to the right of Carrie reads "Eat Chicken Dinner Candy 5¢."

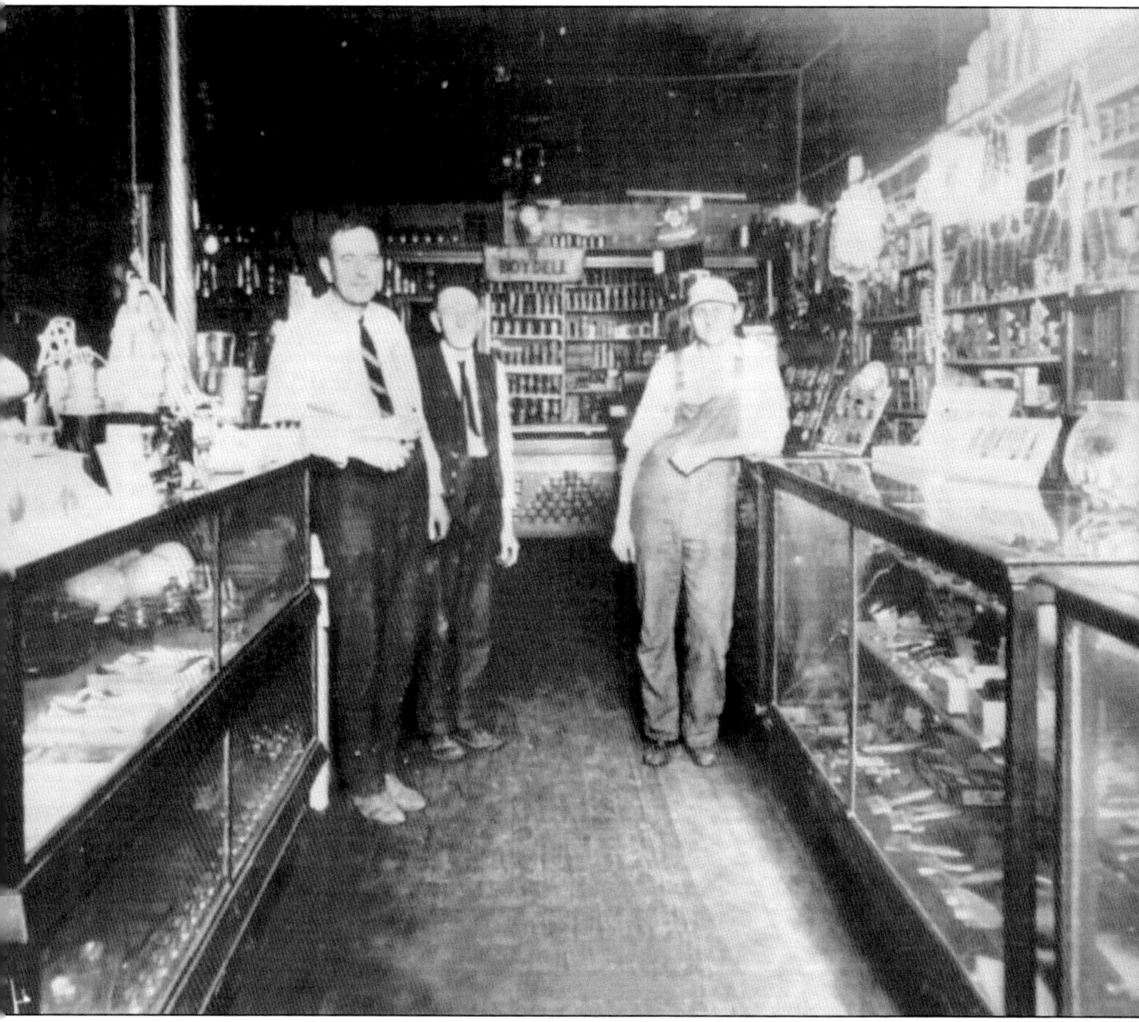

For many years, the McPherson brothers had the largest and most complete hardware store in the Millington area. The building still stands and is now an antique shop. From left, William, Clarence, and George McPherson are pictured in the 1920s.

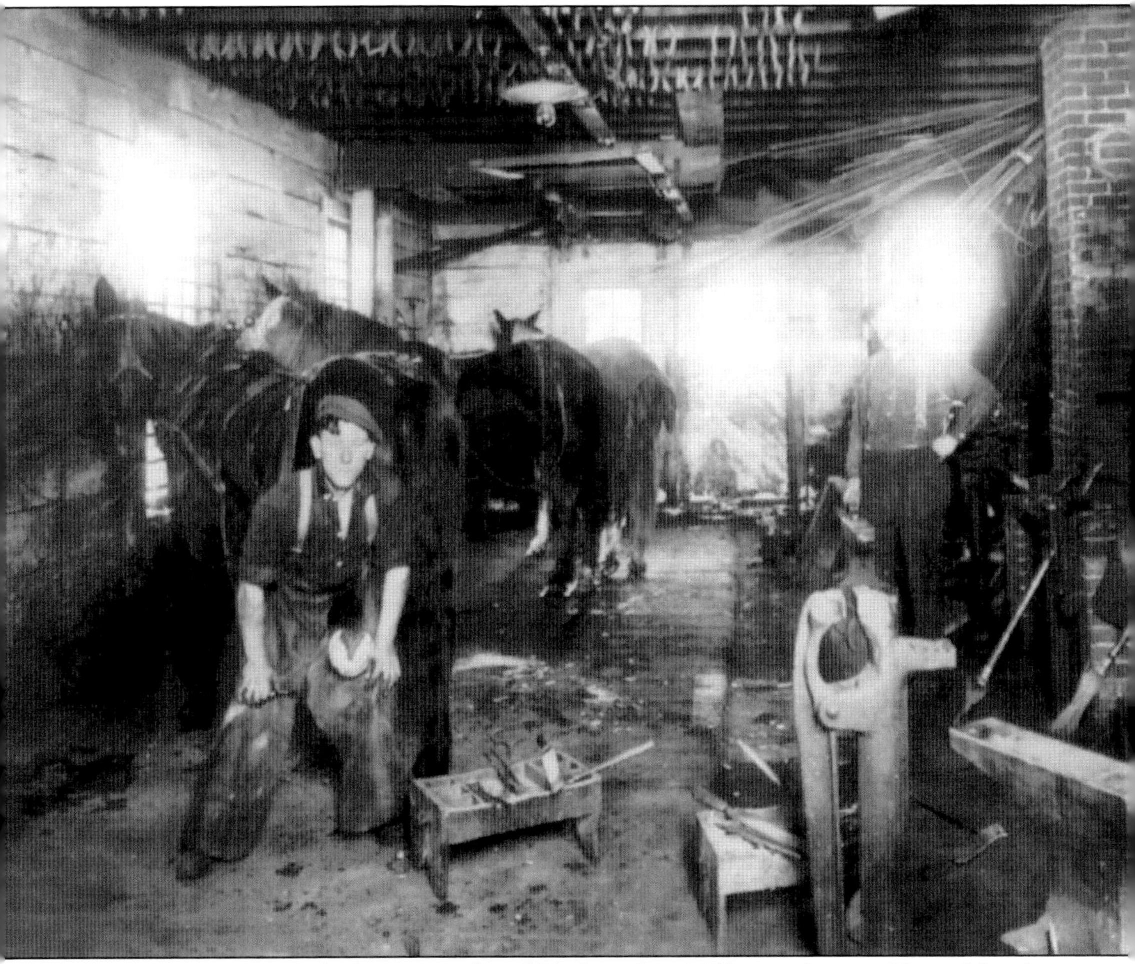

Bobby Taylor is probably the best remembered blacksmith in Millington history. He could and would do anything to get what you needed. In this 1920s photograph, he is shoeing a horse with one of his "homemade" horseshoes.

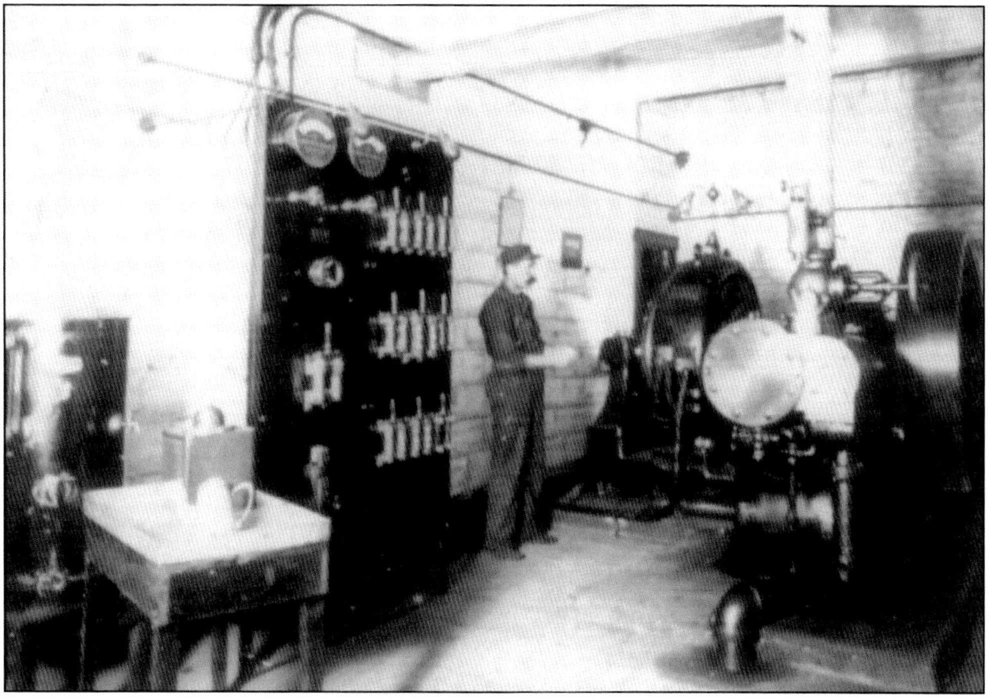

At one time, Millington had one of the earliest power plants, which supplied electricity to the village. The plant was sold when the large companies like Detroit Edison began to produce the "so-called" cheap power.

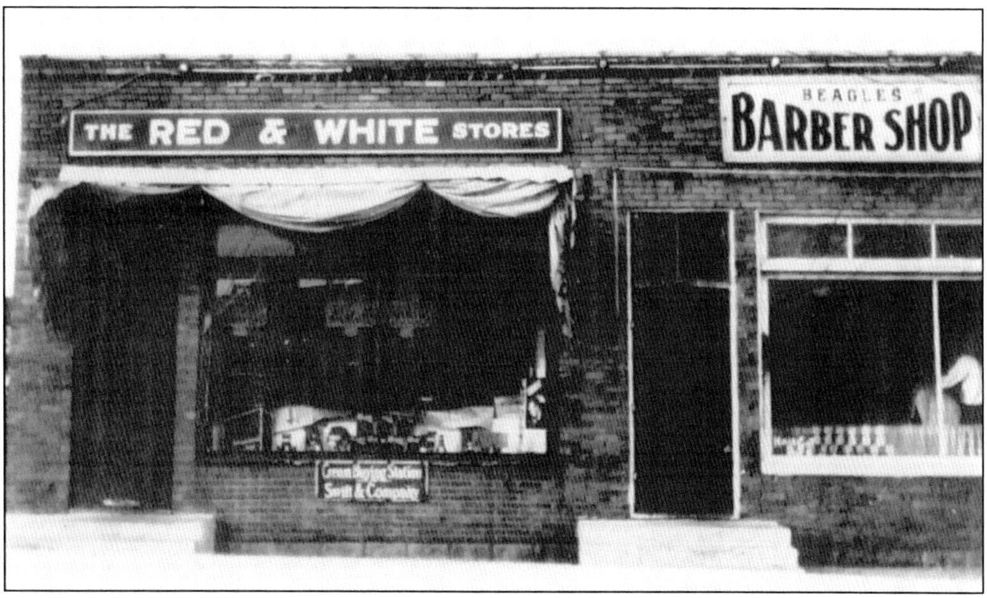


Millington's first dime store was adjacent to Beagles barber shop. With haircuts for only 25¢, you could get a year's worth of haircuts for the price of one today.

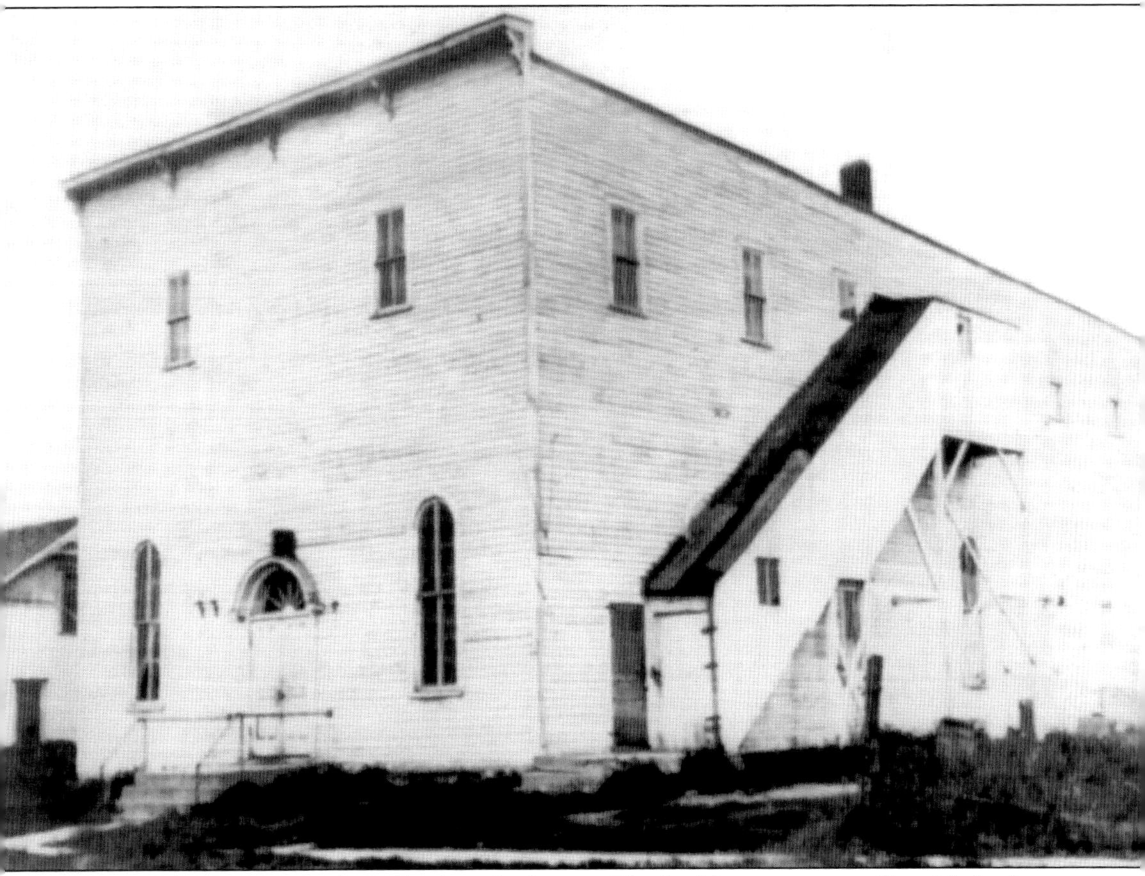

The Capitol Theater was the village's only theater. The building was originally a Methodist church. Notice the curved church-style windows in the front. The building was sold to the Macabees Club and then acquired by a man who converted it into a movie house. Many stage shows were held there also.

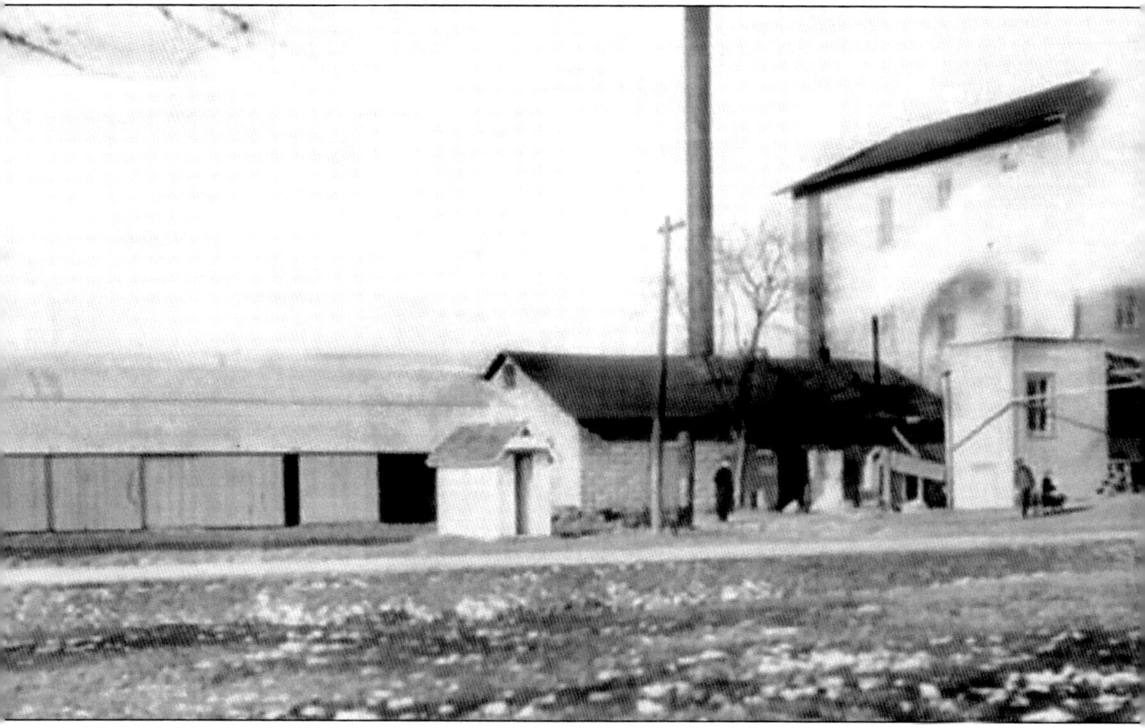

This mill was one of the few steam-powered mills in the area. Located on East Street, it served the community for many years, grinding farmers' grain into animal feed. One of the by-products was many corn cops which were gathered by local boys and sold as kindling for wood and coal stoves.

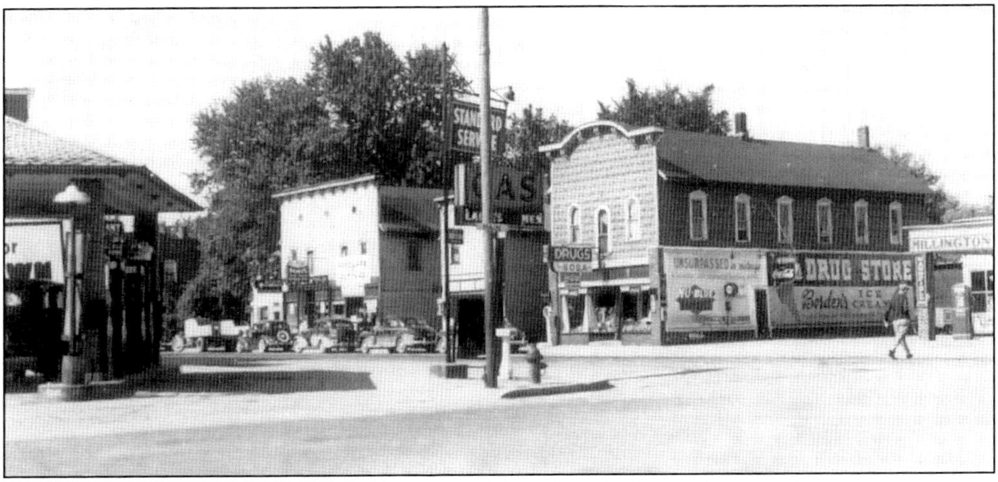


Millington's Standard Gas station was owned by Clare Bishop who later became postmaster for the area.

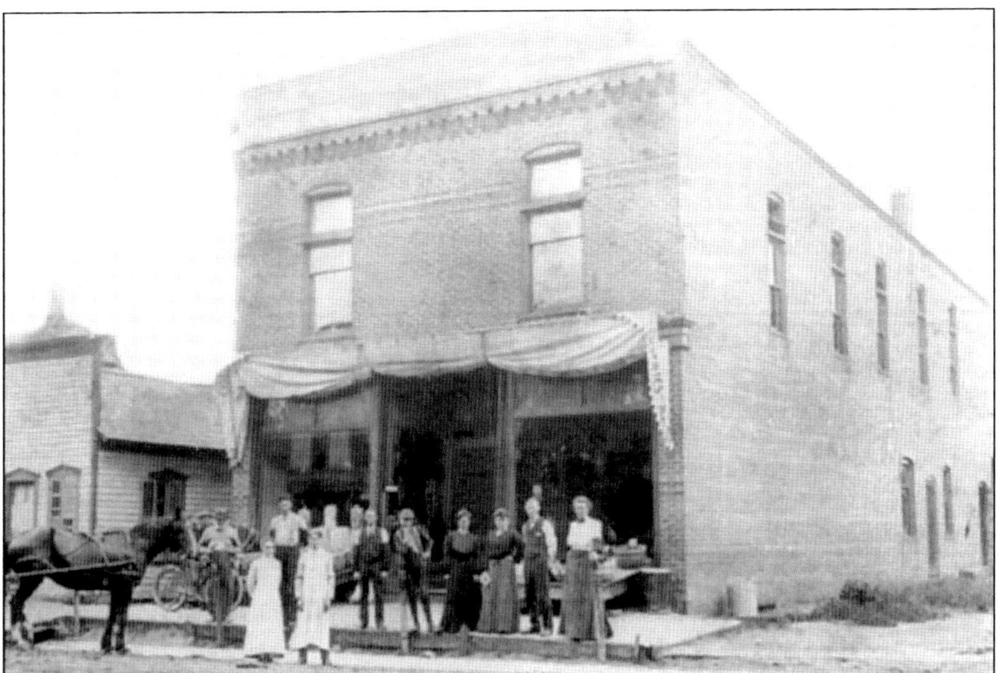

This is the drug store that served the area for many years under two or more families. The building is now vacant, but is soon to reopen with a new business.

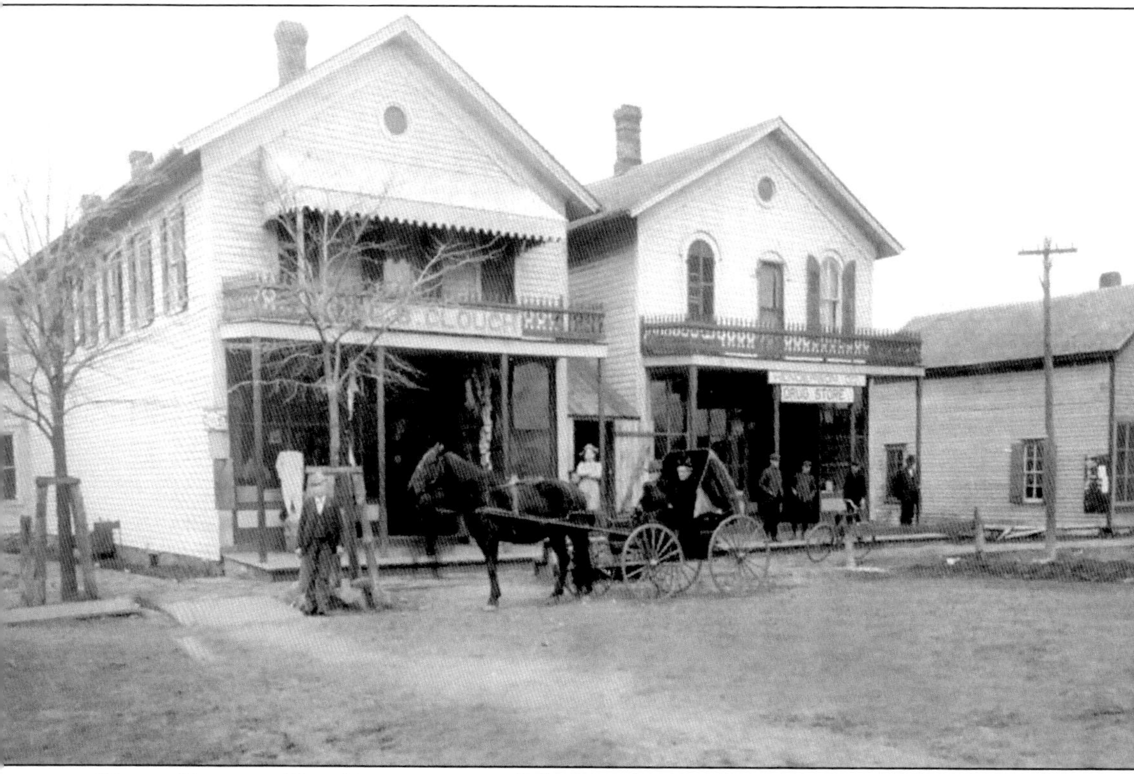


Pictured here are Clouch's variety store (left), Henderson's drug store (center), and the original local post office (right). The drug store building was later moved and became a private residence. The post office was torn down and replaced by a house. The building that housed the variety store is now an antique store.

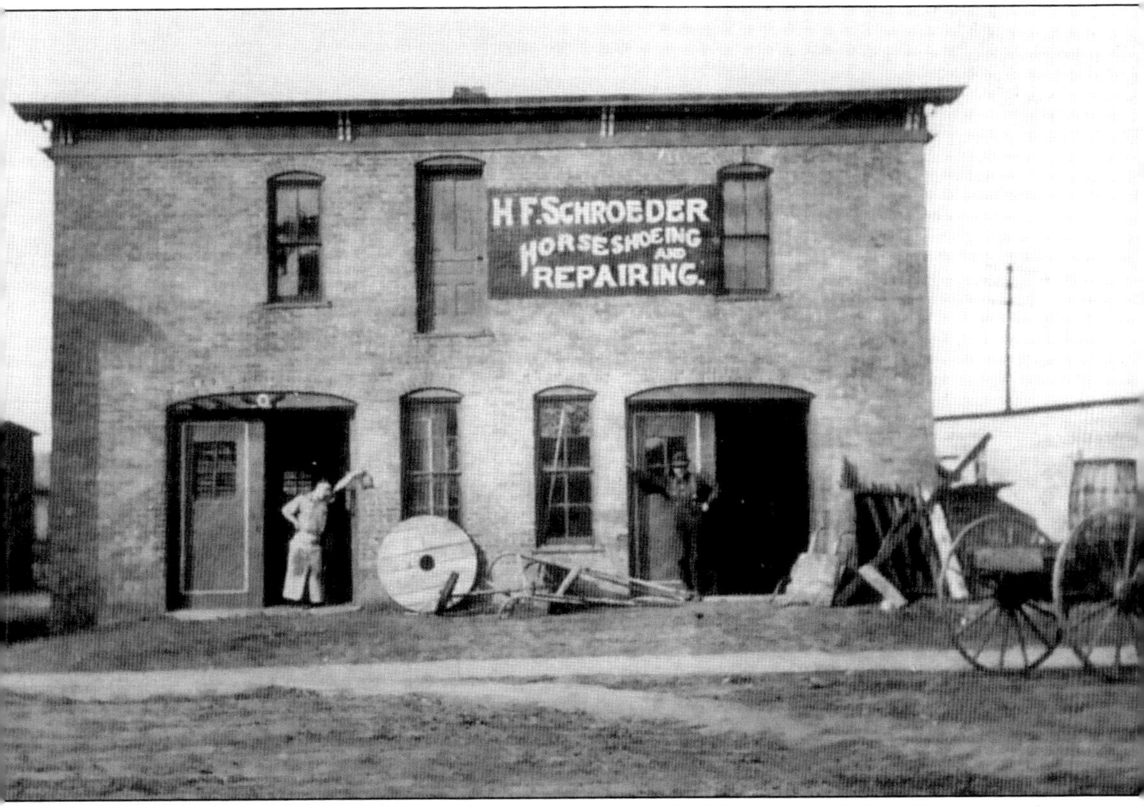


H.F. Schroeder was a blacksmith in early Millington. The building where Schroeder operated his business later housed Bobby Taylor's blacksmith shop.

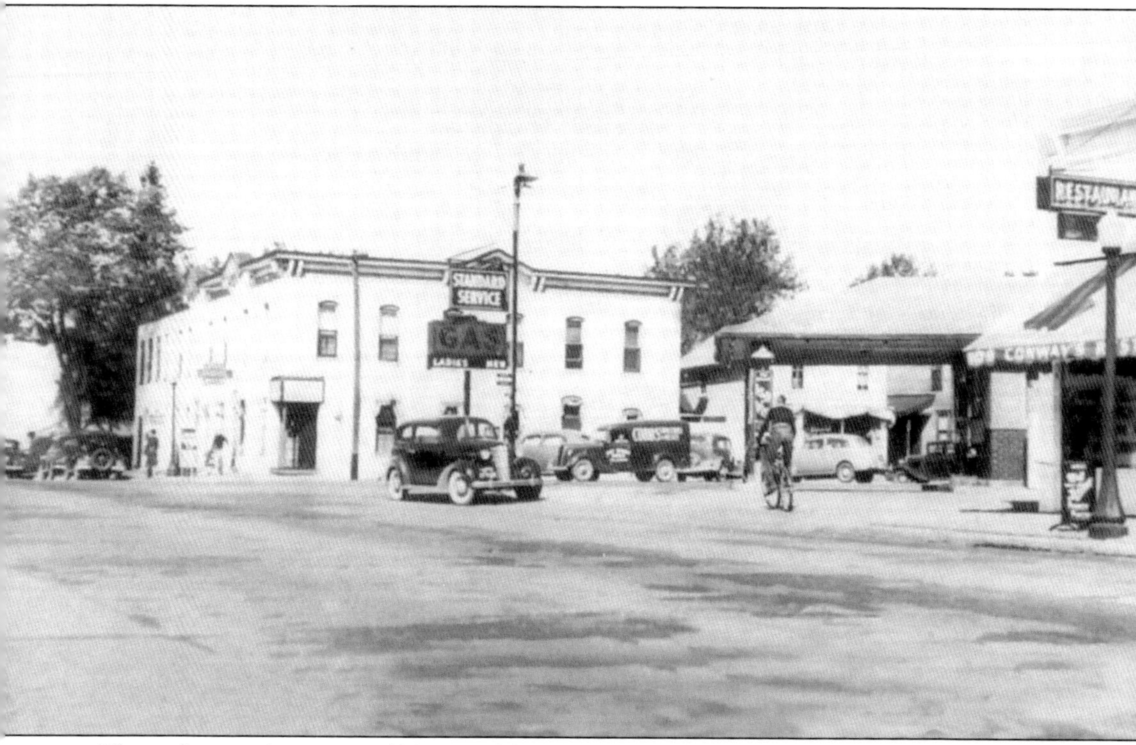


This is the popular corner of Main and State Streets in the 1930s. Note the Capitol Theater in the left rear. The Cobbs truck (center) was likely being driven by Ivan McPherson.

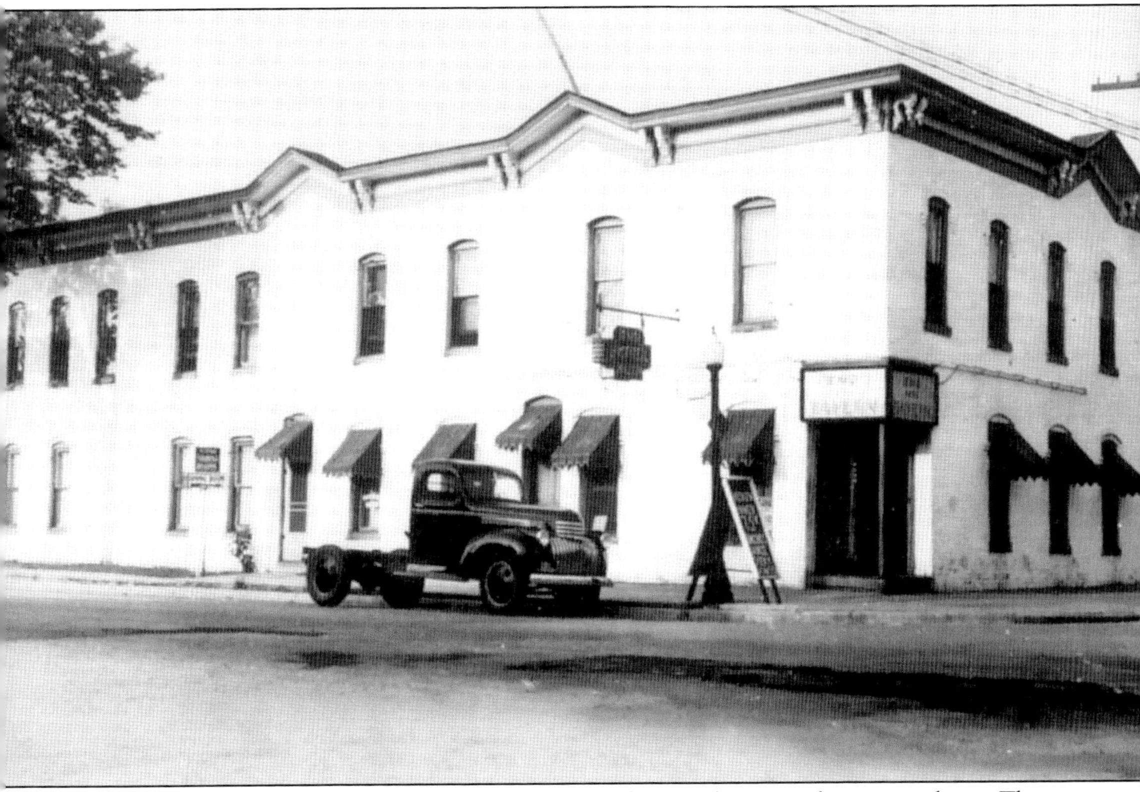

This is the Eno Hotel and Tavern, which later suffered an explosion and was torn down. The side door led to the restaurant and ballroom where many local teens spent their Saturday nights.

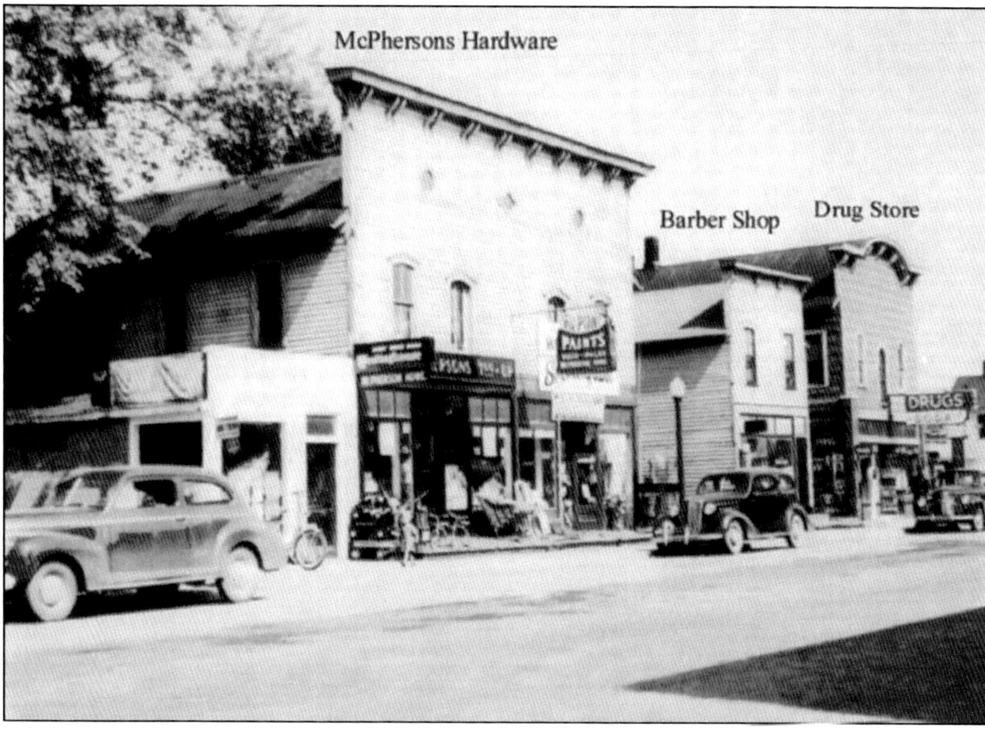


These three buildings have been landmarks for many years. At the present time, they are home to (from left) an antique store, a beauty shop, and a tanning parlor.

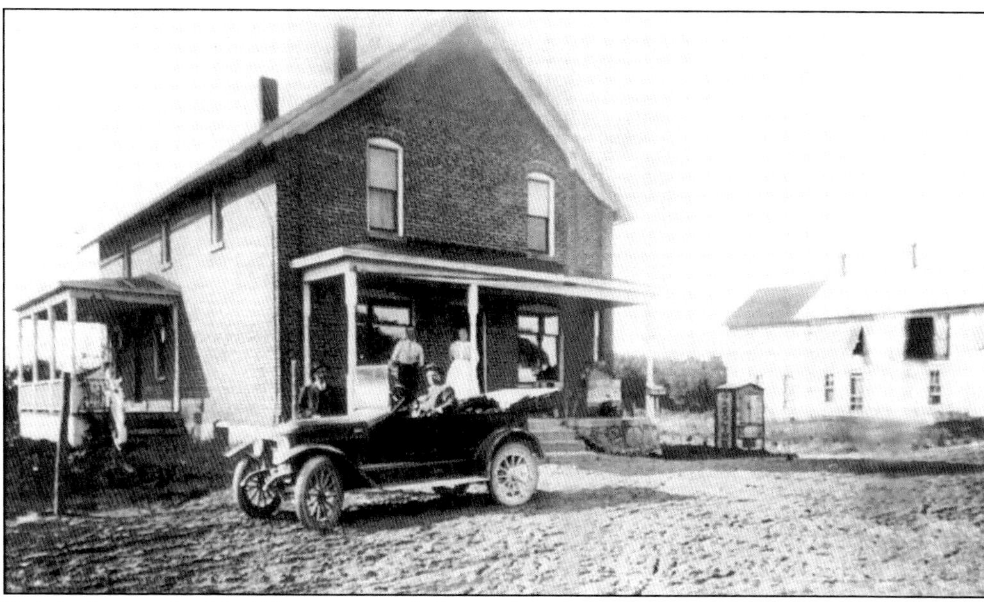

This is the popular Neal Frost store and cheese factory, located at Birch Run and Bray Roads. From time to time, residents would stop in to stock up on supplies and chat with Neal and his wife. It was Arbela's most popular stopping place.

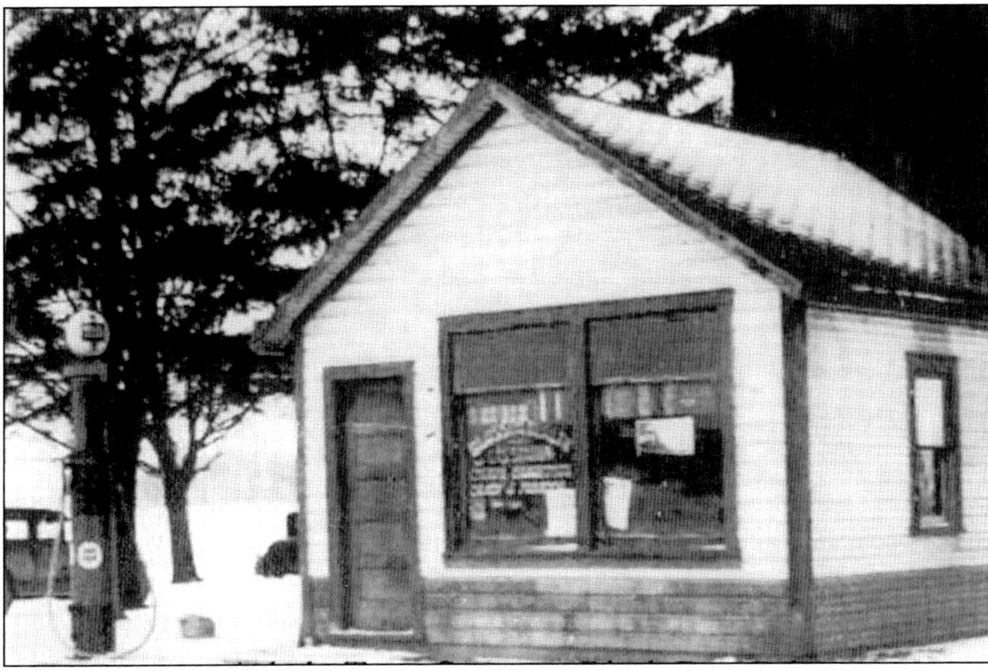

This Arbela store on Birch Run Road no longer exists but served the needs of the community at the time.

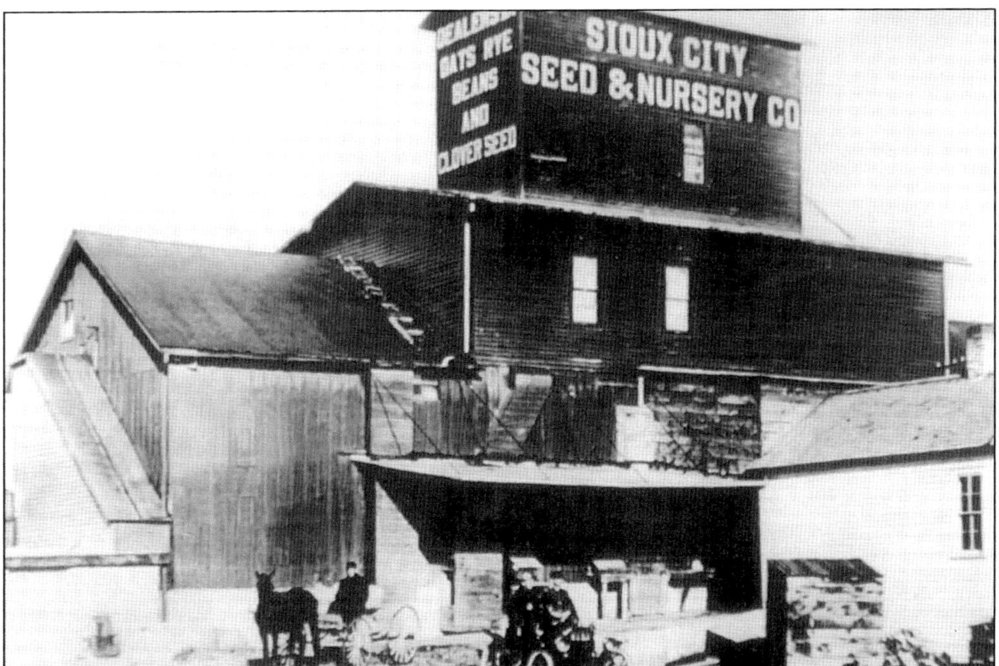


This business, the Sioux City Seed & Nursery Co., was operated by H.B. Johns and flourished for many years. It is currently active as the Millington Elevator and serves the needs of the farming community.

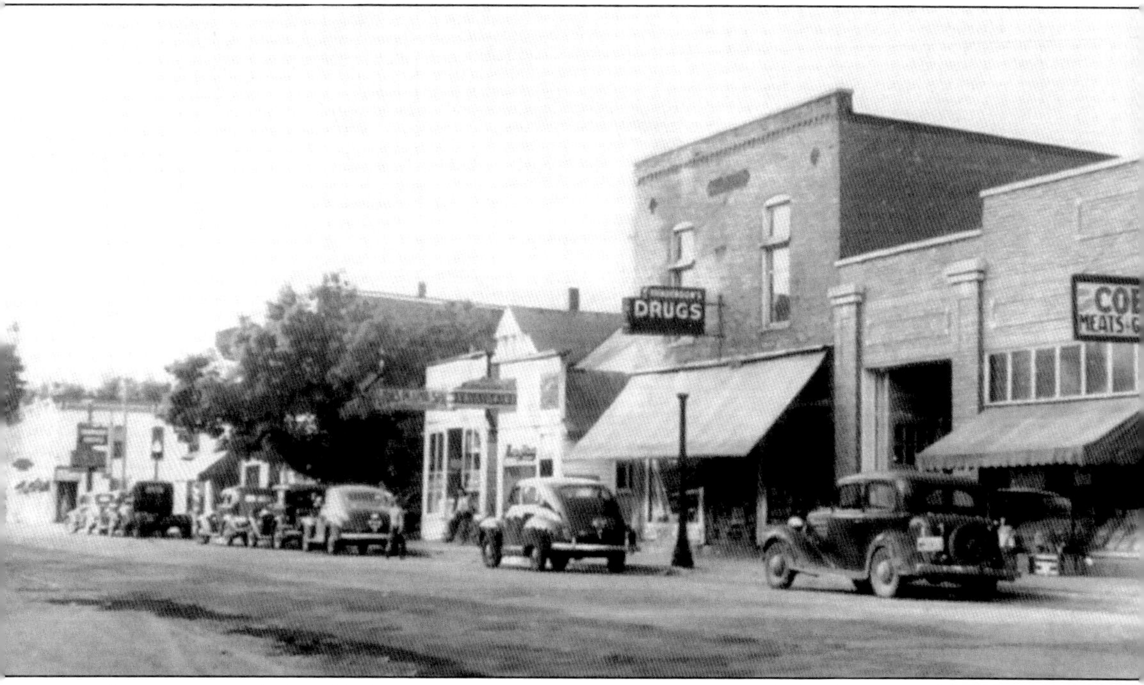


Cornerstones of the 1930s community were Cobbs Grocery (which also sold dry goods), Henderson Drugs, Red Drapers Appliance Shop, and Van's Plumbing. The photo shows looks north on State Street to show these businesses.

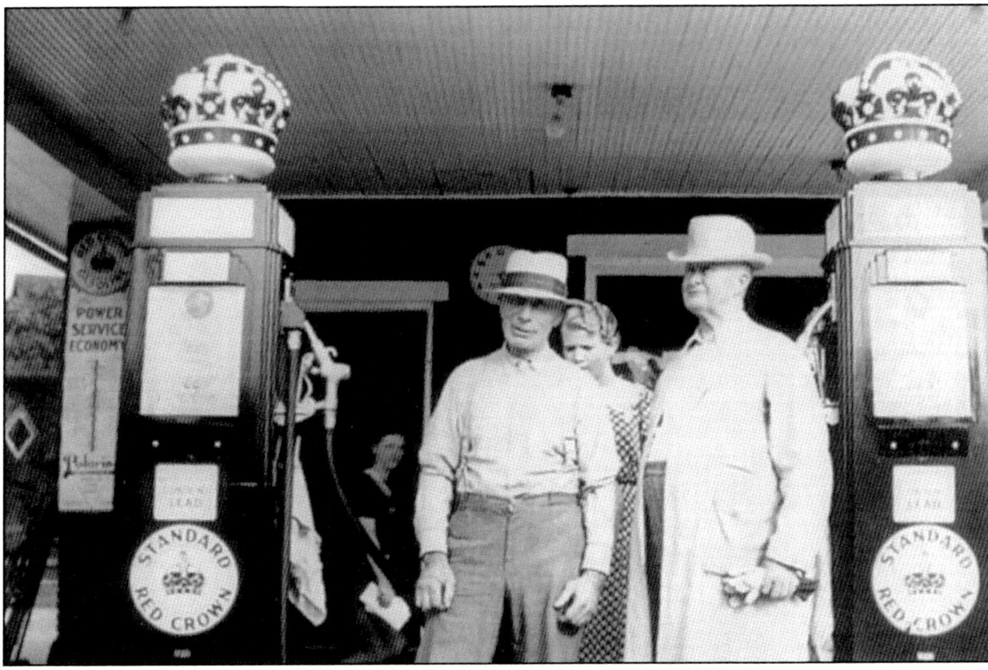


Two residents stand outside of Standard service station, a popular place to stop and chat. Orie Cardwell is in the long coat, and beside him is Ed Gunnel.

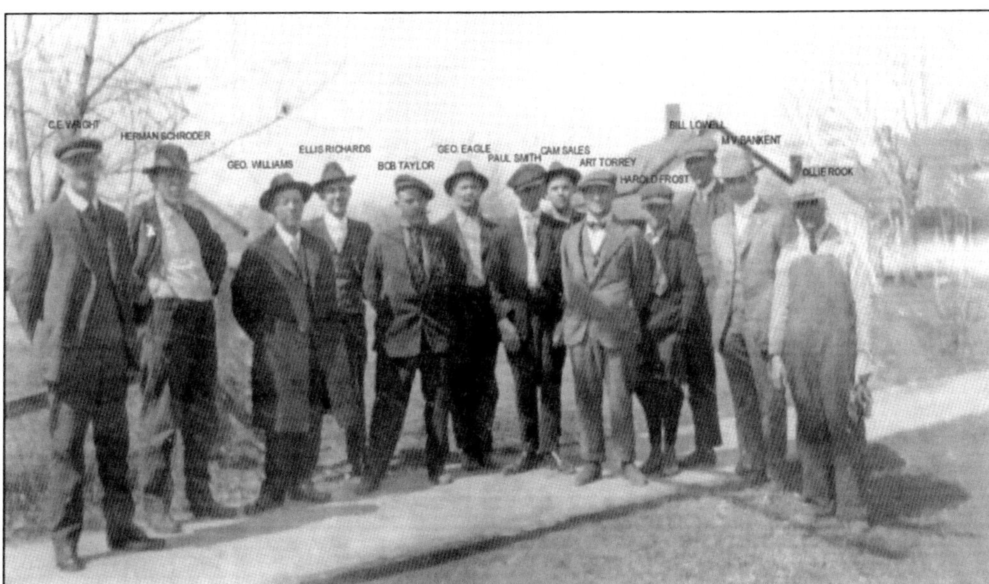


Early village businessmen pose for this picture, taken in the 1920s. They are, from left to right: C.E. Wright, Herman Schroder, Geo. Williams, Ellis Richards, Bob Taylor, Geo. Eagle, Paul Smith, Cam Sales, Art Torrey, Harold Frost, Bill Lowell, M.V. Bankent, and Ollie Rook. Note that they are dressed in suits, the business dress of the time.

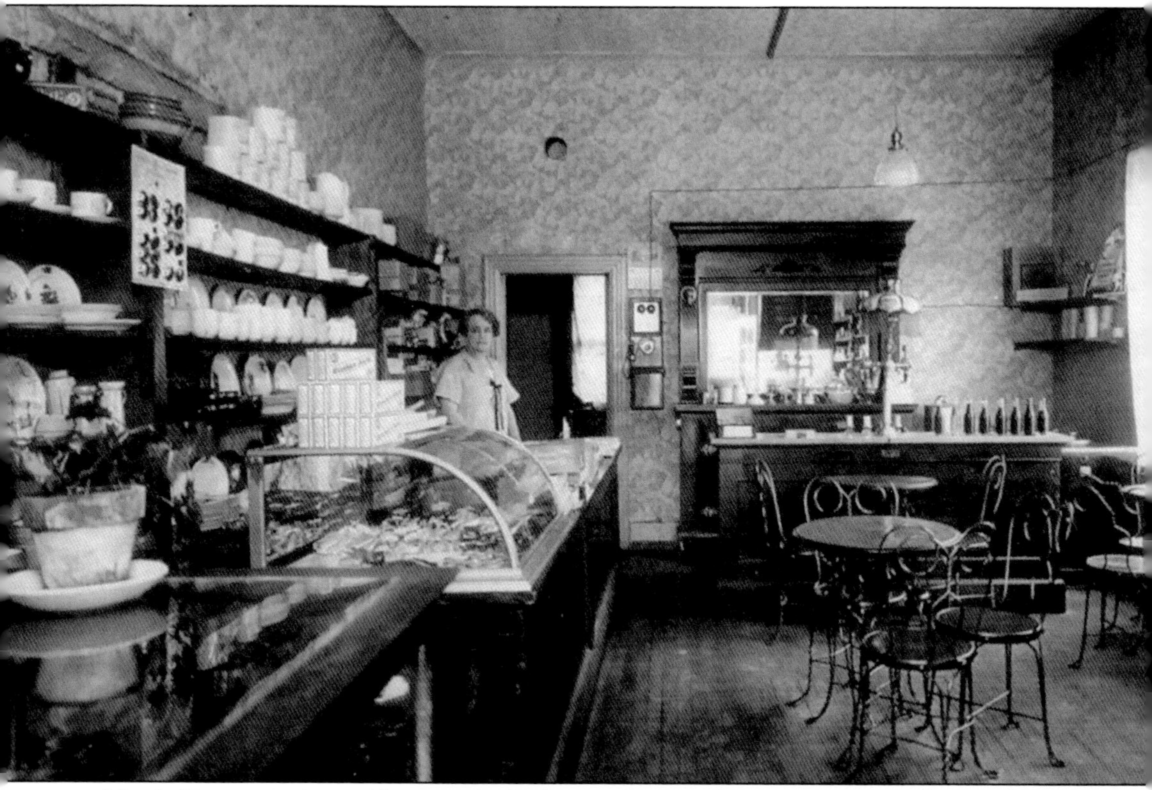

Myrtle Conway is pictured here inside the famous Conway Restaurant. It was a favorite hangout for townspeople, especially the younger crowd.

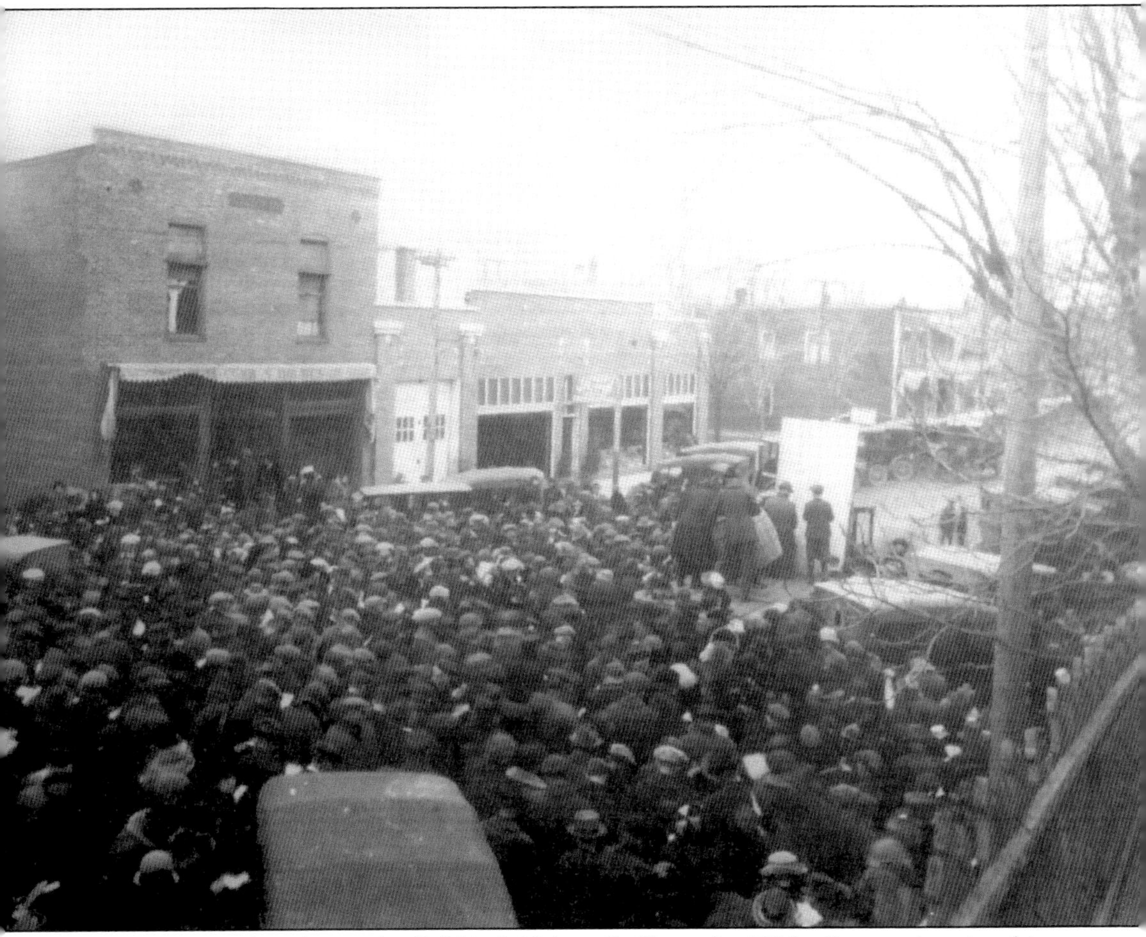

This picture was taken during the Cobb's & Holmes Raffle in the 1920s. Can you imagine this many people attending a raffle? Note that the mass of people prevented auto traffic.

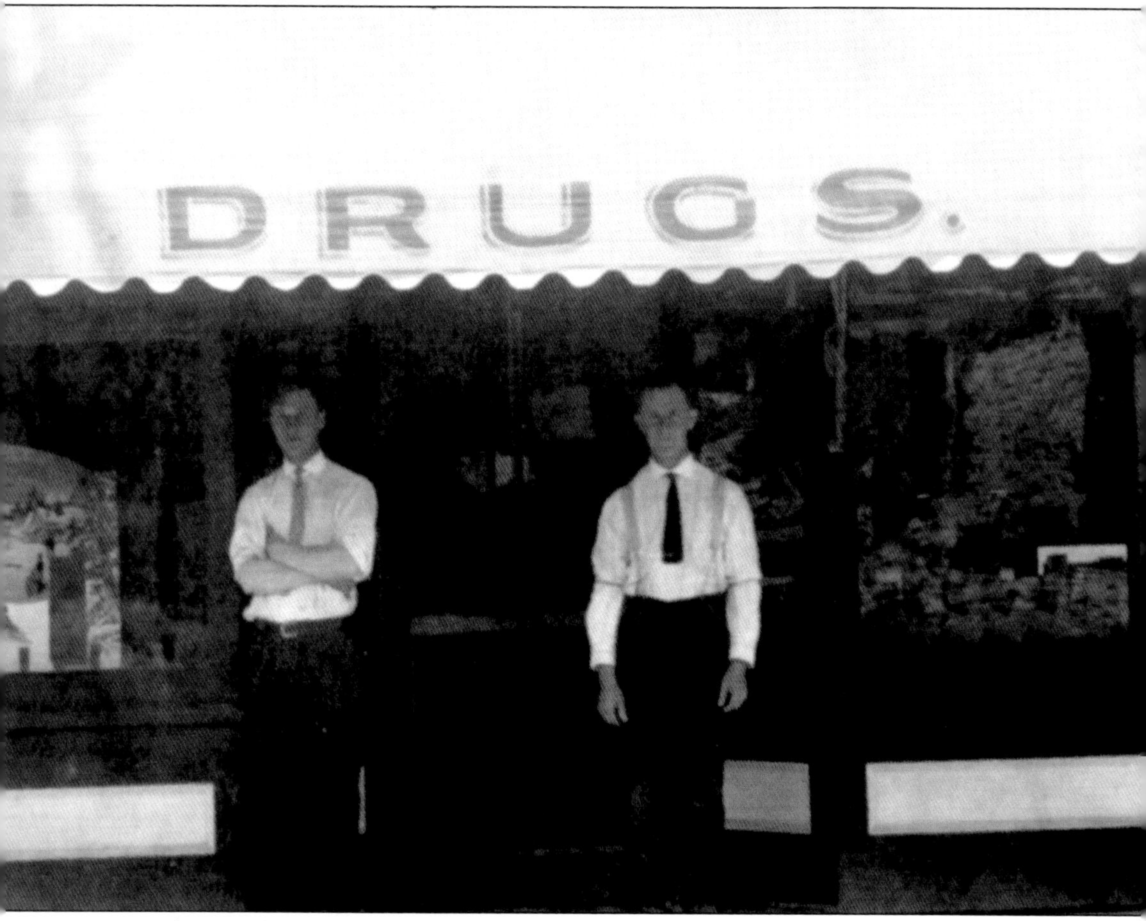


Kennedy's was the place to get medical supplies in Millington. Kids would also load up on candy if their parents approved. The store was located on West State Street.

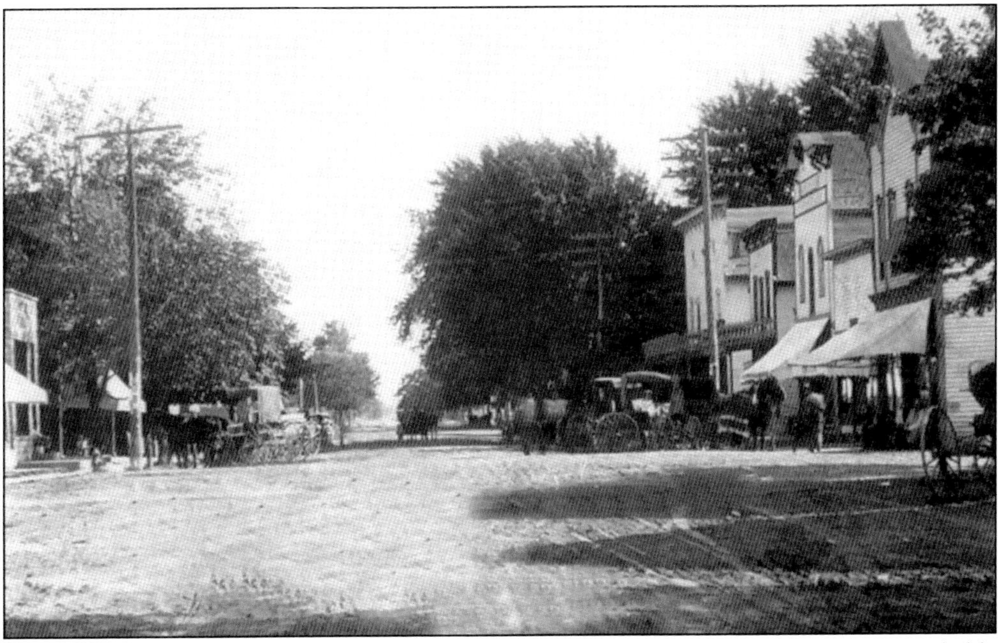

This photo shows State Street looking south during Millington's early days. It was probably taken on a Wednesday or Saturday judging by the number of people in town.

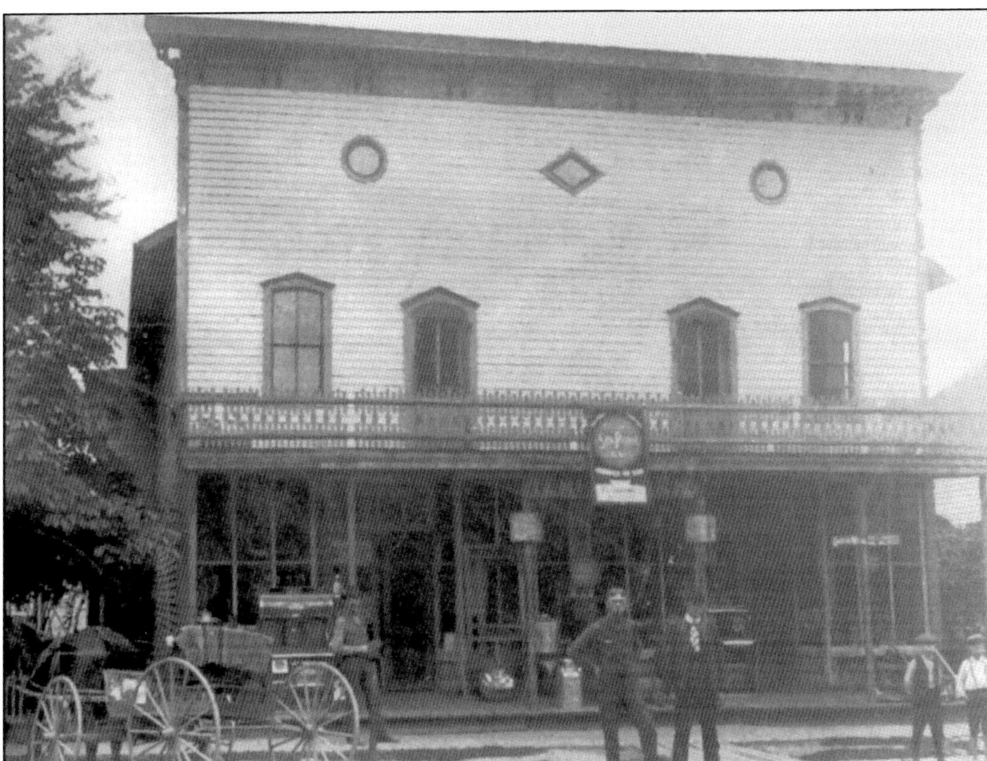

Cardwell Hardware preceded McPherson's Hardware in the same building. The photo is from the 1920s.

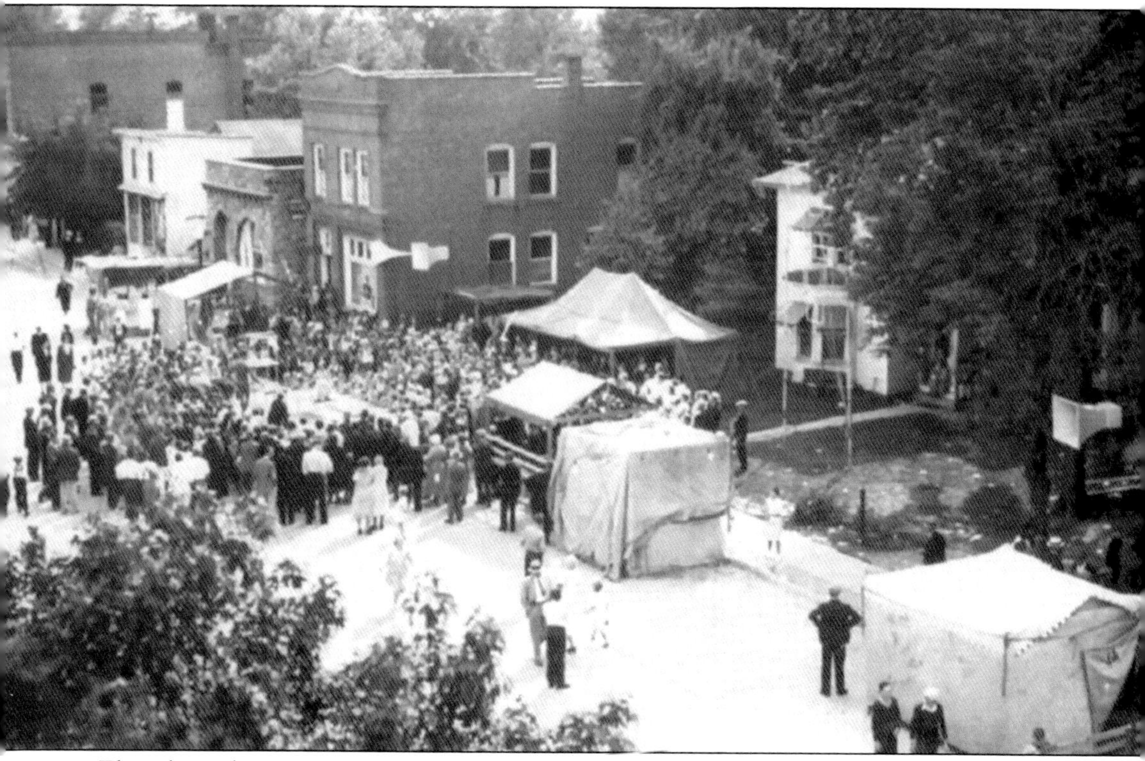

This photo shows a 1930s Millington Homecoming celebration, with crowds gathering at the booths. Tents in front of the funeral home were usually for an ice cream social with homemade ice cream and cakes. The picture was taken south of the hardware store.

# *Eight*
# SPORTS

School sports have been a large factor in the development of the present community. Some of our school players went on to become College and Professional players. Others stayed on and played with village teams. In the following pictures, we try to portray some of these teams. You should be able to recognize many of these people.

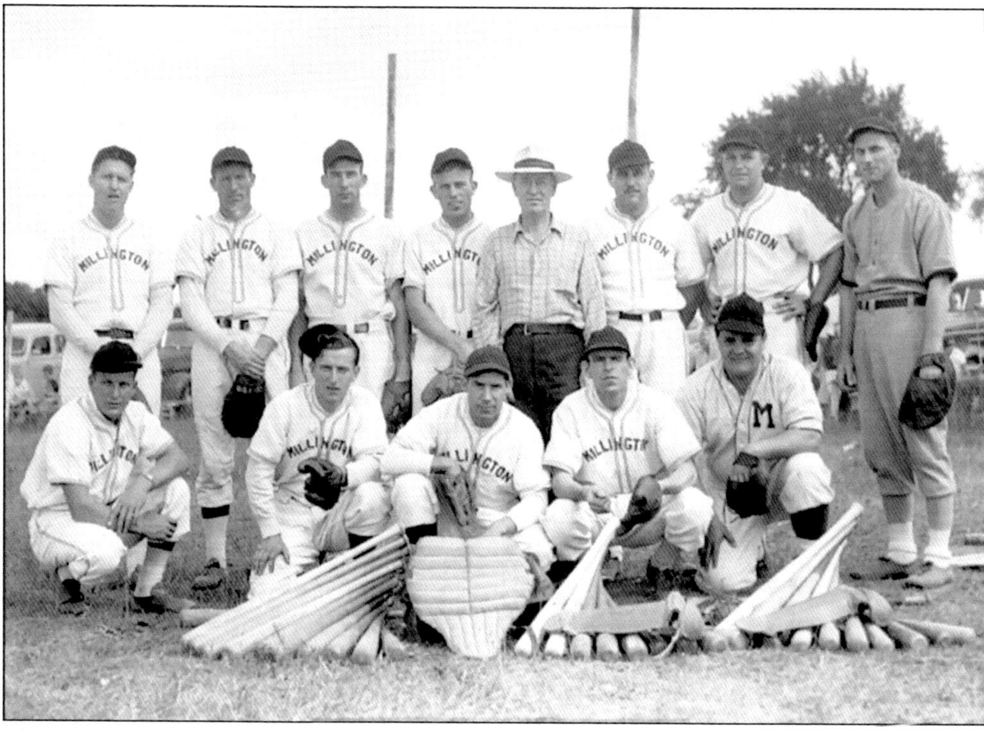

This team, coached by Nate Ross, played in many games in the thumb. They were the 1946 Eastern Michigan League champions.

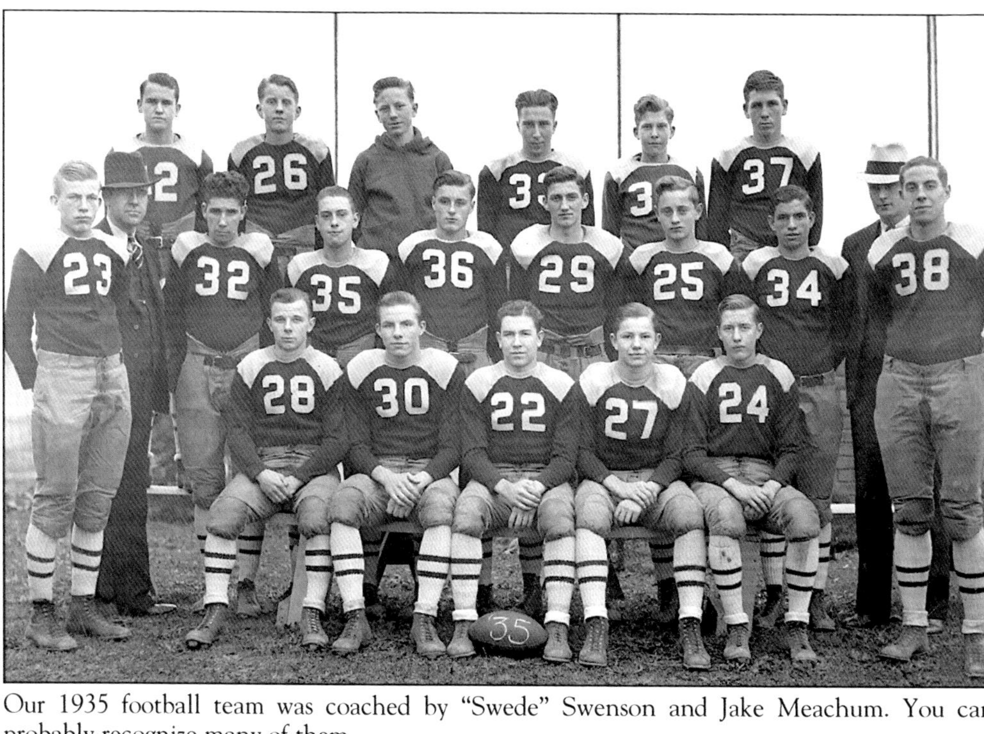

Our 1935 football team was coached by "Swede" Swenson and Jake Meachum. You can probably recognize many of them.

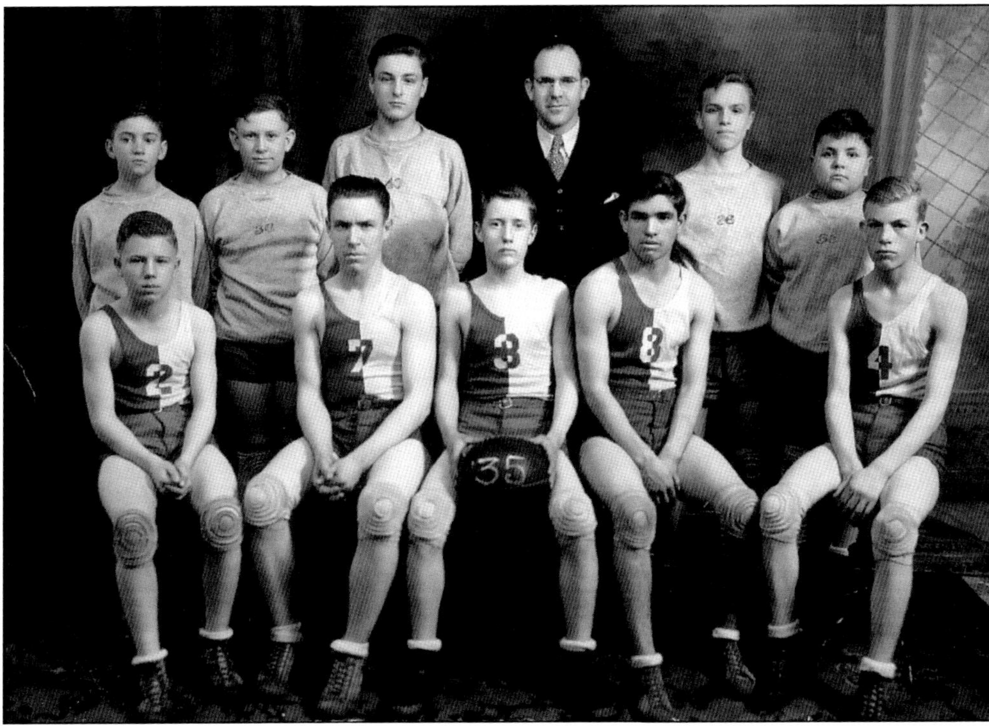

The 1935 "midget" basketball team was coached by Jake Meachum. They won many championships.

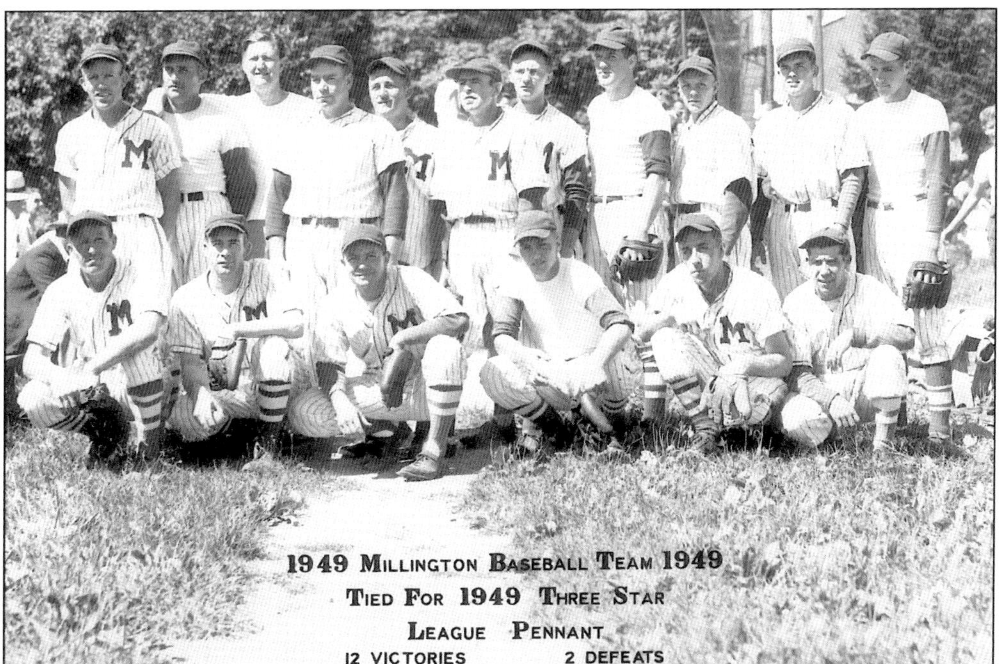


This is the Millington baseball team of 1949. They took the pennant that year and had many more winning seasons.

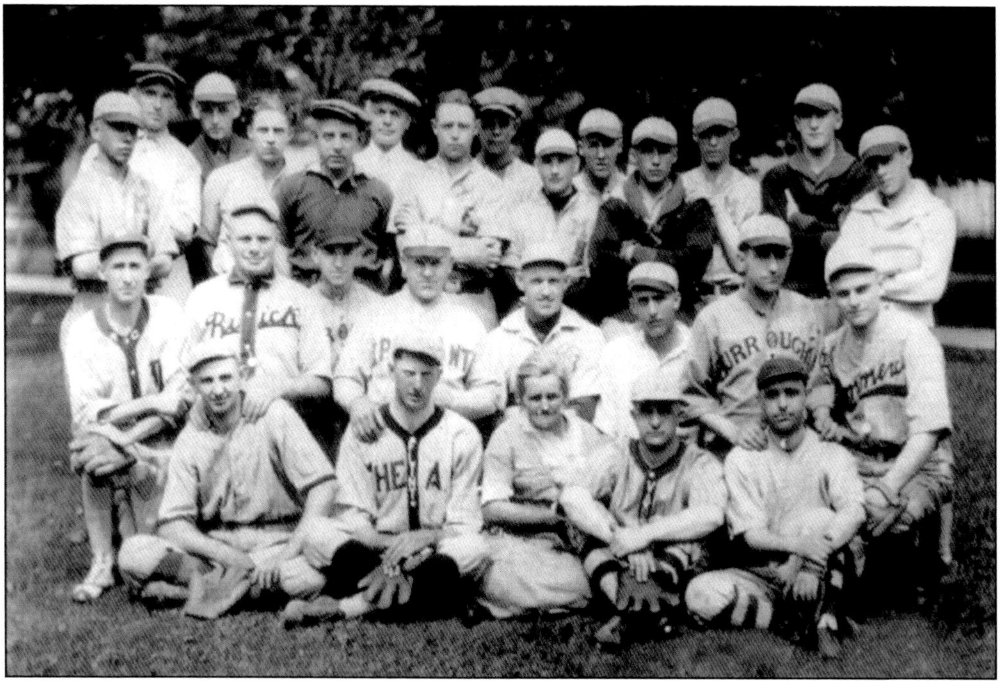

The 1912 and 1922 baseball teams are pictured together. Both teams were very successful. Millington baseball fan Lizzie Richards is pictured in the center of the front row.

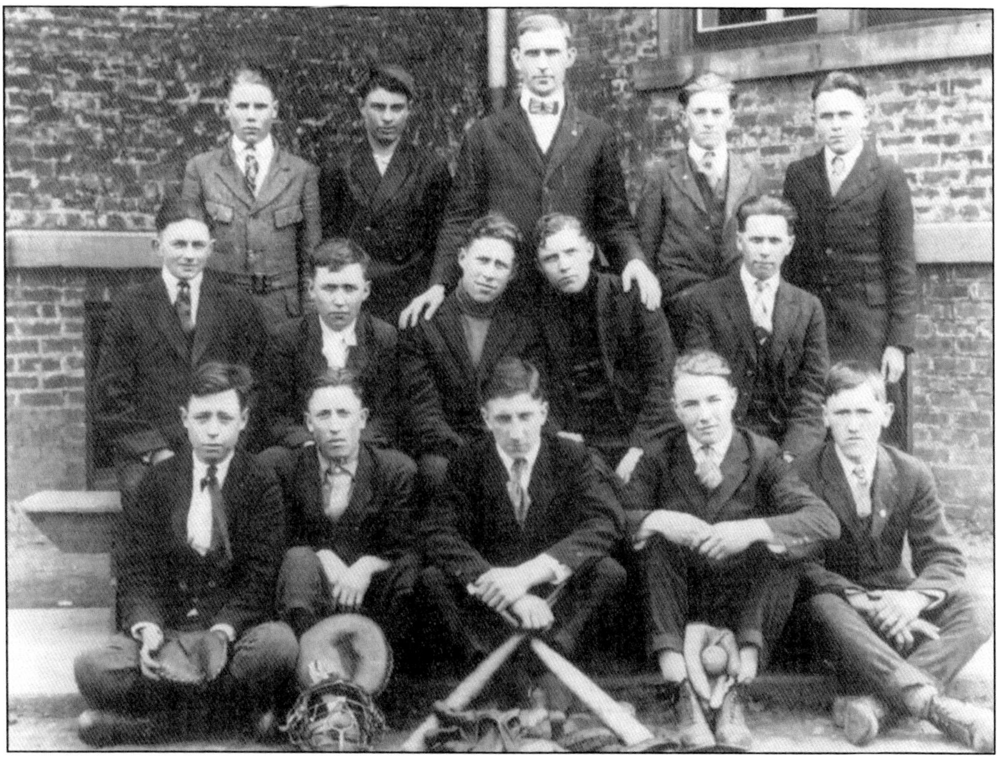

This is a Millington High School baseball team from the 1920s.

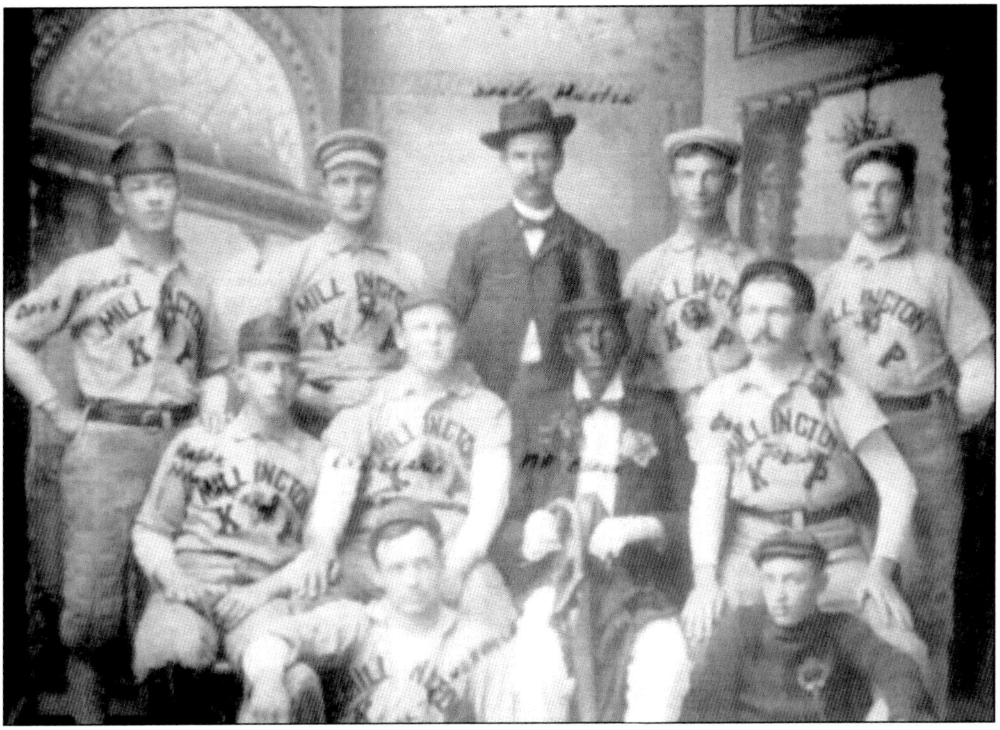

This is another early Millington baseball team.

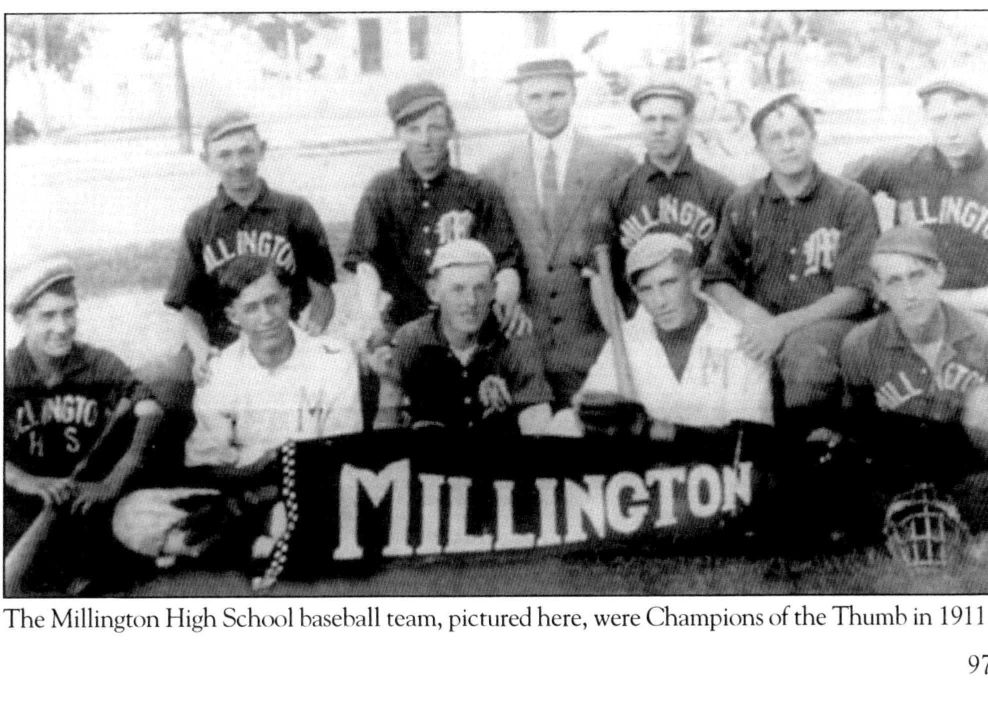


The Millington High School baseball team, pictured here, were Champions of the Thumb in 1911.

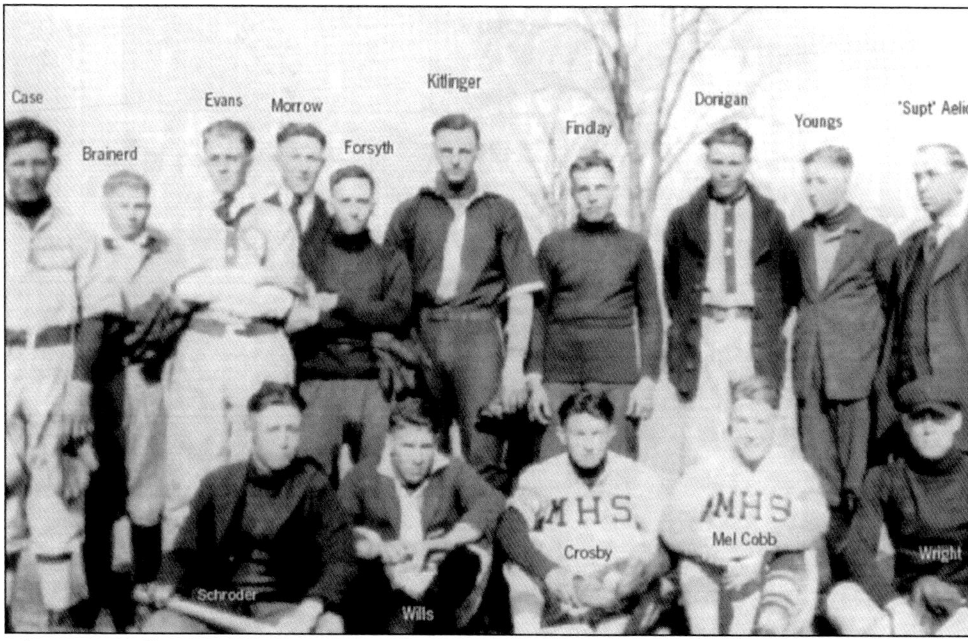


The 1920 Millington High School baseball team is shown here. The players are identified, from left to right, as follows: (back row) Case, Brainerd, Evans, Morrow, Forsythe, Kitelinger, Findlay, Donigan, Youngs, and "Supt" Aelick; (front row) Schroder, Wills, Crosby, Mel Cobb, and Wright.

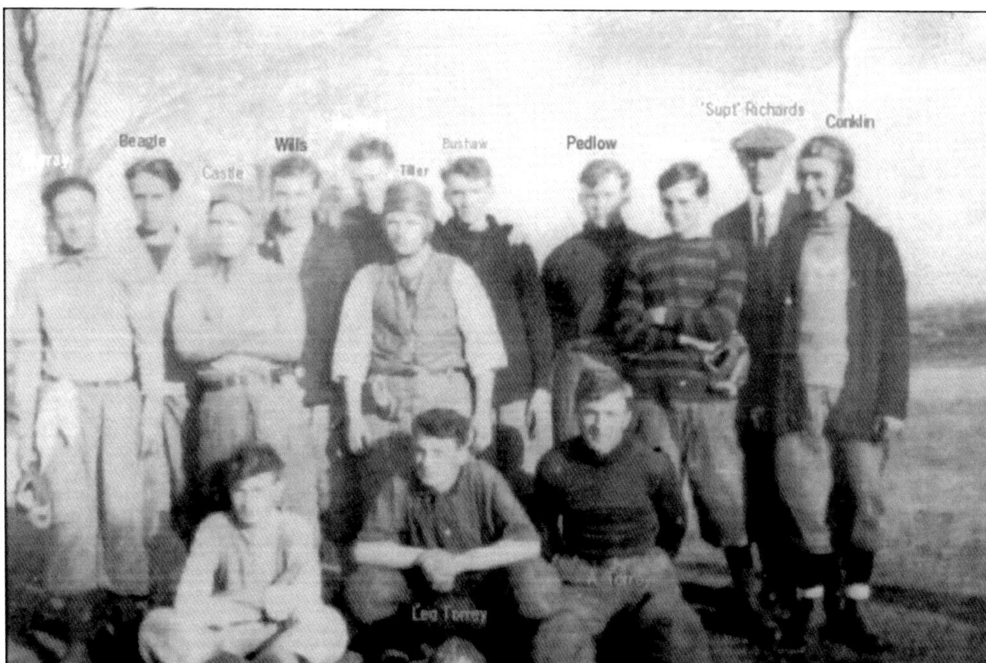


Members of the MHS football team from the 1914–1915 school year are, from left to right: (back row) Murray, Beagle, Castle, Wills, Huston, Tiller, Bushaw, Pedlow, Supt. Richards, and Conklin; (front row) Art Torrey, Leo Torrey, and A. Torrey.

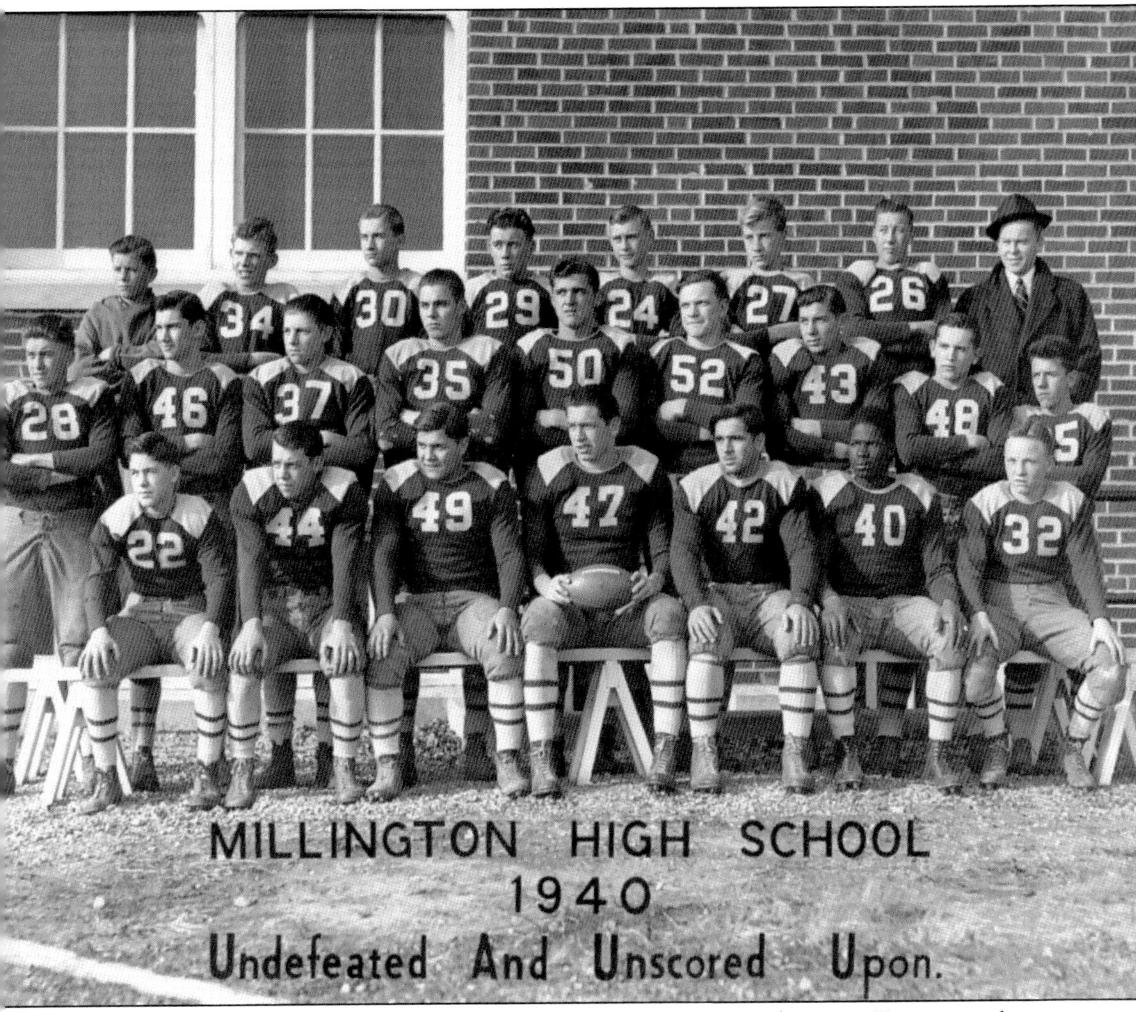


The 1940 Millington championship football team went unscored upon. Team members included, from left to right: (front row) Hilton Foster, Bray Billyard, Norman Castle, Edward Drubin, Max Coon, LeeRoy Clark, and George Youngs; (second row) Jim Laing, Robert Farnum, Earl Betz; (third row) manager Alburton Rosencrants, Harold Gleason, Gaynord Farnum, Ed Gilchrist, Hatty Martin, Fred Green, Bill Wolfington, and coach Steve Glaza. (Photo courtesy of Bill Worth and Jerry Hanlin.)

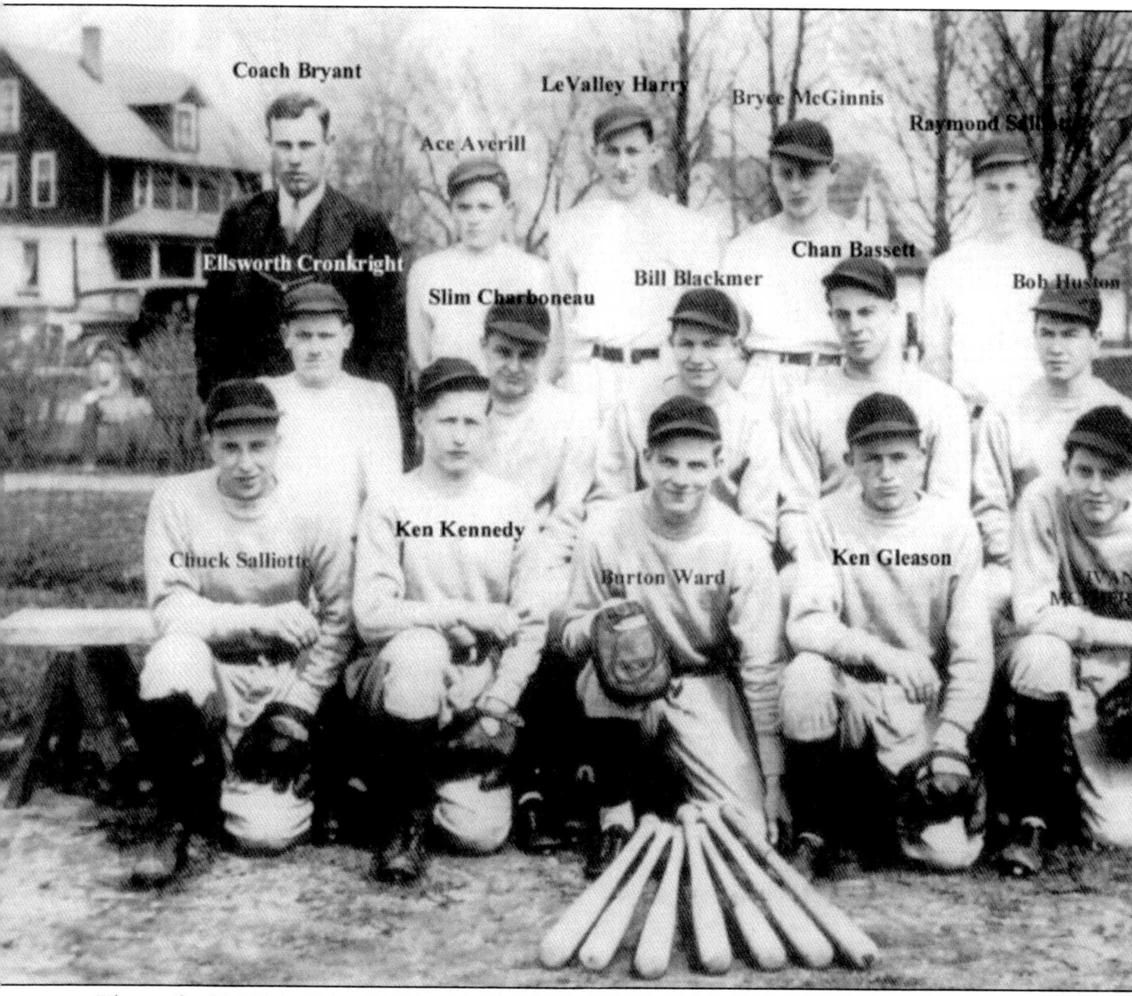


This is the 1936 MHS baseball team. They are identified from left to right as follows: (back row) Coach Bryant, Ace Averill, LeValley Harry, Bryce McGinnis, and Raymond Salliote; (middle row) Ellsworth Cronkright, Slim Charboneau, Bill Blackner, Chan Bassett, and Bob Huston; (front row) Chuck Salliotte, Ken Kennedy, Barton Ward, Ken Gleason, and Ivan McPherson.

# *Nine*
# Founding Families

Early settlers in the Millington-Arbela area came from a variety of backgrounds. Many came from Canada and were descendants of Tories who had moved to Canada from Eastern states when England was defeated in the Revolutionary War. Others came more directly from European countries. They were stalwart, self-sufficient individuals.

Tuscola became a county in 1840 but was still an uncharted wilderness. Lumbering the virgin timber and cork pine was the main occupation. Many individual businesses were also present.

According to a handwritten account, one enterprising homemaker saved her potato peelings while traveling to Michigan. When she arrived, no land had been cleared for a garden. So she planted her peelings in a rotten log and harvested potatoes in the fall.

Included in this chapter are condensed histories of some of the early families residing in the Millington-Arbela area. Many of the complete histories can be found at the Historical Museum in Millington.

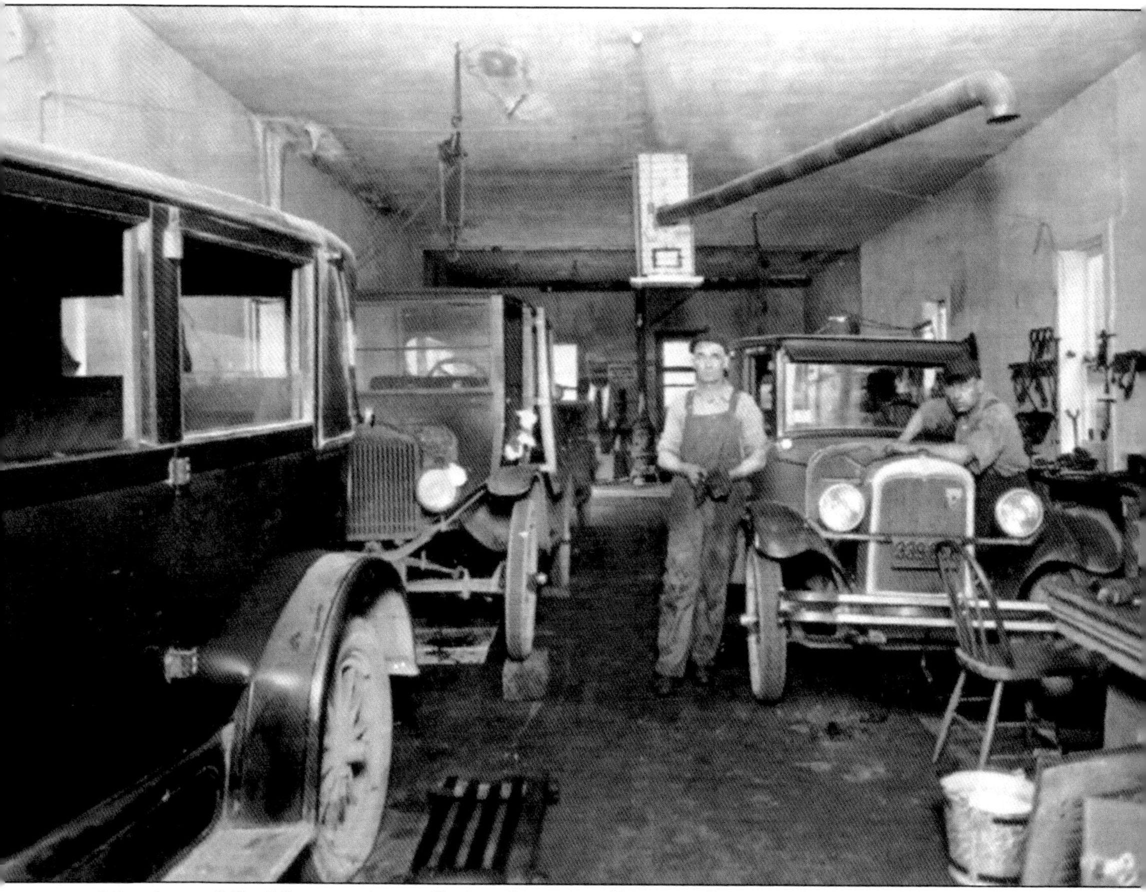

Members of Carl Lavern Aurand's family originally came from Germany. Johannes Aurandt, a blacksmith, arrived in Philadelphia in October of 1753. He purchased land from Thomas and John Penn, the son and nephew of William Penn, and soon Aurandt owned 2,000 acres of prime virgin timber.

Daniel Aurand, great-grandson of Johannes and grandfather to Carl L. Aurand, moved to Michigan in 1845 or 1846. Carl Aurand was born August 29, 1893 in Otisville and died February 13, 1983 in Millington. He had married Alice Thompson and they had three children.

Carl worked many jobs including as a mechanic and driver for Dave Evans, a banker. He also worked on the railroad. Later he had an auto repair shop, and after that, a Ford dealership. In 1941 the Carl Aurand family moved to a farm one-half mile south of Millington and became dairy farmers.

Both Carl and Alice were community-minded and served in many organizations in Millington. Carl was a charter member of the Rotary.

Their children were: Alma (1915–1988), who married Gabriel A. Difore II; LaVern (1918–1973), a metallurgist at A.C. who married Mary Lois Rock; and Alice (b. 1928), a registered nurse who married Victor DeLand.

A large antique silver watch made in Paris and dated 1649 was brought to America by Johannes Aurandt. The watch was passed down through generations of Aurand sons, and is now in the possession of Paul Harvey Aurand, a newsman, author, lecturer, and fourth generation grandson of Johannes.

In this picture, Carl Aurand and Bill Harter are at work in their auto garage, c. 1920s.

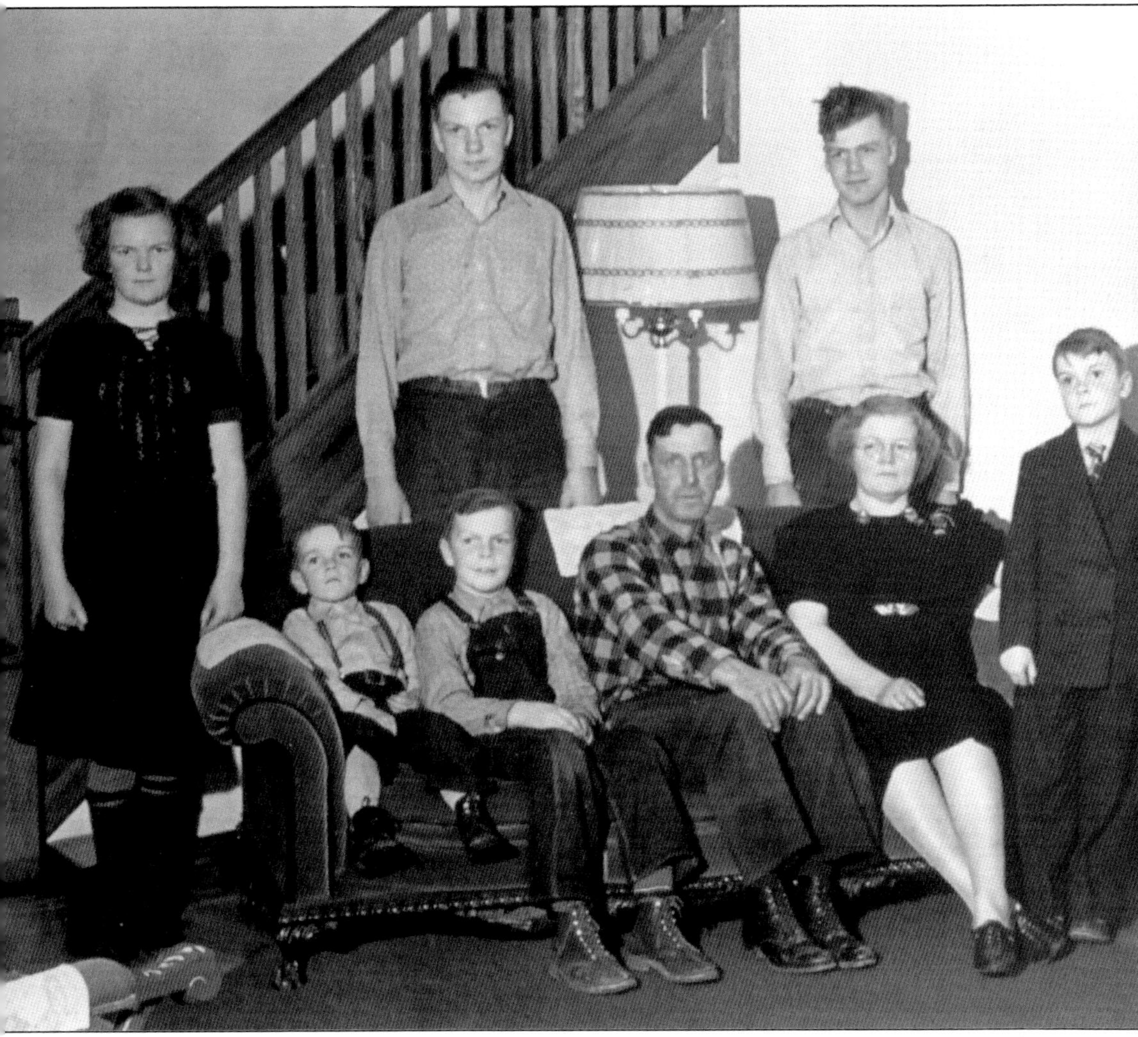

The Robert Burns family came to Millington Township in 1903 from Sarnia, Ontario, Canada. Robert and his wife, Margaret, bought a 40 acre farm on West Arbela Road. They had two sons: Russell and Harry. Both boys graduated from Millington High School. Russell became a career Army officer. Harry married Mildred Bush in 1919 and they purchased a farm on Irish Road.

Harry started a hatchery business, which supplied chicks to local farmers. In 1930, he went into commercial egg production. The business grew from an initial number of 100 chickens to a hatchery that produced 120,000 eggs every day of the week. Harry and Mildred had six children: George, Alfred, Norman, Lloyd, Lyle, and Viola. In 1956, the four sons and their father organized the family corporation known as Burns Poultry Farm. These four men, each with a son of their own, continued to produce and market eggs until recently.

Harry passed away in 1985. Over 30 of his descendants are presently living in the Millington area.

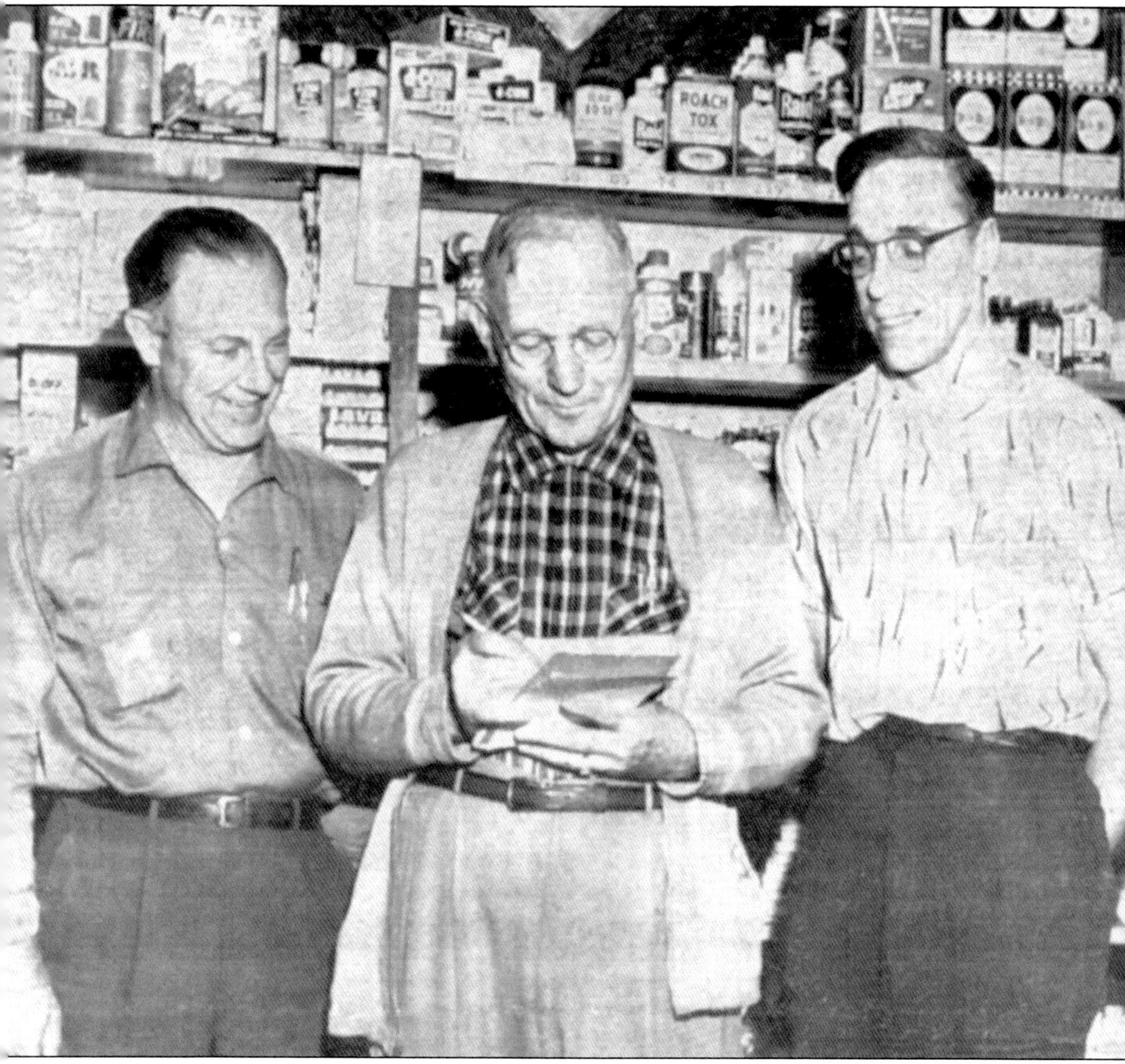


Albert Henry Cobb was born June 21, 1887, to Melvin and Frances (Reid) Cobb. There were nine boys and one girl born to the family. Some of Albert's brothers who lived in the Millington-Vassar area were Orville, Harold, Ty, and John.

Albert married Lily E. Holmes in Caro, Michigan, in 1908. Her parents were John and Lucy (Price) Holmes. Albert and Lily had two children, Cleo and Arlene. Cleo married Marie Buecher. They had five children: Richard, John, Michael, Maryann, and David. Arlene married Albert Rock. They had two children, Ruth and Daryl.

This clipping from the May 17, 1962 edition of the *Millington Herald* shows Cleo Cobb (left), Albert Cobb (center), and Albert Rock upon the 47th anniversary of the A.H. Cobb Company. The caption explains that they celebrated the anniversary with a store-wide three-day sale.

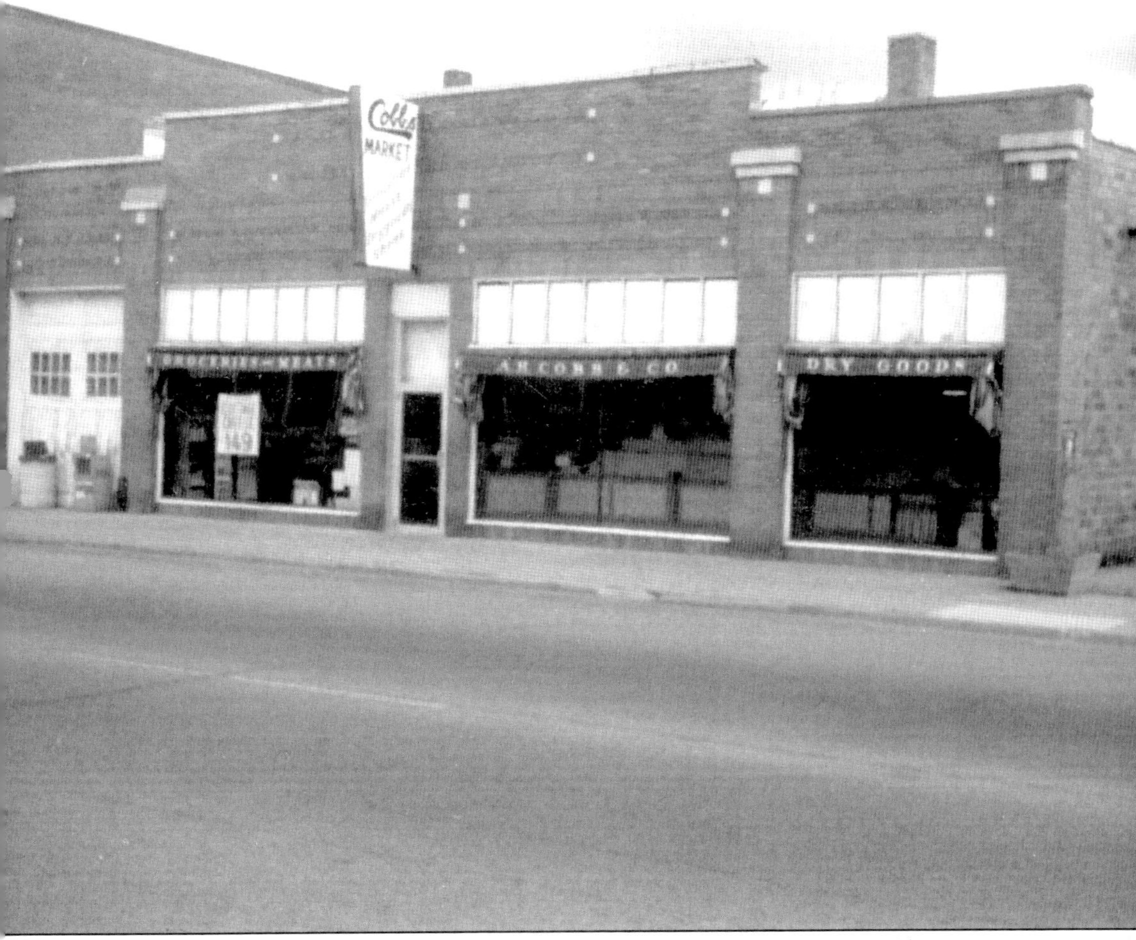


Albert Cobb began his business career by trading fish for farm produce. In 1915 he went into the meat business with Mr. Ed Gillman and in 1916 he opened a grocery store with his brother-in-law, Albert Holmes. After serving the public in four different locations he purchased the final location from D.J. Evans (Ford dealership and garage). In 1969, his son Cleo and son-in-law Albert Rock became partners in the A.H. Cobb & Co. business. Albert Cobb was in business longer than anyone else in Millington—54 years. In 1970 he was chosen to receive the Most Honored Citizen Award. He was the first person to receive the award.

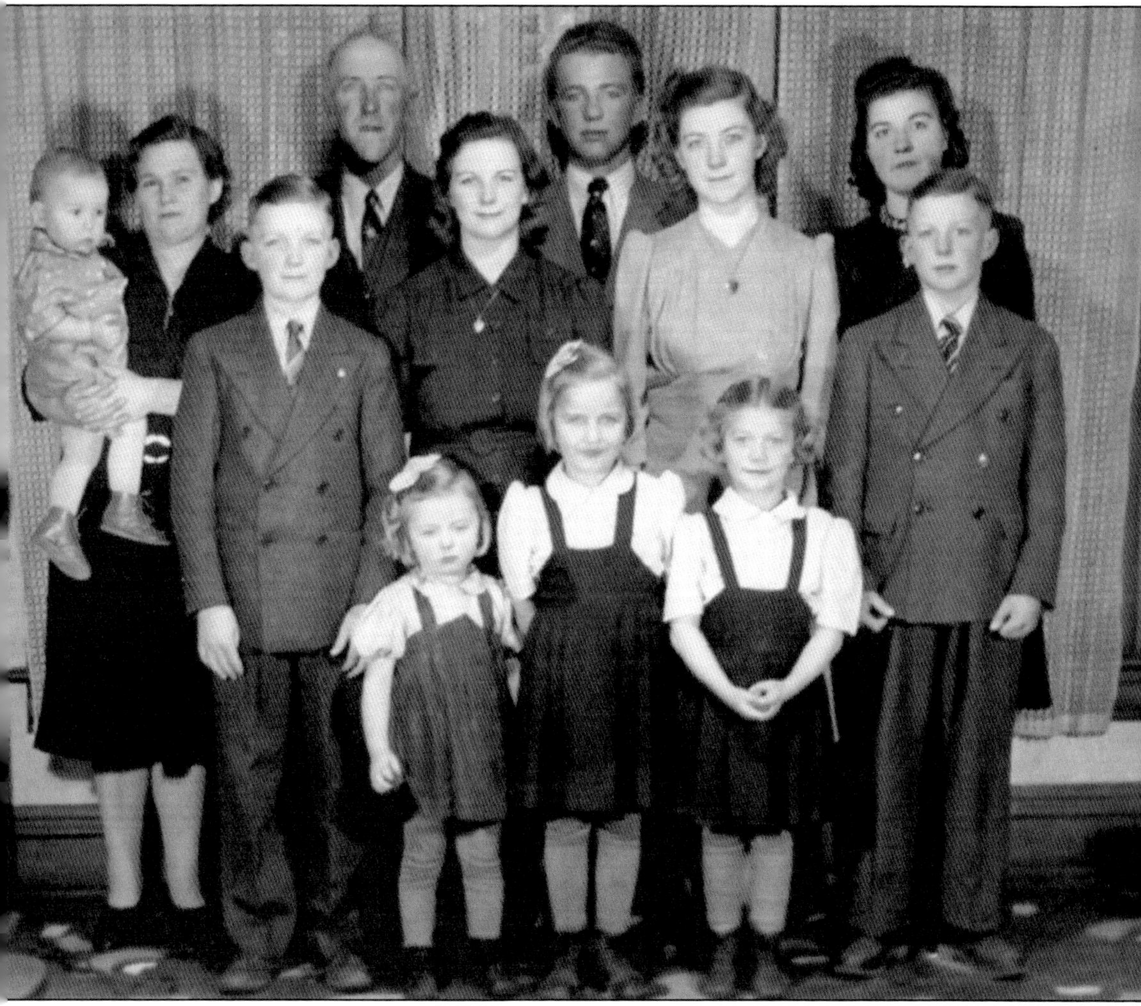

After leaving Canada, Henry Forsyth and his wife, Mary, and their 11 children, arrived in Millington Township prior to 1880. Their first home was a log cabin on the corner of M-15 and Birch Run Road. In 1882, they purchased an 80 acre farm on Fulmer Road.

The second generation Henry Forsyth had three children. They raised beef cattle and hauled the meat to Bay City.

The third generation Henry Forsyth was a dairy farmer and spent time training horses. Henry married Minnie Mamerow and they had ten children: six girls and four boys. Their names are Gertrude, Albertine, Henry, Helen, Burton, Norman, Elinor, Carolyn, Wilma Jean, and James. Six still live in the Millington area. Henry passed away in 1971 and Minnie lived on the family centennial farm until 1999.

The fourth generation Henry Forsyth was a family doctor and practiced in Chesaning, Michigan.

# 50th wedding anniversary

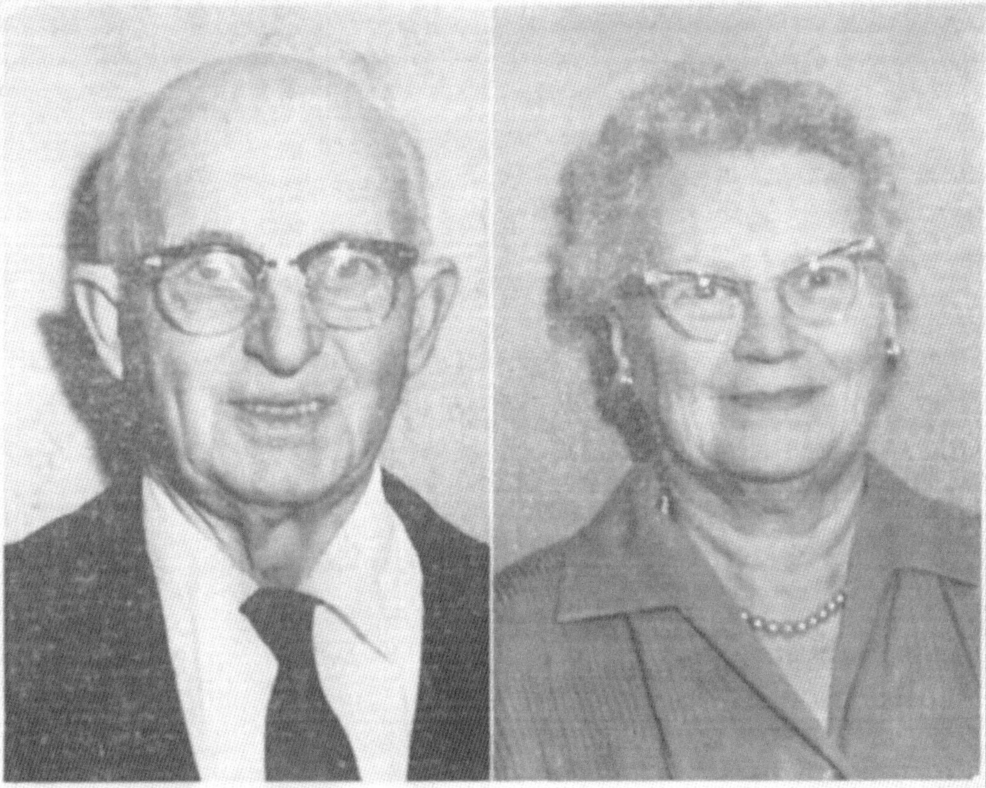

The Golden Wedding Anniversary of Mr and Mrs Albert Holmes will be observed with open house from 2 to 5 pm at the I.O.O.F. Hall, Millington, Sunday, February 12. The Holmes were married February 8, 1911. Both Mr and Mrs Holmes have lived in this area all of their lives. They have two daughters, Mrs Adolph Rittenger, St. Clair Shores, Mrs Donald Davidson, Millington and one son, Mr Carthon Holmes, Anna Maria Island, Florida, and five grandchildren. (photo by Daryl Rock).

Albert Holmes was born to John C. and Lucy (Price) Holmes on February 4, 1885 in Arbela Township. He had one sister, Lily, who married Albert H. Cobb. He married Faye Milliman in Sarnia, Canada, on February 4, 1911. They have three children: Carthon (Pat), Amethyst, and Anna Marie. Amethyst married Donald Davison and lived in the Millington area all her life. Pat was married to Vera Holbrook and lived in Florida. Anna Marie was married to Adolf Rittenger and spent time in St. Clair Shores and Florida.

Albert began in the business world as a partner with A.H. Cobb. Together they started the Cobb & Holmes store. Albert Holmes later became president of Millington Bank. Following his banking career he became a real estate broker. He was a lifelong member of the Millington F & AM Lodge and a lifelong resident of Millington. He died August 7, 1966 at the age of 81.

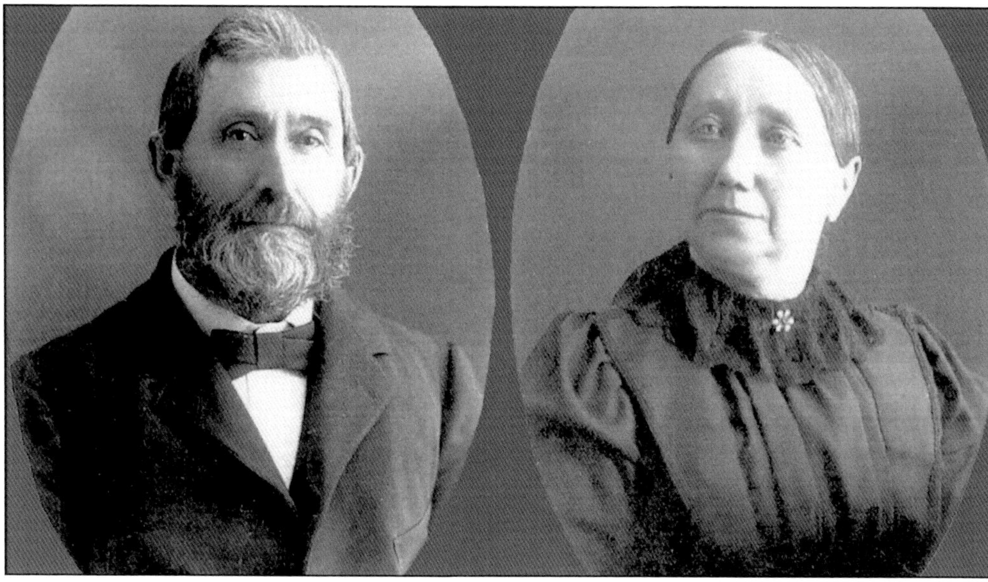

Henry and Henrietta Jensen arrived in Millington in December of 1869 from their native Schleswig-Holstein, Denmark. They bought 60 acres of uncleared wilderness two miles south and three and one-half miles west of Millington. Clio was the nearest town and Henry carried supplies home from Clio.

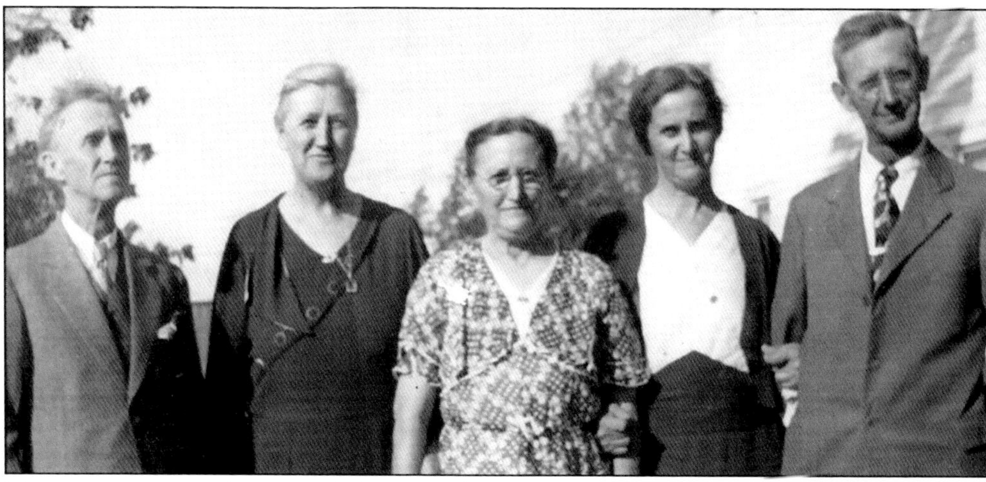

Henry and Henrietta Jensen had children whose names are familiar in the area. Mina (born on the ship coming to America) later married Charles Kurpsel. They had two sons, Norman and Elmer. Emma married Frank C. Koch (not Frank H.) They had three daughters: Edith, Elsie, and Alta. Marcus Jensen married Allie Wilcox. Their children were named Maxwell, Audra, Wilford, Carl, and Thurman. Frank married Bertha Reynolds and they were the parents of Harold. There are now five generations descending from Frank: Harold, Donald, Dianne, Jenelle, and Joah. After Bertha's death, Frank married Florence (McDowell) McClew. Mary married Glen Wing and they were the parents of Harry. Carl married Gertrude McNeal and they were the parents of Ruth Taylor. Anna married Charles Donigan. Their children were Dorothy, Darlene, AnnaMarie, and Harold.

Henry and Henrietta are buried in Gunnel Cemetery. The other Jensens who have passed away are buried in Millington Township Cemetery.

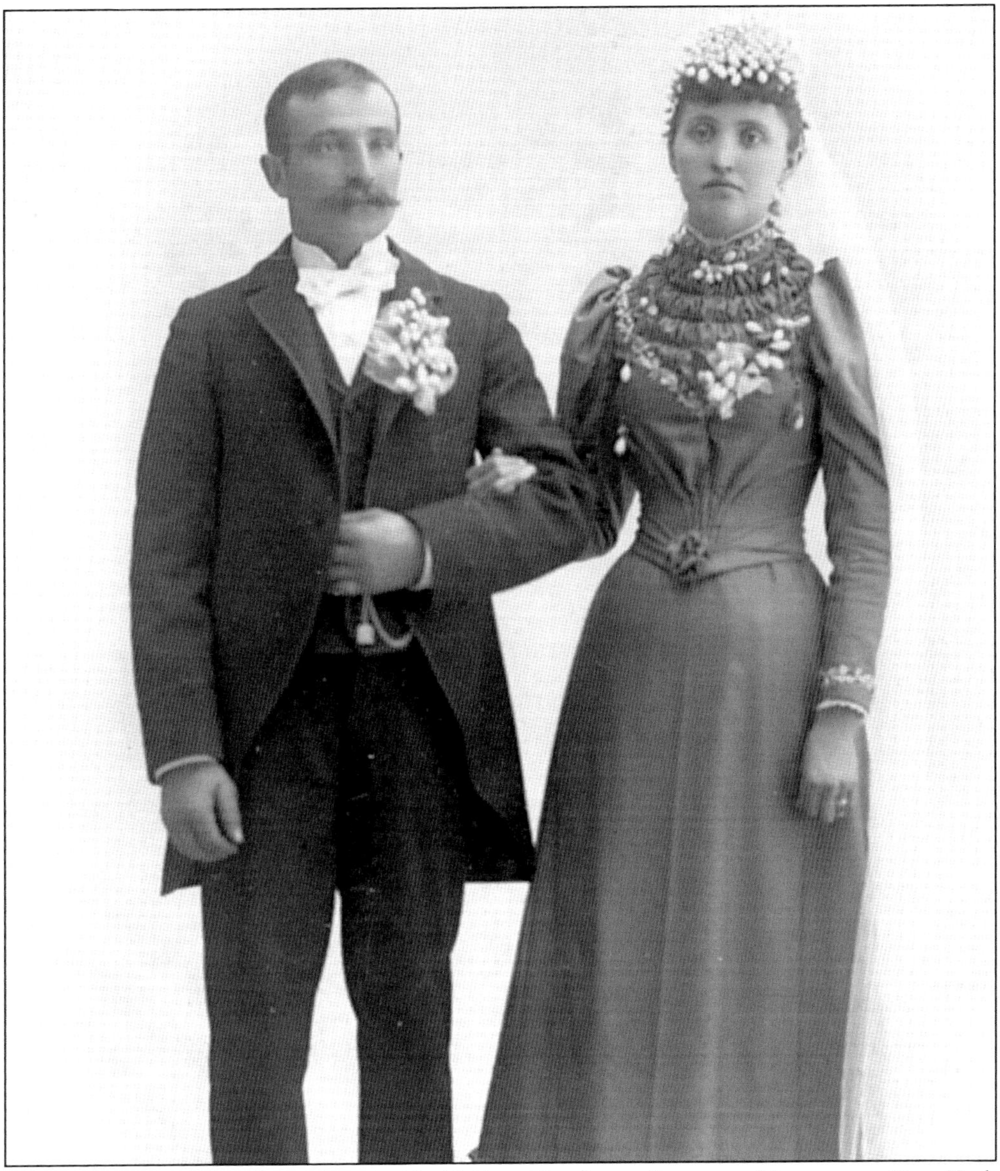

Charles F. Kurpsel was born August 27, 1864 in Hamburg, Germany. He came to New York City with two brothers and two sisters to escape wars and fighting in their homeland. Charles was 18 years old when he arrived in the U.S.

Charles, a small man in stature, was a farmer all his life. He married Almina E. Jensen on November 1, 1893, and they purchased a farm on Birch Run Road. They had two sons, Elmer and Norman. The sons farmed together and were known as the Kurpsel brothers. Elmer married Edith Stockwell and they had one daughter.

Norman married Ottille Petzold. They purchased a farm on West Birch Run Road. They had four daughters: Lela, Vera, Edna, and Lola. The girls helped with the farming, and even the milking until the cattle were replaced with Hereford beef cattle.

Lela married Arnold Higgins. Vera married James Kern. Edna and Ralph Ferber married. Lola married Roger Wendt and they now reside at the former Charles Kurpsel homestead which now serves as the home of Wendt Catering.

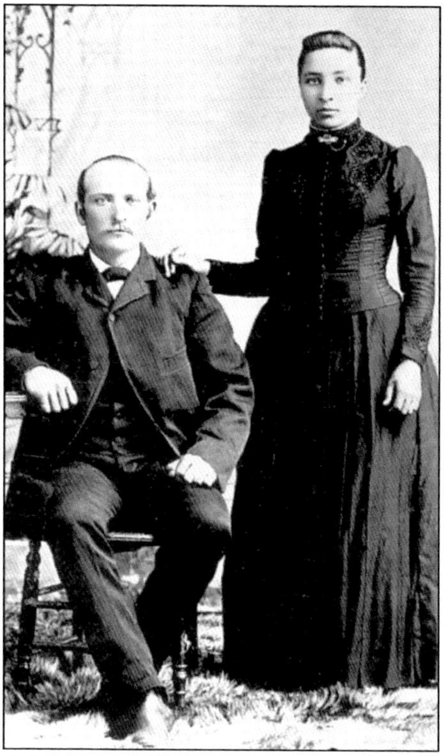

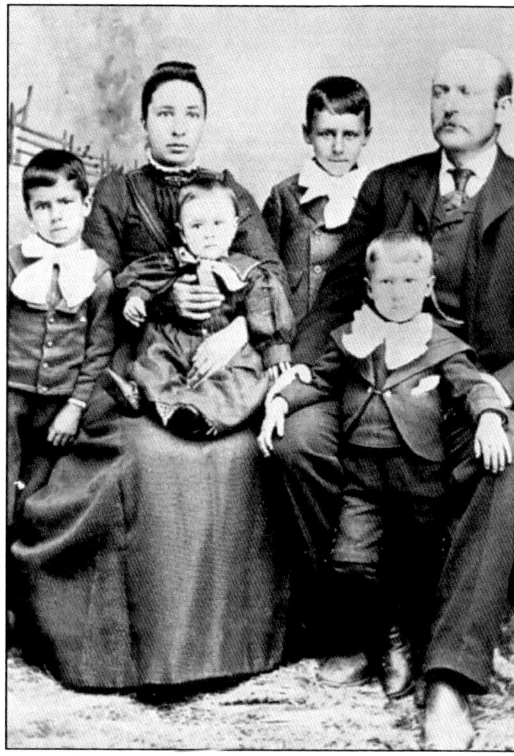

Adolph Rudolf Ill was born in Baden, Germany in 1864. His parents were both born in Germany. His mother was buried there, and his father was buried in Canada. Adolph married Anna E. Petzold in 1892 in St. Thomas, North Dakota. They had 11 children. The first two were born in North Dakota, and the rest were born in Arbela Township, Michigan.

Adolph came to Arbela Township between 1894 and 1896. He worked as a farmer his entire life and died in 1927. Both Adolph and his wife Anna are buried in Millington Township Cemetery. Anna Elizabeth (Petzold) Ill was born in Manitoba, Canada, in 1874. Her parents were both born in Canada. Her father died in 1890 and her mother died in 1921.

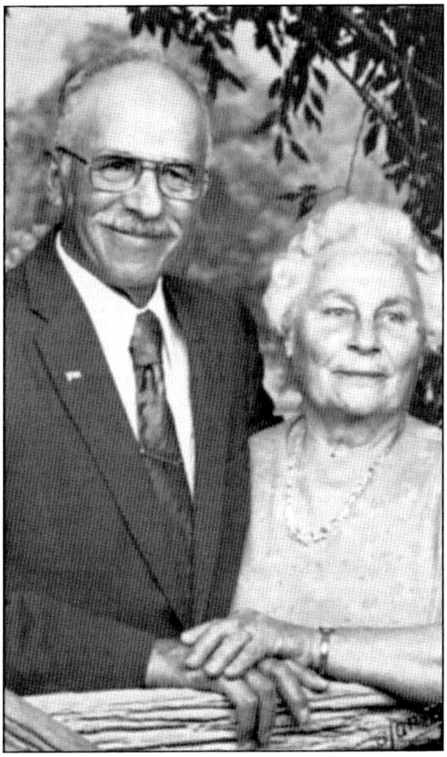

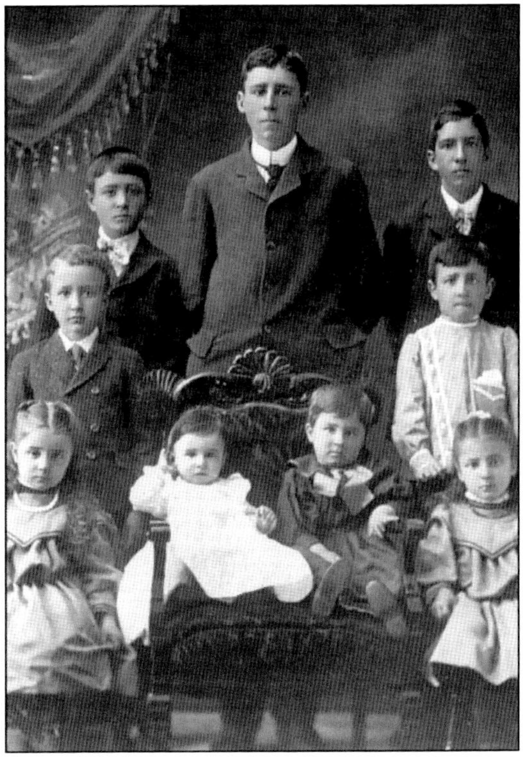

Arthur Arnold Ill was born in Arbela Township in 1905. He is pictured here with his wife Agnes F. (Weber), whom he married in 1929. They had four children: Raymond, Janith, Eunice, and Victor. Arthur was a farmer all his life. He is buried in Pine Grove Cemetery, Arbela Township.

Alma (Reinert) Ill was born in Birch Run Township in 1892. Her parents were born in Michigan. She married Ewald Ill, the oldest child of Adolph R. and Anna E. Ill. He was a farmer in Arbela Township, and they had two children, Herbert and Esther. Alma is buried in Millington Township Cemetery.

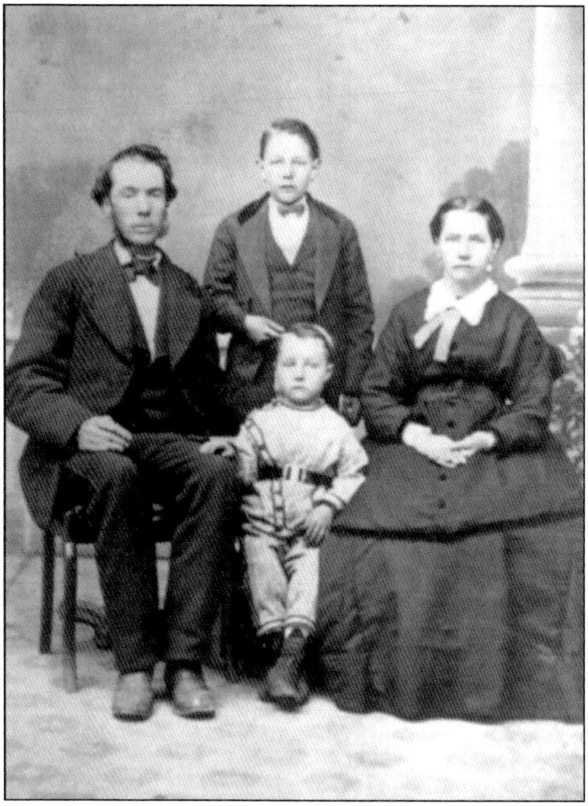

McPhersons have lived in Millington since the 1850s and many descendants populate the area. All the ancestors can be found in the Millington Township Record Book.

Henry Harlow McPherson's ancestors came from Scotland in 1783. They were Tories and fought with the British during the Revolutionary War. They were forced to live in Canada for a number of years. Henry H. McPherson moved to Millington in the 1850s. He married Cornelia DeWitt and they had two sons, William A. and Harvey E. Both sons lived and worked in Millington their entire lives.

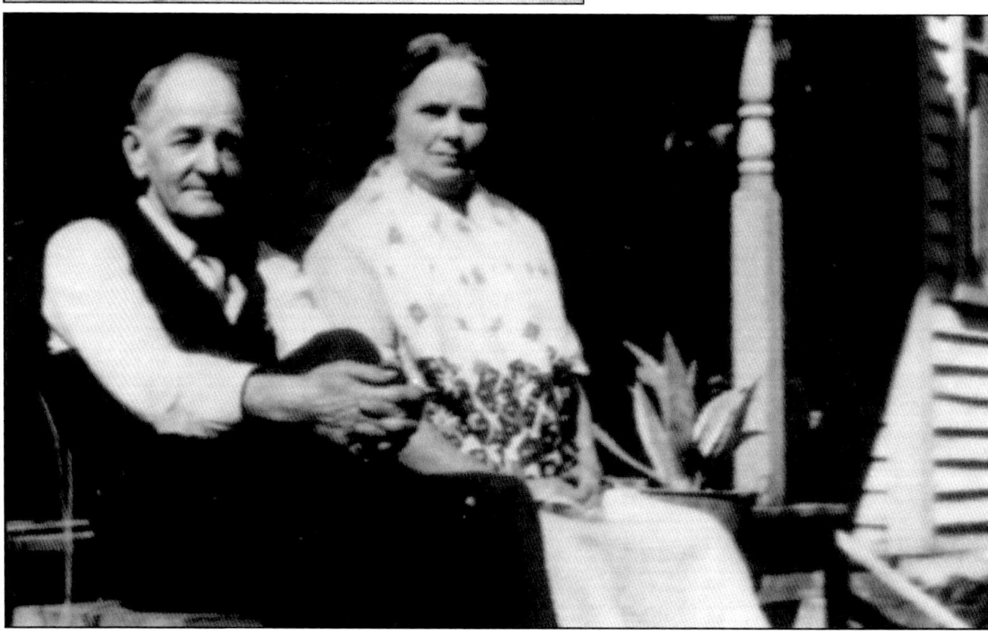

William Arthur McPherson was born in 1861. He had a grocery and hardware store in Millington. Many will remember McPherson's Hardware, which was later owned by his grandson, George. William married Elizabeth Dunn and they had four children: Harry, Clarence, Hazel, and Phil. The boys stayed in Millington and raised families here. William died in 1930.

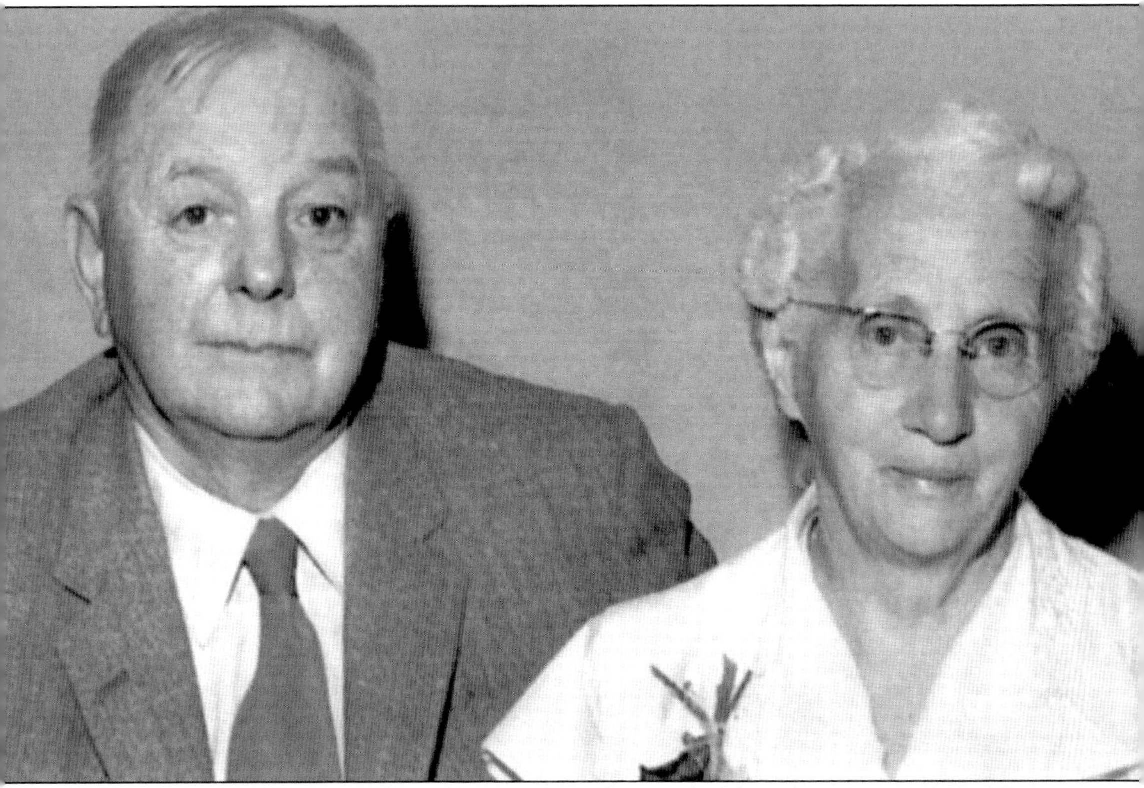

Harry McPherson married Myrtle Hadden in 1905. They worked for a short time at A.C. Allen Store and then moved to a farm northwest of Millington to raise their family. After World War II they moved to Cedar Lake but returned to Millington after a few years. Their children were George, Lloyd, Vivienne, Harry Jr., Ivan, and William (Bill).

George married Esther Berry. They had two daughters, Natalie and Hazel Mae. He served as the owner of McPherson's Hardware for many years.

Lloyd was a 1928 graduate of Millington High School and lived in Millington but worked at foundries in Vassar and Waterford. He married Doris Gunther and they had a son, David.

Vivienne graduated Millington High School in 1927 and attended the County Normal School at Caro. She later taught at Comstock School. She married LaVerne Draper, and they were the parents of LaVerne Jr. and Karen. They operated Red's Appliance Store in Millington.

Harry Jr. married Lena Rosenstangle and together they had four children: Harry Jr. III, William, Sandra, and Connie. He worked at a factory in Frankenmuth but lived in Millington. His grandchildren presently operate a restaurant and tractor sales and auto repair businesses.

Ivan, a 1937 graduate of Millington High School, attended business college in Battle Creek, Michigan. He served in the Navy for four years during World War II, and was general manager of Millington Truck Body in Millington and Huntington, Indiana, for 40 years. He married Rosemarie Charno of New York City. Their children are Judith, Greg, and Kim—all Millington High School graduates.

William (Bill) graduated from Millington High in 1937. He enlisted in the Navy and was present at the attack on Pearl Harbor December 7, 1941, on the U.S.S. *California*. He survived that ship's sinking and spent the rest of his time on the U.S.S. *West Virginia*. He was awarded the Pearl Harbor medal among other honors. He married Alverna Church, and they had two daughters, Lanna and Lourie. They lived in Millington and Caro and now live in Florida.

The McPhersons have now scattered throughout the United States. Their complete history is available at the Millington-Arbela Historical Museum.

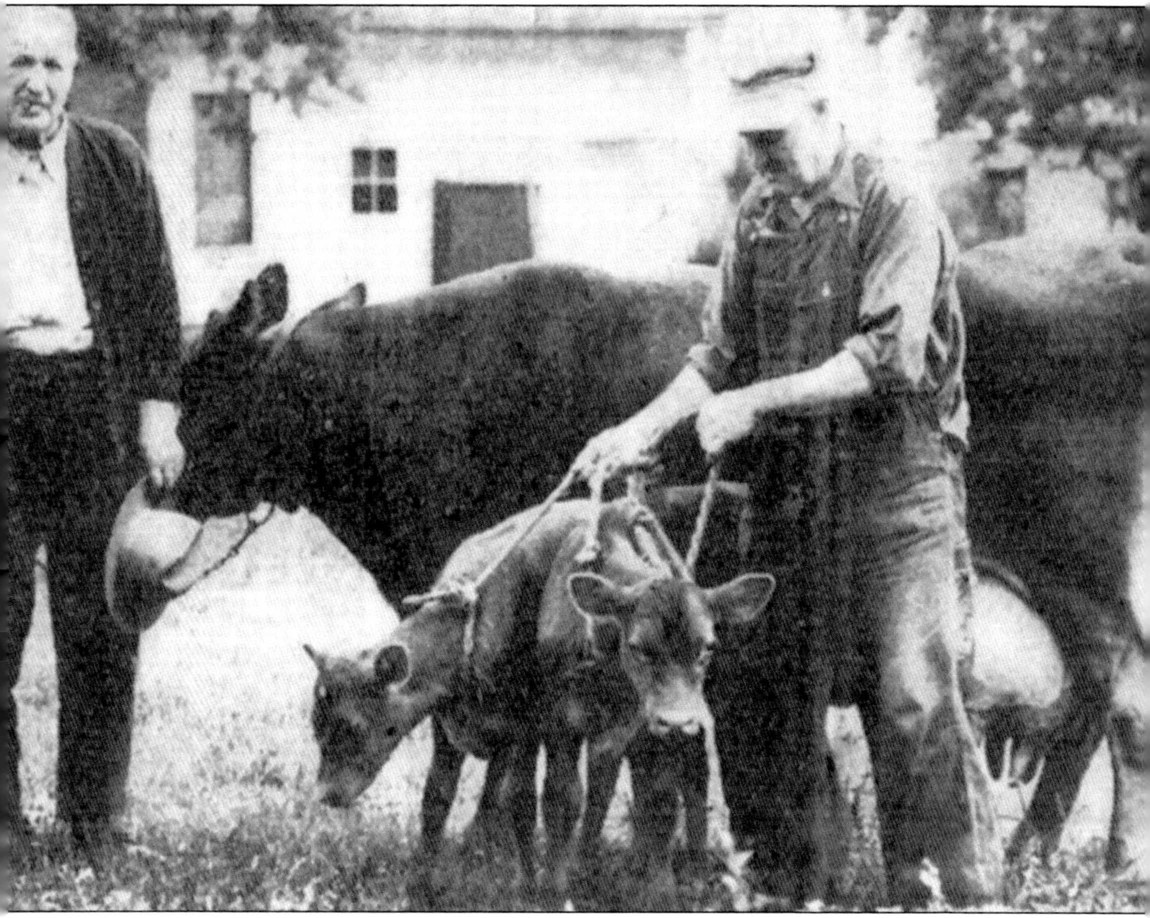

Lincoln Milliman was born in Sanborn, New York, on October 18, 1863. He came to the Millington area with his parents Nicholas and Cynthia Milliman. Lincoln married Lydia V. Bush on September 19, 1887 in Pendleton Center, New York. Lincoln and Lydia lived on their 40 acre farm, three miles west of the present Village of Millington, for 52 years. Lincoln was a veterinarian for 35 years. A road was named in his honor. Their daughter, Hazel Faye, married Albert Holmes and gave them two granddaughters, Amethyst (Davidson) and Anna Marie, and one grandson, Carthon (Pat). Lincoln Milliman is pictured in this newspaper photo with one of his Jersey cows. The man holding the twin calves is Henry Shaver.

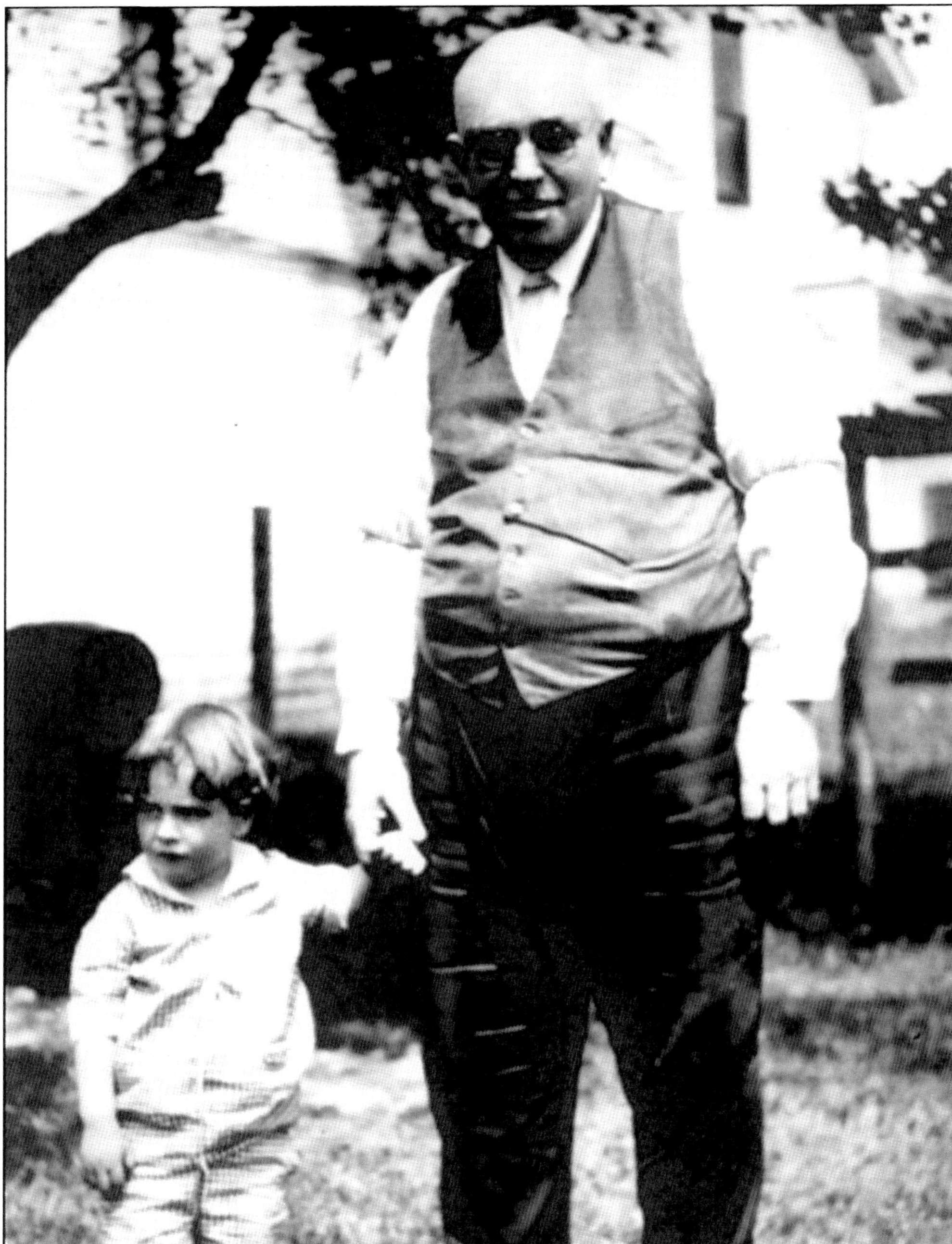

Charles A. Valentine was born July 5, 1855 and came to Millington with his parents, William and Maryette, from Brighton in 1867. Charles clerked in the store owned by his uncle, Homer Beach, which was the first store in Millington. He later opened his own store on the corner of State and Center Streets, managing it until his death on September 13, 1927. He also served as Village President and School Board President for many years. Millington's first telephone office was upstairs in the Valentine building. Charles was also involved in bringing electricity to Millington. He married Frances Adelaide Mead on May 14, 1895 and the couple had six children, but only two survived, Max and Mary.

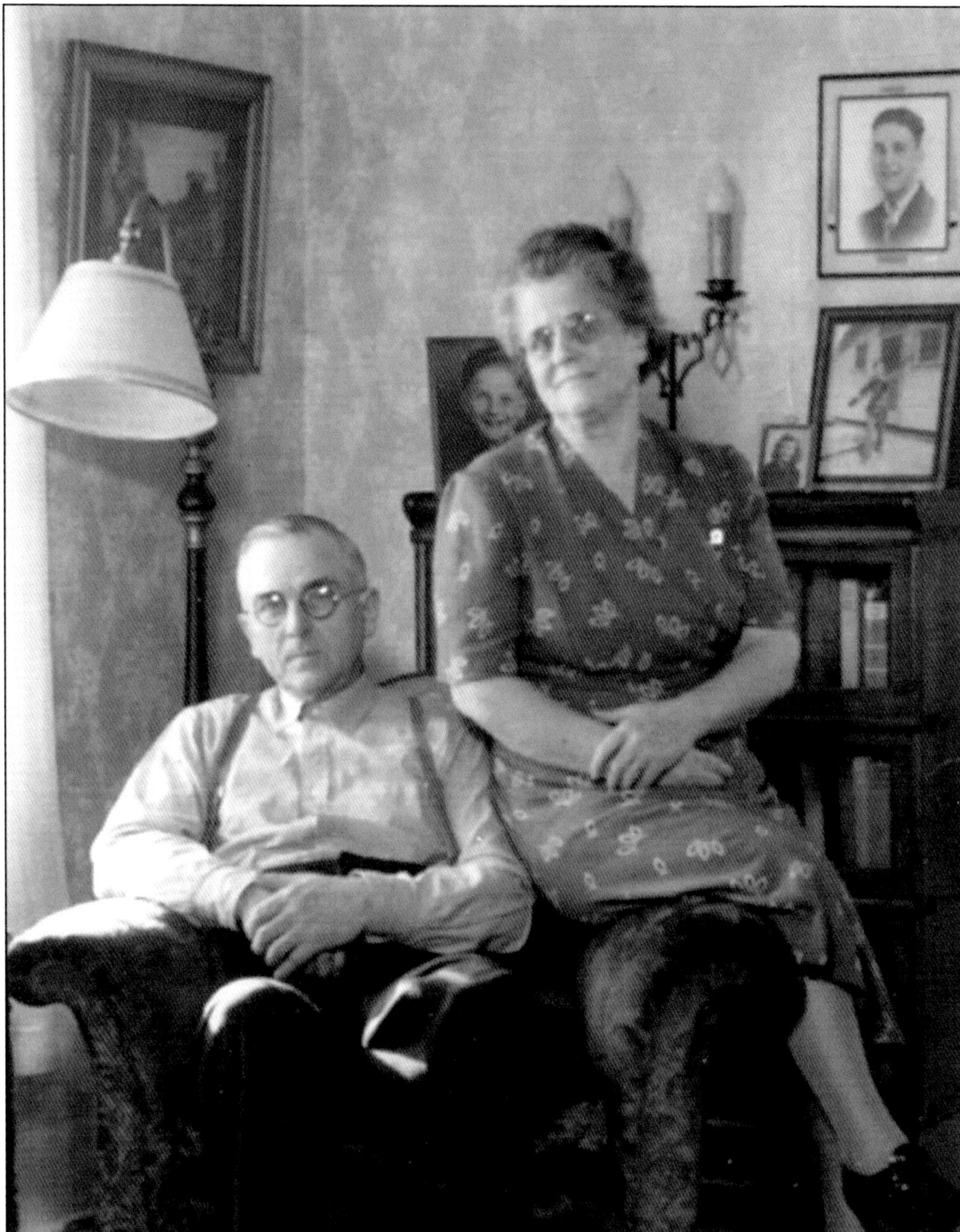

Max C. Valentine, son of Charles and Frances, worked for his father. Max's children were Charles, Ruth, and Robert. Charles had an appliance store and later an electrical business in Millington. He married Iva Lanfear. They had four sons: Keith, Kenton, Kermit, and Jim. Charles and Iva both served in township government. Charles' sister Ruth married Thomas E. Jones and moved near Detroit, later moving back to Millington. Robert married Doris M. Seelye in 1946 and moved to Detroit. They later returned to Millington and Robert served the village government for 19 years. Three of the Valentine men served as President of the Village of Millington: Charles A., Max C., and Robert H.

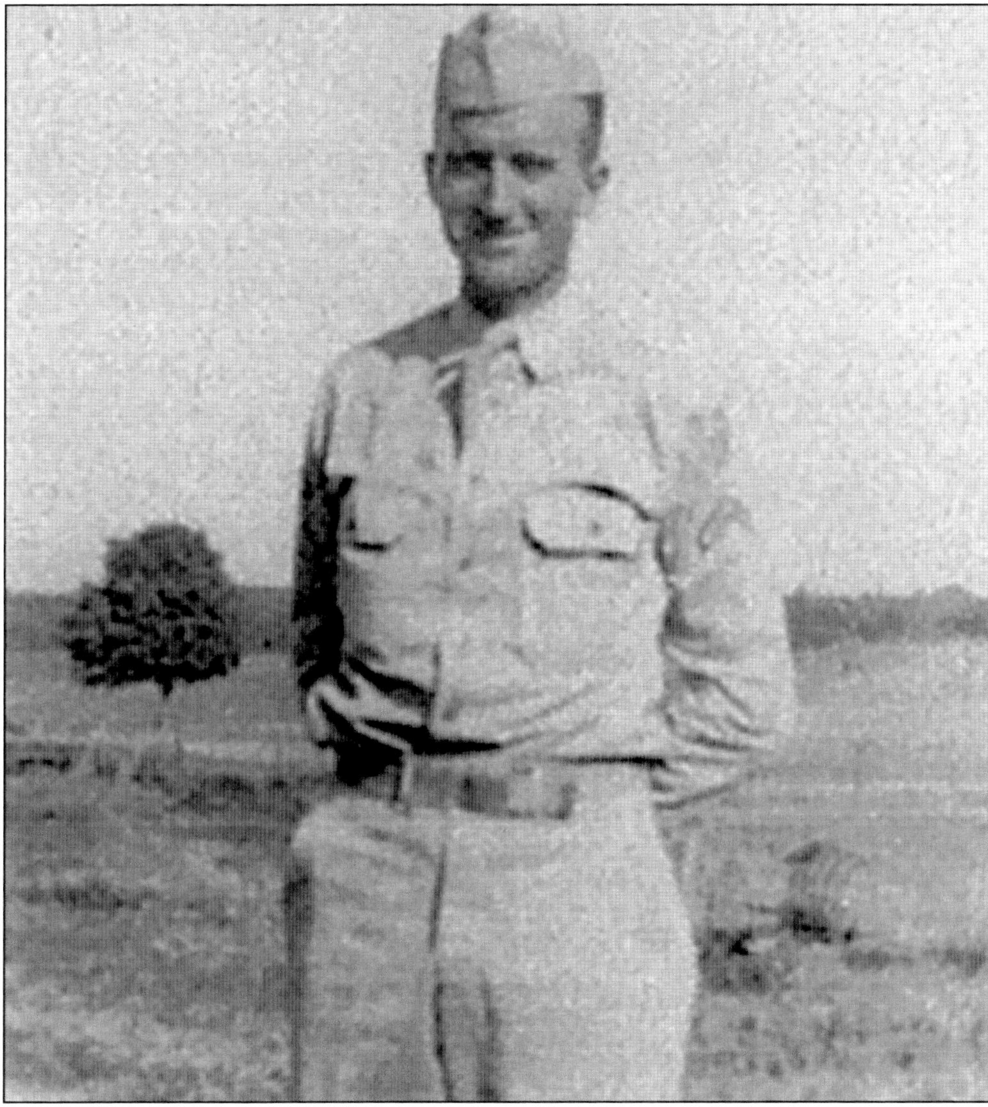

John King Jr. was born January 6, 1629 in England. He married Sarah Holten in Massachusetts. John was a tanner, also a representative to Colonial Congress. The seventh generation of his family resulted in Asabel, who was born in 1812 in New York state and died in 1862 in Genesee County, Michigan. He and his wife Ann Marie Hart (1815–1913) had four children: Ellen A., Mary E., William H., and Frances. Ellen A. King was born in 1838 in New York state. She married Moses Farnum in 1857. Moses had a dry goods and grocery store in Millington. Ellen had the first millinery in Millington. Together they had six children. After Moses died, Ellen married Samuel Atwood in Tuscola County in 1873. He built a hotel in Millington and was the first sexton of the cemetery in Millington.

Otis K. Farnum, son of Ellen King Farnum, was born in 1866 and died in 1937 in Millington. Otis married Lottie Brink in 1891. Otis, or "O.K." was an auctioneer. He and Lottie had two daughters, Dorothy Jean Stader, of Caro, and Virginia Isabelle Roger, as well as two sons, Vernon and Paul. Vernon served in World War I. Paul served in World War II and died September 24, 1944 of wounds to the head. He was buried in France but was later returned to Millington for burial. Paul had a daughter born in Flint on June 8, 1934.

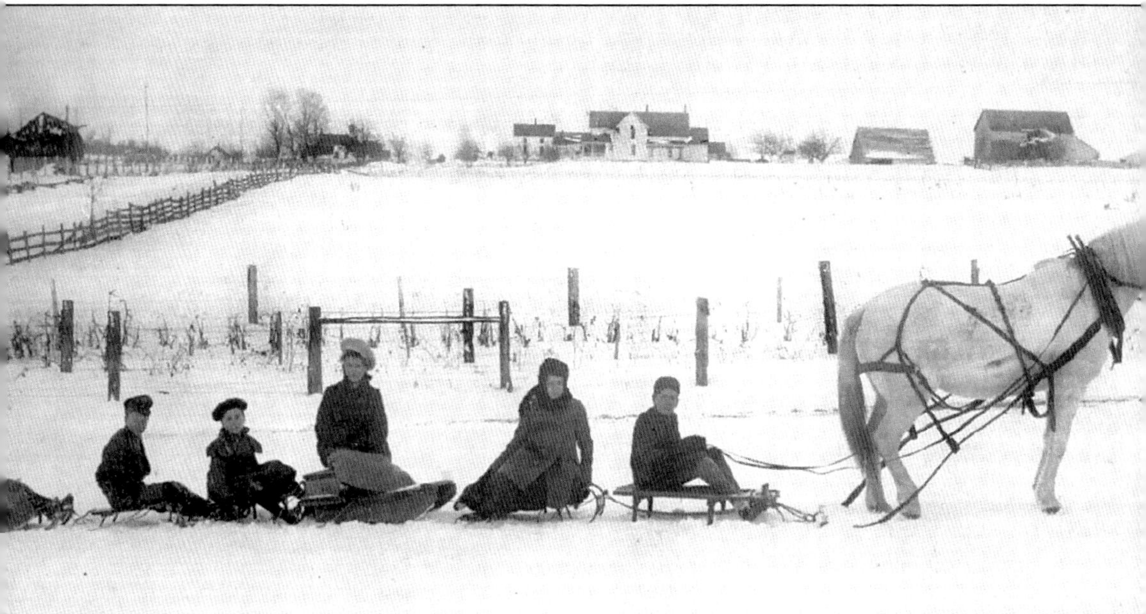

Lora Beach Castle was born February 19, 1897. She was the daughter of Frank Beach (1862–1931) and Carrie Bostick Beach (1864–1924). Lora graduated from Millington High School at age 16. She married Cy Castle at age 20. He was a rural mail carrier for many years.

Lora's grandfather, Homer Beach, came from Brighton in 1853 and was one of Millington's first settlers. He ran a dry goods and grocery store and was also a Highway Commissioner with Alfred Foster and Allen Glynn. Homer built several homes in the area, including his own. It later became the Castle home. He also built the home presently owned by Don Jensen.

This photo shows members of the Beach family on the Beach farm in the early 1900s. They are, from left to right: Lora Beach, Glen Mead, Leila Rice Braurer, Fay Milliman Holmes, Ethel Beach Garner, and Bernie Beach.

*Ten*

# The Area Now

This final chapter is to give you an insight into what the area looks like now. First are some aerial views. We include a view of "Millie," our water tower with the smiling face. We have also included various views of the Village of Millington and the Arbela Township Hall and the surrounding area. See how many things you recognize. There is also a large industrial park at the northern village limits. We have also included some of the area's older homes as they currently appear.

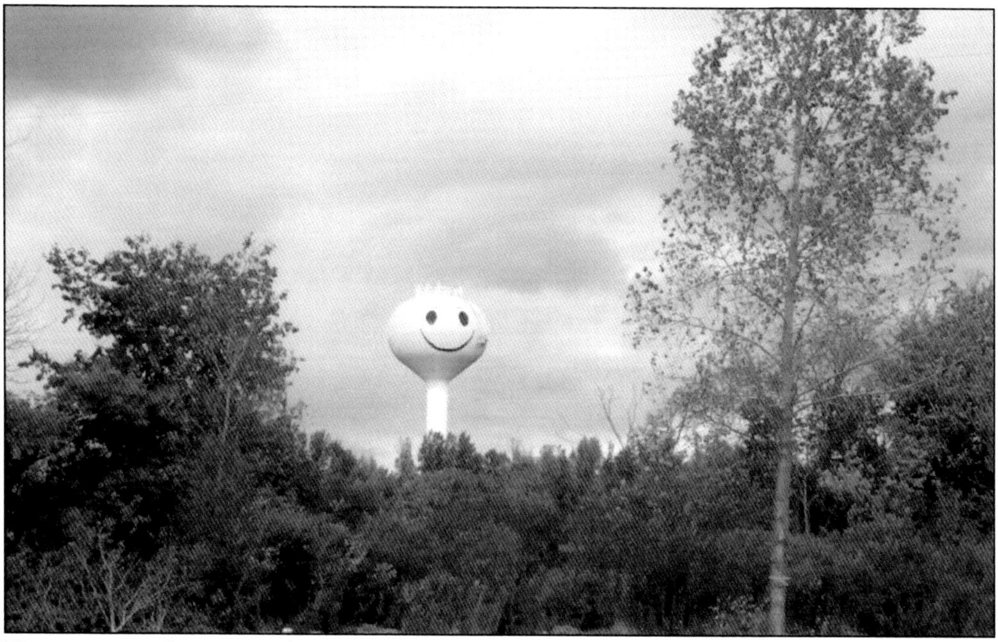

This is our newly repainted water tower. A contest was held to name the tower and the most popular name was "Millie." From another view, the smiling face sports a bow tie, inspiring the comment: Millie with a bow tie?

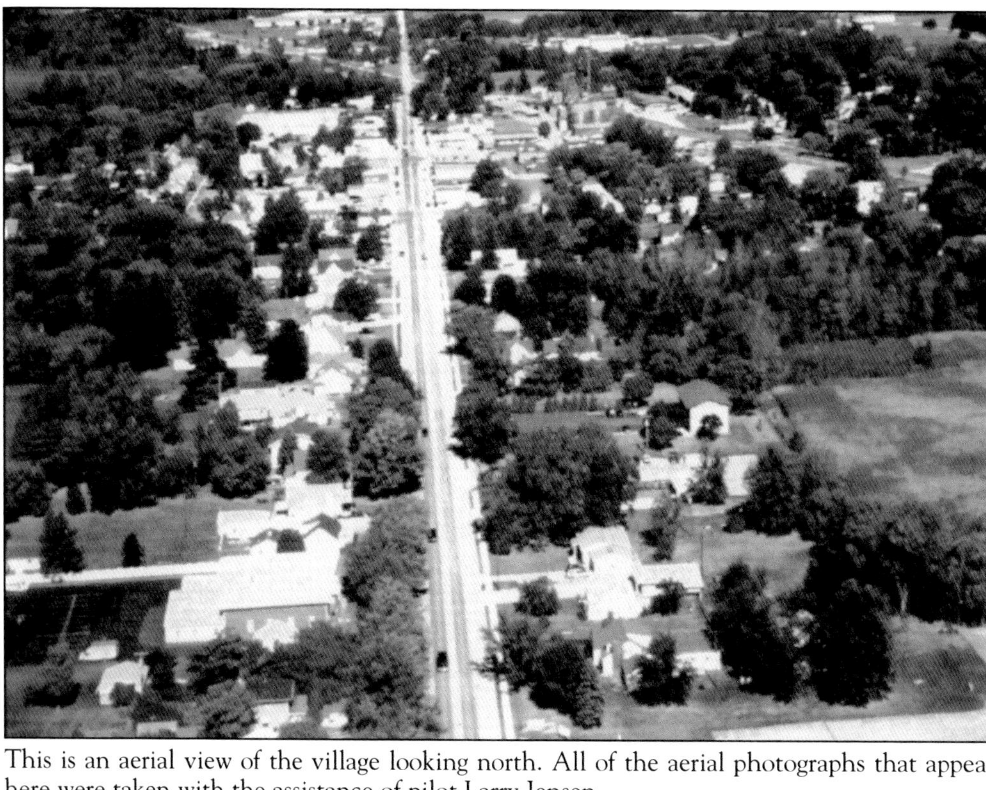

This is an aerial view of the village looking north. All of the aerial photographs that appear here were taken with the assistance of pilot Larry Jensen.

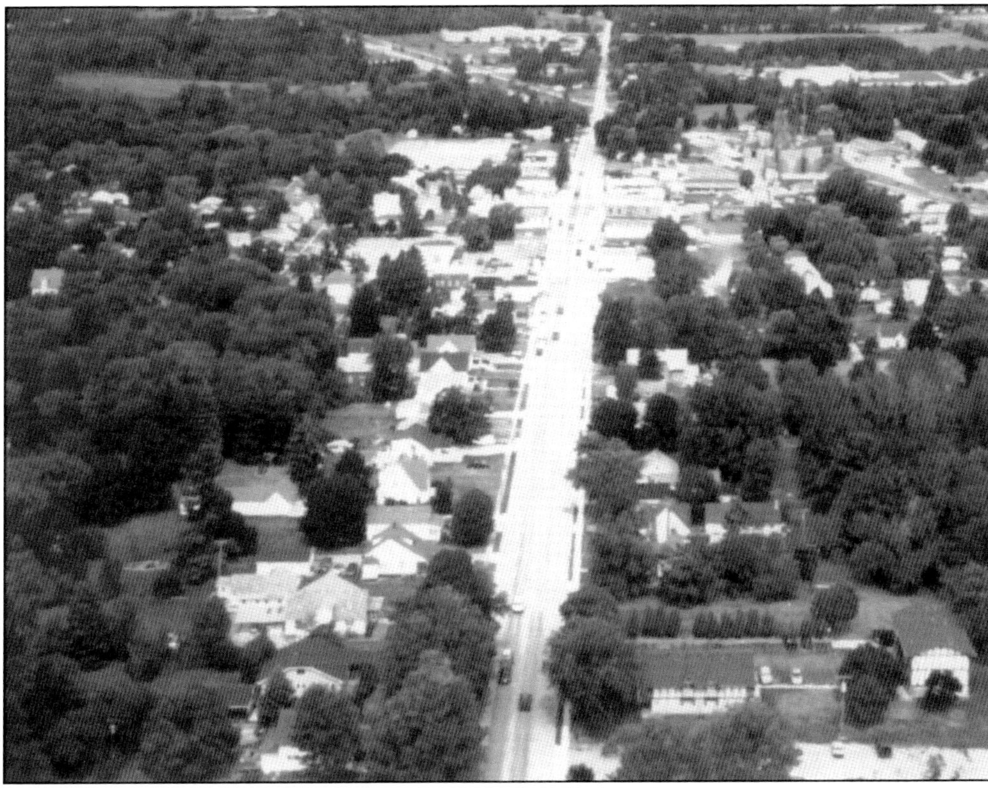

Another aerial view from the south shows more detail of the business area.

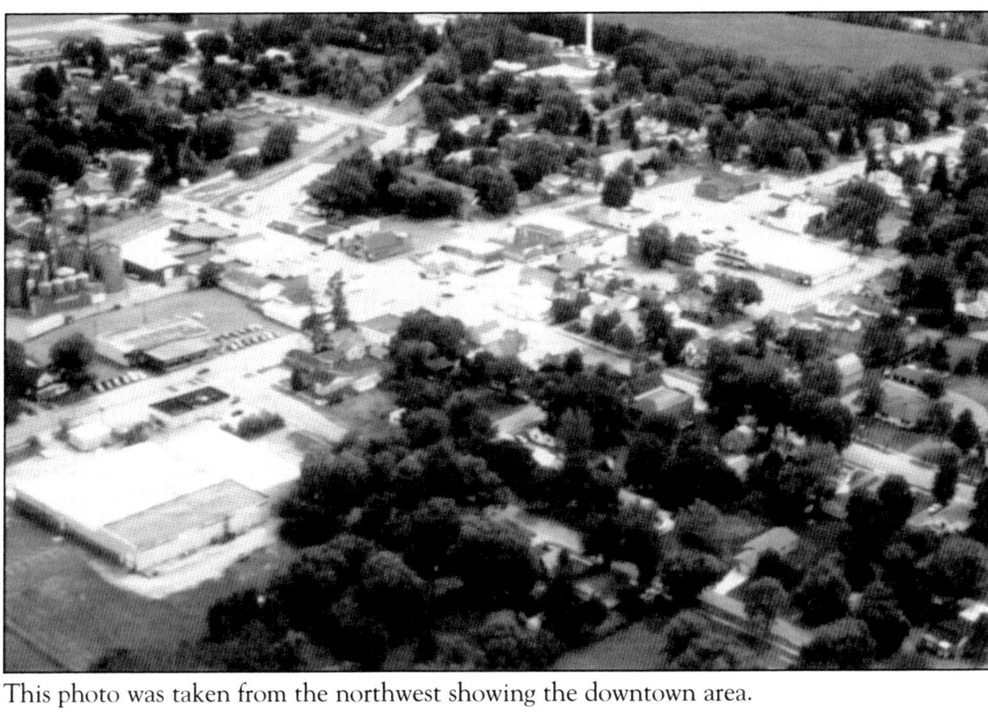

This photo was taken from the northwest showing the downtown area.

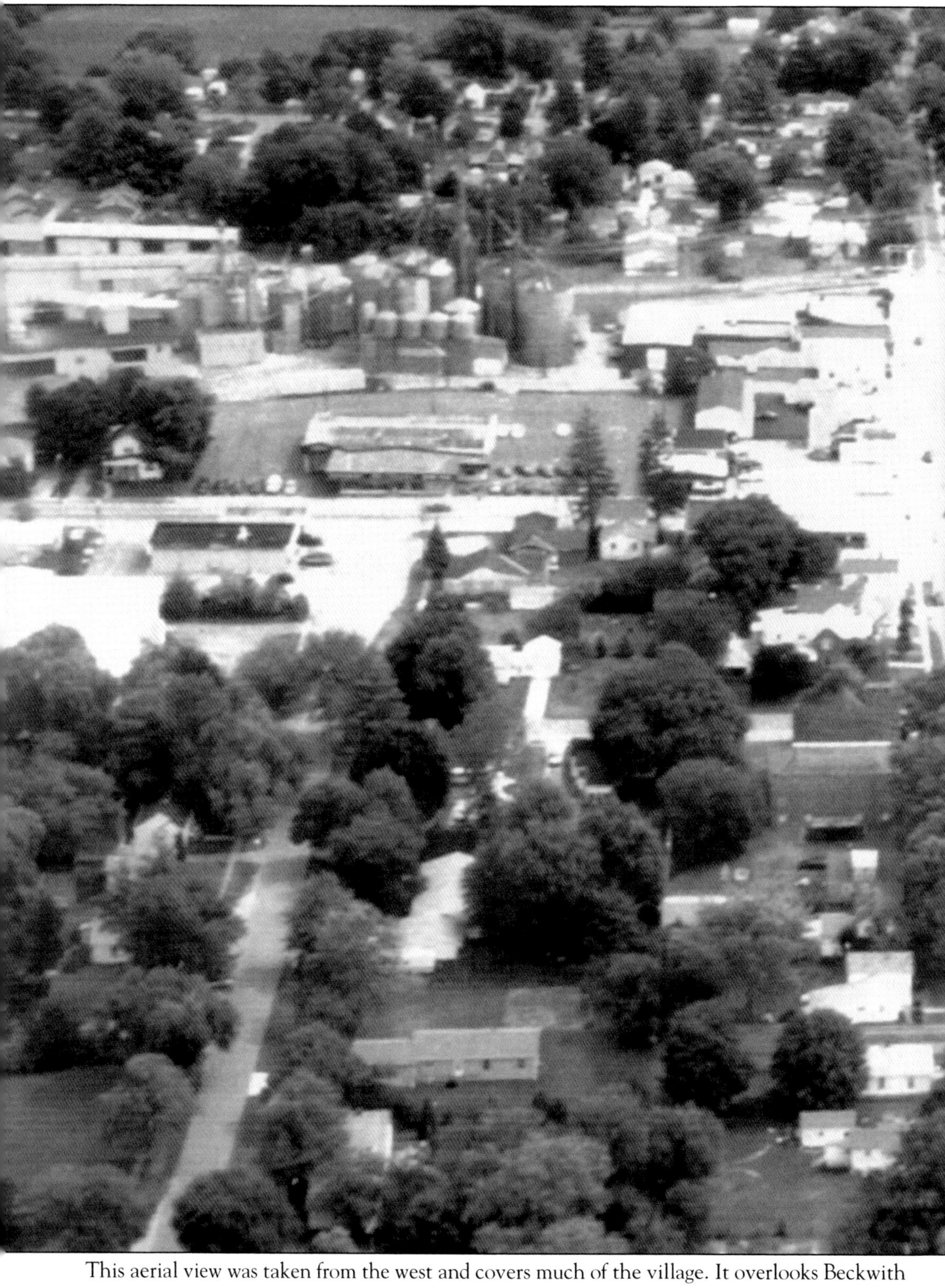

This aerial view was taken from the west and covers much of the village. It overlooks Beckwith

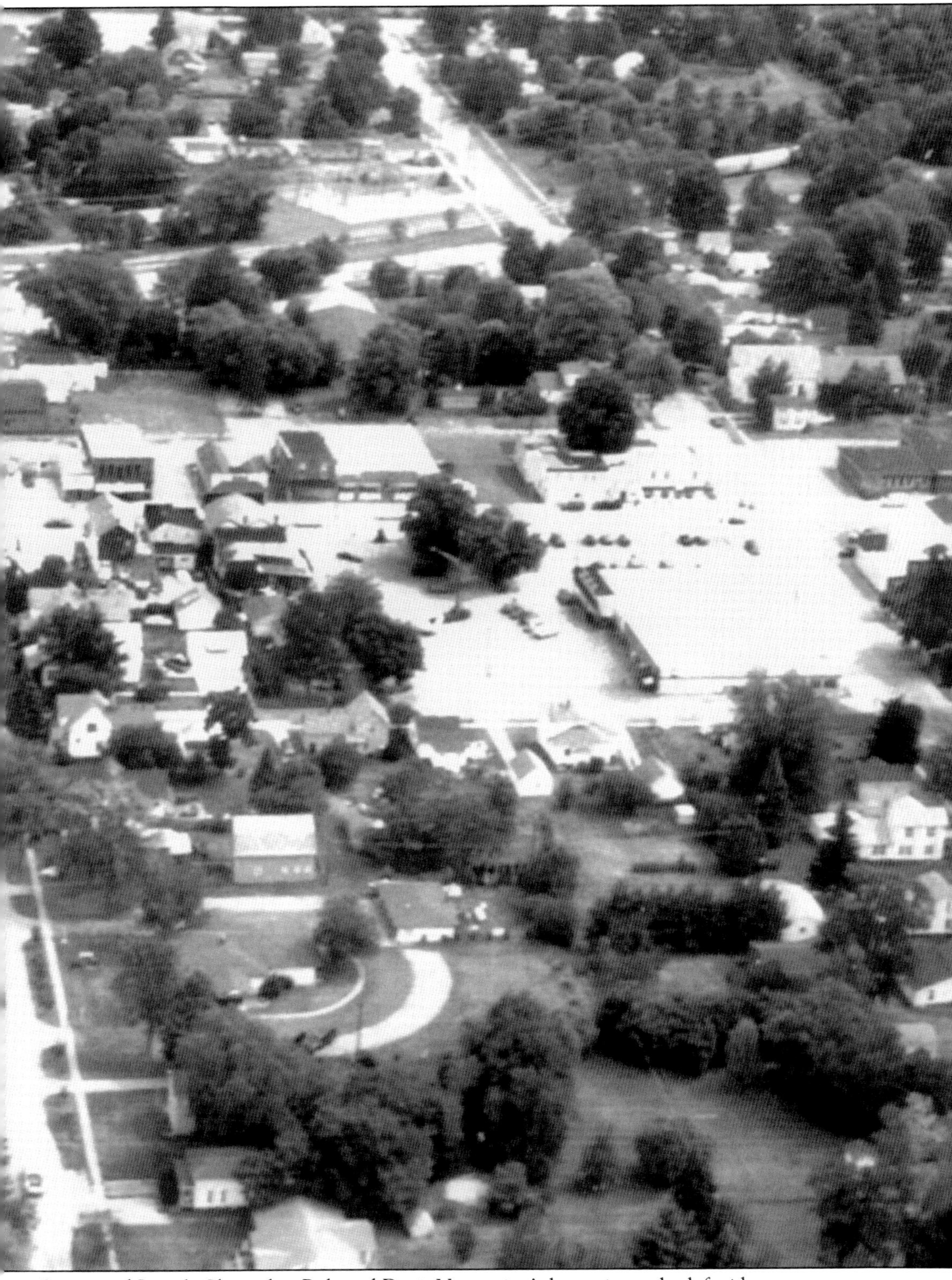

Street and Joseph Chevrolet. Bob and Doris Vanentine's home is on the left side.

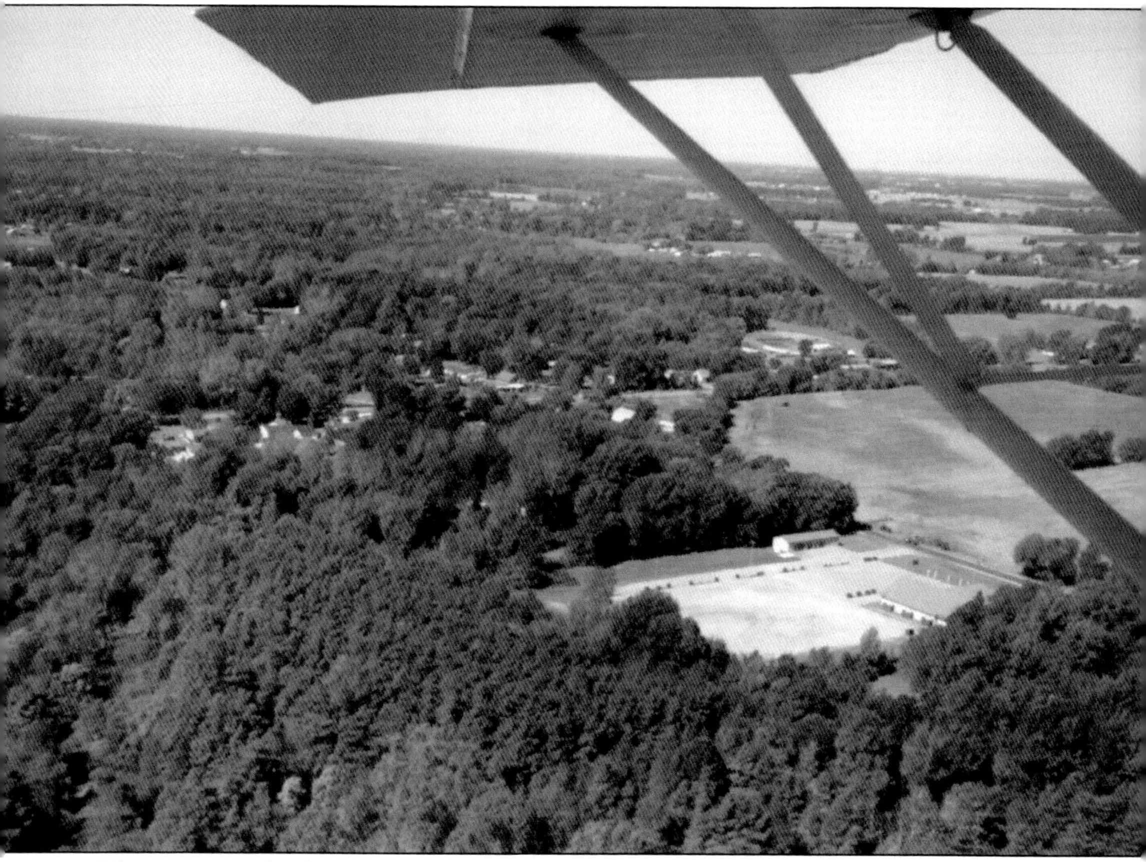

This is a view of Arbela Township Hall taken from the north.

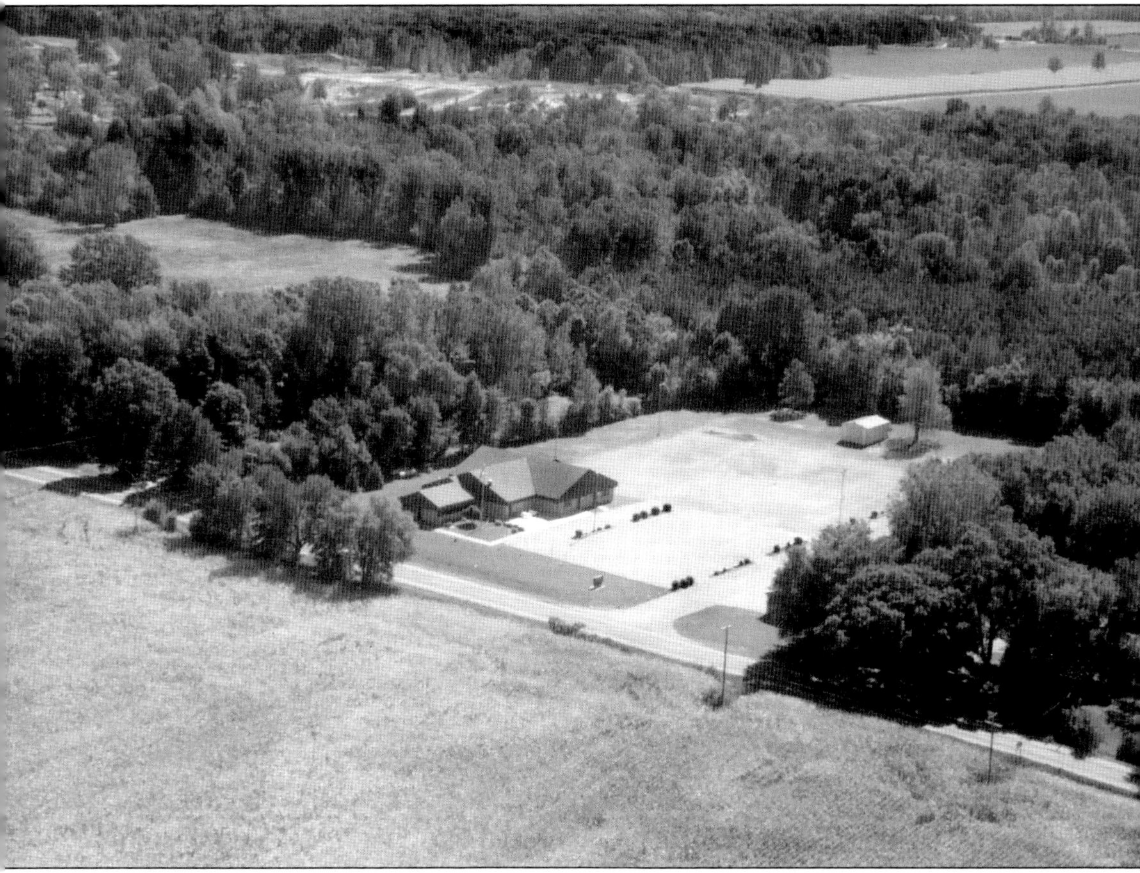

This is a view of Arbela Township from the east, showing the location of the NIEL Frost store in center of the picture.

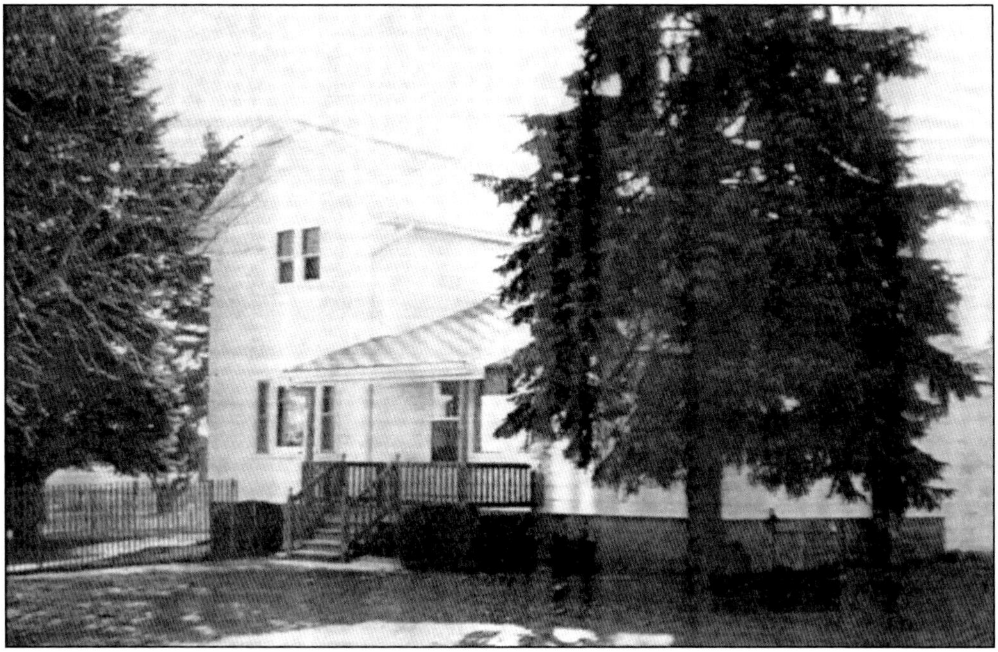

This is the rural home of the Ill family. For over 100 years, it has been owned by the same family. Located at 8729 West Barnes Road, it was built in 1900 by Adolph Ill. Its present owner is Agnes Ill.

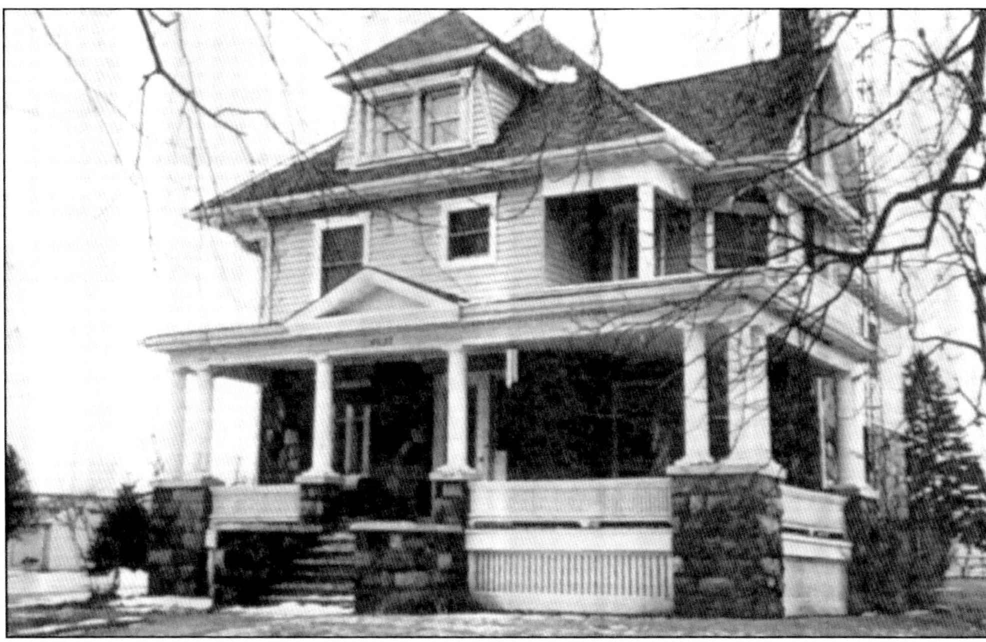

The well-known Seymour House on Main Street was built by David Evans in 1904. It is located at 4627 East Main Street and is now owned by Charles Kroll.

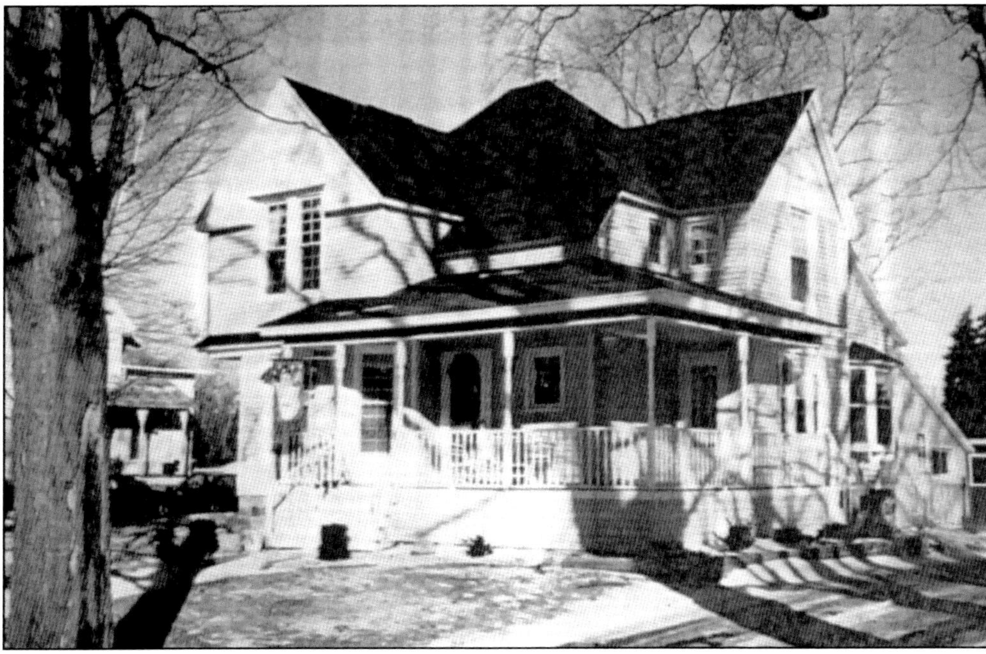

The Lennox House is at 4828 West Center Street. It was built in 1898 by William Carson. Jack Shreve, its current owner, has recently restored the home.

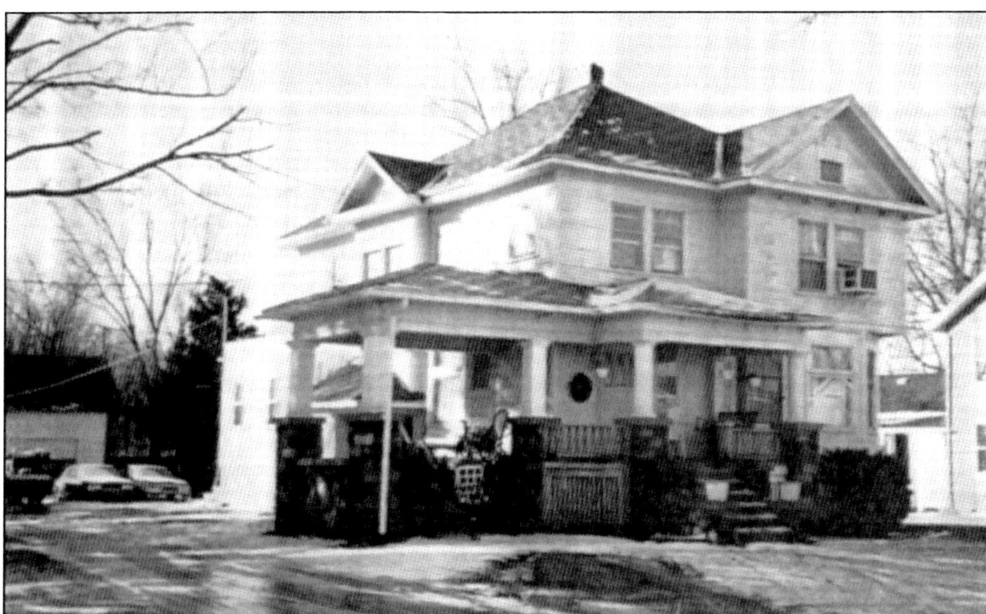

The Johns House is located at 4785 West Center Street. It was built *c.* 1900 by H.B. Johns, and is currently owned by Wayne Leix.

# ACKNOWLEDGMENTS

The Millington-Arbela Historical Society wishes to acknowledge the following people who made this publication possible: the society members who submitted written material and pictures for our use, as well as the people who strived to get this material in order and consolidate it into this book. The people who worked on putting this book together are: Bob Valentine, Clayton Betzing, Ina Greenfield, Virginia Jensen, Betty Johnson, and Ivan McPherson.

# BIBLIOGRAPHY

Millington Centennial Committee, Centennial Booklet.
Church, Fred. Publisher, *Millington Herald* Newspaper.
Many publications from the Millington-Arbela Historical Society archives.